# The Official
# Duke Nukem® 3D
# Atomic Edition
## Strategies & Secrets™

by Jonathan Mendoza

SYBEX

SAN FRANCISCO    PARIS    DÜSSELDORF    SOEST

| | |
|---|---|
| Associate Publisher | GARY MASTERS |
| Acquisitions Manager | KRISTINE PLACHY |
| Project Editor | RONN JOST |
| Production Coordination | LABRECQUE PUBLISHING SERVICES |
| Developmental Editor | TERRENCE O'DONNELL |
| Copy Editor | MARK WOODWORTH |
| Proofreader | RACHEL FUDGE AND TORY McLEARN |
| Book Design and Production | WILLIAM SALIT DESIGN |
| Cover Designer | ARCHER DESIGN |

Library of Congress Card Number: 97-65001

ISBN: 0-7821-2095-4

Manufactured in the United States of America

10 9 8 7 6 5 4 3 2 1

# DEDICATION

To Diana, for her undying faith, and the members of The Saturn Five, who fight for justice and vow to usher in a new golden age of rock in a future too uncertain.

# ACKNOWLEDGMENTS

Writing a strategy book might seem like a lonely activity. Hunched over the keyboard, my face lit by the glaring monitor, I spent many hours writing and playing and playing and writing. And while at times I might have felt overwhelmed by looming deadlines and the unstoppable roaring of the press, in reality I had the support and goodwill of many associates and friends. First, I thank Scott Miller and George Broussard, Apogee and 3D Realms bosses, for making themselves accessible and keeping in touch during a hectic release schedule. Then there's *GameSlice Weekly*'s Geoff Keighley, who shared a most insightful interview with us. Without Gerard Harbour's help, I'd still be piecing level maps together. My girlfriend Diana's beauty, intelligence, grace, and modesty kept me inspired. Terry O'Donnell's watchful eye and sound judgement kept my writing in check. Ash, my cat, kept me humble and subserviant. Gary Masters, associate publisher at Sybex, emanated relentless energy, drive, trust, and a good measure of poise. But most importantly, you, the true gamer, gave me ample reason to write and attempt to honor and do your enthusiasm justice.

Jonathan Mendoza
jonathan@sunscape.com
CompuServe 73771,1637

# TABLE OF CONTENTS

**CHAPTER 4**

# Mapping Out Strategy and Winning

**46**

## PART II: Duking It Out

**5 6**

**CHAPTER 5**

# L.A. Meltdown

**58**

## CHAPTER 6
# Lunar Apocalypse       116

**CHAPTER 7**

# Shrapnel City

206

**CHAPTER 8**

# The Birth

**290**

## PART III: Duke Nukem's Cognoscenti    398

**CHAPTER 9**

# Modifying Level Maps, Cheating, and Using Command Line Parameters    400

**CHAPTER 10**

# The Bosses of Apogee    406

**APPENDIX A**

# Installation and Setup    416

**APPENDIX B**

# Multiplayer Tips and Online Resources    422

# ntroduction

The fun jumps to almost ridiculous highs in *Duke Nukem 3D: Atomic Edition*. But

the alien threat and the battle for our babes also escalate alarmingly. With the orig-

inal *Duke Nukem 3D*, we marveled at a wonderfully original comic-book character

who thundered with a big-bang in the virtual reality, action game genre. To this day,

we still feel the reverberations.

Sputtering a string of arrogant, albeit clever, one-liners, Duke kicked alien butt, saved
humanity, and, inevitably, warmed his way into our hearts. Duke's easy-going manner, good-looks, and confidence helped us cling to hope during the worst days of
the alien invasion. With the *Atomic Edition*, the latest *Duke Nukem 3D* release, you
experience all three of the original episodes— L.A. Meltdown, Lunar Apocalypse,
and Shrapnel City. But
more significantly, you
get to write a brand
new chapter in the
annals of Duke's leg-
endary exploits: The
Birth awaits your
arrival. This book, as
3D Realms' official
guide, covers all four
fantastic episodes to
make your foray into
Duke's world complete
and absolute.

## NOTE

*Duke Nukem 3D: Atomic Edition* is the latest version of *Duke Nukem 3D*. It combines the three episodes in the original—L.A. Meltdown, Lunar Apocalypse, and Shrapnel City—with The Birth, a new, exciting, but deadly mission consisting of 11 highly alluring levels. If you own the registered version of *Duke Nukem 3D*, you can upgrade to the *Atomic Edition* via a patch known as *The Plutonium PAK*. But if you don't have the original, don't fret. You can simply get *Duke Nukem 3D: Atomic Edition* and not miss a beat.

The Atomic Edition also features a new dreadful foe, the protector drone, and of course, the mother of all aliens and the ultimate boss, an alien queen no less. The pig cops also acquire a new mode of transportation and effective means of destruction, the pig cop tank. On the hardware side, the *Atomic Edition* lets your shrinker double up as an expander when you find the right ammo.

# WHY BUY THIS BOOK?

You can justify getting this book for dozens of reasons. For one, you could be helping restore America's economy. Or maybe there's a gap in your bookshelves. Or perchance you know a Duke aficionado who would kiss your feet for a copy. But it could also be that you like to be well informed about a matter you consider essential to life: your enjoyment of *Duke Nukem 3D: Atomic Edition*, an action game unlike any other known to humankind this side of *DOOM* or *Quake*. Whatever the case, this book covers the basics of the game, while it guides you through the perils that await you. Let it be your trusted and faithful companion.

Another compelling reason to consider this book is the frank and earnest interview with Apogee and 3D Realms visionaries and partners Scott Miller and George Broussard (from *GameSlice Weekly* magazine). Find out what goes on in the minds of two key industry players who are helping shape the future of PC games. Incidentally, these gentlemen and the entire Duke team at 3D Realms are also responsible for getting this tome in your hands. They helped to write it, and much of the information in these pages was lifted directly from their brains through an X5G Think-o-matic War Computer.

# THE LOAD-DOWN ON THE SOFTWARE

*Duke Nukem 3D: Atomic Edition* contains four episodes:

- 💣 L.A. Meltdown
- 💣 Lunar Apocalypse
- 💣 Shrapnel City

♦ The Birth

Each episode, in turn, contains a number of levels. L.A. Meltdown has 5 levels and 1 secret mission (for a total of 6 levels). Lunar Apocalypse and Shrapnel City each have 11 levels (2 of which are secret). Finally, The Birth has 11 levels, 1 of which is a secret level. Altogether, then, *Duke Nukem 3D: Atomic Edition* gives you 39 fascinating and compelling virtual 3D environments to explore and conquer.

# THE STORY SO FAR

*Duke Nukem 3D: Atomic Edition* is the natural and explosive conclusion in the Duke saga. Duke made his first stellar appearance in the endearingly original side scrolling game called simply, *Duke Nukem*. In his first foray as a public figure, Duke defeated the evil Dr. Proton and his legion of mechanical minions. From the beginning, Duke won fans who related to his can-do attitude, agility, and clever ways to overcome adversity. Also, how could anyone not like a former surfer with blond hair, an impossibly square jaw, and a self assurance that defies easy definition?

In *Duke II*, while giving a television interview, our hero is suddenly snatched by aliens. Millions watch in horror as Duke vanishes in a blue beam while promoting "Why I Am So Great," his latest autobiography. The aliens (who insist on being called Rigelatings) have a keen interest on Earth and they wish to extract whatever knowledge they need from Duke's brain to help them enslave humanity. Only Duke's resourcefulness and the cleverly hidden explosive in his molar save him from a fate worse than death, a brain drain at the claws of the aliens' highly touted X5G Think-o-matic War Computer. Duke manages to free himself, kick butt, and escape in a tiny alien space probe, just as the alien's mother ship is blown to stellar confetti.

In his 3D incarnation, as *Duke Nukem 3D*, Duke returns to Los Angeles, expecting a hero's welcome. But instead, his small craft is shot from the Angelino skies. Ejecting in time to escape a fiery death in a plummeting piece of alien junk, Duke lands safely on top of a sky scraper. He is just in time to witness a ghastly alliance of hostile aliens attempt to subjugate the Earth for their own fiendish ends. The aliens also have a strange and unspeakable fascination with human females. Hundreds of helpless women are trapped in slimy, green, leathery cocoons all over the city. Duke sets out to explore, find answers, and, hopefully, save humanity.

It doesn't take long before Duke begins to glean the aliens' machiavellic agenda. They intend to crack the Earth apart like a giant walnut and reap her bountiful mineral resources. The aliens' plan is most deplorable and cruel, albeit cleverly ingenious. By aiming their weaponry on California's San Andreas fault line, they expect nothing less than to render planet Earth into a pile of rocks for their subsequent interstellar mining operation. In other words, they plan to pound our home planet with the equivalent of a cosmic wrecking ball. But even more disturbingly, the aliens have more than a curious interest in inter-species bio-genetics and our females seem perfectly suitable for their experiments.

Overcoming insurmountable odds, Duke is somehow able to survive and to anhilate what he thinks is the last front of the alien menace. But in reality, that only leads to another beginning, The Birth, the last episode, which you can only experience with the *Atomic Edition*.

Summoned urgently by an army colonel covered with medals like some bellicose Christmas tree, Duke is briefed on a latest, most disturbing development. An army operative, explains the colonel, managed to film a harrowing scene of a human female inside an alien laboratory. The army recovered the film, but the operative is considered missing in action and presumed dead. The stern looking colonel runs the film and stops talking.

The film rolls and Duke watches. A helpless female lies on what looks like a medical table of some sort. She is surrounded by dozens of protective drones, an alien type you haven't seen before. These tall aliens have leathery skin and move with fast, jerky motions like those of a striking snake. The poor woman kicks and groans in desperation and in the throws of what appears to be a most painful labor. And then, just before the unfortunate and ghastly offspring is able to poke through, the grainy film stops. But you have seen enough, anyway. Our chicks are in more danger than ever. Donning your 20th century vintage Ray Bans, you say with cool determination, "I'm coming in."

# HAVE YOU GOT THE RIGHT HARDWARE?

Besides nerves of steel, finely tuned reflexes, and above-average intelligence, to play the *Atomic Edition* you need the following:

- 486/66 CPU or better (Pentium or 686 is recommended)

- 8MB of RAM minimum

- VGA graphics card

- Sound card (Gravis UltraSound, Sound Blaster, WaveBlaster, or similar)

You can also play in higher resolutions—up to 800×600—if you have a VESA-compliant video card. (Most of these cards have adequate drivers. But if you experience video problems, try using UNIVBE, a driver widely available online.) Depending on your playing style and preference, you might consider using a Gravis Gamepad or joystick—though most players do quite well with the keyboard alone.

# WHY *DUKE NUKEM 3D:* *ATOMIC EDITION* IS SO GREAT

Consider a few of the reasons why *Duke Nukem 3D* soared all the way to number one on the Internet's top 100 games list, just days after its shareware release.

## IT'S THE 3D ENGINE, DUDE

Considering the level of the competition and the magnitude of the stakes, upping the ante in the electronic, 3D action game realm is not inconsequential. But 3D Realms, Apogee's brainchild (spawned solely to create advanced 3D games), has done just that with its Build engine, the powerhouse behind *Duke Nukem 3D*. As a 3D-rendering workhorse and development tool, the Build engine gives its creators myriad new ways to construct convincing, interactive, and creative virtual architectures. That's why, in the *Atomic Edition*, you can experience:

- **Floors above floors**—Although games like *DOOM*, *Heretic*, and *Dark Forces* let you climb or descend, their playing field doesn't allow the existence of one floor above another. In *Duke Nukem 3D: Atomic Edition*, you have complete freedom to roam. You can visit and explore areas directly above or below you.

- **Underwater movement**—To solve certain puzzles, you will have to cross dangerous underground sewage systems or traverse the length of long, sinewy bodies of water. You'll be surprised to find how realistic your movement and displacement become when you're submerged.

- **A third-person perspective**—An optional *virtual camera* view allows you to see the unfolding action from a third-person perspective in the Chase mode, as if you were following Duke Nukem with a camera mounted on your shoulder.

- **Slanted floors and surfaces**—No longer restricted to flat areas, Duke Nukem can climb along steep, angular terrain.

- **The ability to look up and down**—Your viewing vantage point is not restricted to a flat plane. You can actually look up and look down. In fact, while hovering with a jetpack, you can get a bird's-eye view of your environment.

- **The ability to jump and duck**—Your movement in your new virtual environment is more lifelike. Unlike other first-person games, as Duke Nukem you can jump high and duck low. This seemingly simple maneuvering adds tons of realism and possibilities as you take running jumps over crates and other obstacles. Because you can crouch low, you can also hide behind objects and come out pouncing on your enemies.

## DUKE IS ONLY AS GOOD AS HIS TOOLS

Besides the merits of *Duke Nukem 3D*'s Build engine, the game has other nifty innovations that have made it an instant mega-hit.

- **Support for up to eight players in an IPX network, which is common in most office settings**—Depending on your point of view, installing *Duke Nukem 3D: Atomic Edition* on the office network could be seen as a productivity drain, or as a cathartic and ultimately beneficial release of energy. *Duke Nukem 3D* and the *Atomic Edition* are featured attractions of Dwango and TEN, online platforms for multiplayer games. (The shareware version supports only four players.)

❧ **A dazzling assortment of weaponry and equipment**—Your arsenal runs the gamut from semiautomatic hand pistols, pipe bombs, and rocket-propelled grenades, to crystal-powered shrinker weapons, a freezer gun, and wall-mounted laser trip bombs. (The last three weapons are available only in the game's full version.) In the *Atomic Edition*, your shrinker also acts as an expander when you find the right ammo. Among the useful nonweapon items you can score are scuba gear for diving, jet-packs for hovering over the scenery, night vision goggles for optimum vision in dark conditions, protective boots for running or crossing over toxic canals and pools, and even testosterone-laden steroid pills for sudden power surges.

❧ **Build, a map tool editor**—This tool can let you create additional *Duke Nukem 3D* levels in real time and in 3D. Modifying existing levels is also a breeze with this tool. Even if you've never so much as decorated a room before, you might discover there's a hidden architect inside you waiting to be freed.

❧ **ArtEdit, a dedicated bitmap editor**—With this program, you can place new graphic elements into your maps, whether these are new aliens, weapons, or textures. In sharing its development tools with you, the enthusiast, 3D Realms proves in a most convincing fashion that it holds no monopoly in level design and instead wants to "give the power to the users."

# BETWEEN THE COVERS

Written in close collaboration with 3D Realms' and Apogee's designers, coders, dreamers, and artists-at-large, this book is your official handy reference to the coolest, most inventive 3D action game in the 3D shoot-'em-up genre, the inimitable *Duke Nukem 3D: Atomic Edition*.

## NOT ANOTHER SILLY STRATEGY BOOK

*The Official Duke Nukem 3D: Atomic Edition Strategies & Secrets* is not your average hint and strategy guide. This book is chock-full of timely and useful information. Between its covers you're likely to find the knowledge to become a skilled and serious contender, perhaps even a downright formidable one. But beyond any skills you might acquire, there's another reason why having this book will make you feel good. In it, the gracious and talented Duke Nukem team members take a breather from their courageous labor to share with you their own insights, anecdotes, and contributions.

To accommodate both new and experienced players, this book is composed of three parts:

- Part I gives you the basics of playing *Duke Nukem 3D: Atomic Edition.*

- Part II lets you jump right in and duke it out.

- Part III gives you a behind-the-scenes look at the making of *Duke Nukem 3D: Atomic Edition.*

### Part I: Duke Nukem 3D Essentials

This section of the book is required reading for every new player. If nothing else, it can help you avoid an early demise by giving you the basic tools and information to start your foray in Duke's fantastic universe.

For those who just can't wait to get into the action and prefer learning on-the-fly, the very first chapter takes you on a brief, but instructional, tour of Hollywood Holocaust, the first level in L.A. Meltdown. If you're more the studious type, then you might skip the tour and focus instead on Chapters 2 and 3. These chapters get you acquainted with your powerful arsenal and equipment, introduce the unsavory company you will keep, and show you some essential fighting and strategy skills (for both solo and multiplayer modes). You also get a briefing on using the game's menus and controls. Finally, you'll learn how to interpret and understand the set of maps that introduce each level in Part II.

### Part II: Duking It Out

This is where the flying shrapnel from the pipe bomb meets resilient alien flesh. If you're already familiar with the material in Part I, then you're ready to go bust heads, and so you must. Here is where you get to roll up your sleeves, grit your teeth, and get ready for an all-out assault to thwart the aliens' dark conspiracy. This section provides complete descriptions of each level, detailed maps, proven strategies, and other helpful information. Find out the best routes, execute the most effective techniques, and score all the power-ups, weapons, and equipment you possibly can amass. If you want to know every secret in every level, this is the place to go for answers.

### Part III: Duke Nukem's Cognoscenti

The final chapter runs you through the fundamentals of using the Map Editor and ArtEdit. These will guide you as you create your own virtual structures and render some bitmaps.

This section of the book is a bagful of goodies to supplement your *Duke Nukem 3D: Atomic Edition* enjoyment. First and foremost, there is an interview with the cognoscenti (smart guys): the creative talent at 3D Realms and Apogee. Peek inside the heads of some of the most notable forces in the PC gaming industry, and see how ideas and concepts churn in there.

## GET GOING, DUKE

Brace yourself, for you are about to enter the not-so-distant universe of *Duke Nukem 3D: Atomic Edition*. And, with this strategy book, you are going in well prepared and well informed. This book delivers the goods, the information, and the insight to prepare you for what is sure to be a thrilling and most memorable gaming joyride.

# PART

I

# Atomic Edition
# Essentials

Getting down to the basics—that's what Part I is all about. Think of it as your basic train-

ing, your bootcamp, to whip you into shape for the ensuing mayhem. If you're a new player,

the information in Part I is indispensable to your survival. If you're a veteran of past *Duke*

*Nukem 3D* campaigns, you might wish to skip Chapter 1 and read Chapter 2 about your

new adversaries and the new weapon available to you before going on to the meat-and-

potatoes of this book in Part II, "Duking It Out." Here is what you will find in Part I:

- **CHAPTER 1**, "Spare Me the Details, I'm Ready for Prime Time," provides a crash tour of the early goings-on in Hollywood Holocaust, the first level in The L.A. Meltdown.

- **CHAPTER 2**, "Entering Duke's World," covers operating the game's features and controlling the movement and combat techniques of your Duke Nukem character.

- **CHAPTER 3**, "Duke's Enemies, Weapons, and Power-Ups," details the inventory of weapons, ammo, and power-ups at your disposal and runs down the roster of adversaries you'll encounter.

- **CHAPTER 4**, "Mapping Out Strategy and Winning," gives you detailed maps and recommended game plans for tackling each level in The Birth (including its secret level)!

# Spare Me the Details, I'm Ready for Prime Time

Itchy fingers? Say no more. If you have already installed the *Plutonium PAK* or *Duke Nukem 3D: Atomic Edition* and you favor action over words, you're in the right place. (See Appendix A for help.) This lean-and-mean chapter dispenses with formal briefings and introductions, places you smack in the middle of the action, and guides you through some interesting alien encounters as you learn to interact with your new virtual environment.

## YOUR MISSION

Simply stated, your mission in Hollywood Holocaust (as it is in every level) is threefold:

- Build your arsenal with weapons, ammunition, power-ups, and special keycards that grant you access to locked areas.
- Destroy the enemy.
- Find the exit and move on to the next level.

To accomplish your mission, you must rely on quick reflexes, keen powers of observation, and a penchant for holding on to dear life.

## THE CURRENT STATE OF AFFAIRS

After escaping from the tentacles of an alien brain-drain device and destroying the craft where you were held captive, you head back to Earth and your native L.A. But the small alien vessel you escaped in is shot down from the sky. Miraculously, at the last instant, you're able to eject and wind up atop a downtown building. Apparently, while you were gone, another wave of hostile aliens landed and took over the city. Their plans are uncertain, but there's death and destruction everywhere. And the dozens of human females encased in cocoons attest to a bizarre and fiendish alien bio-genetic experiment.

# A CRASH TOUR OF HOLLYWOOD HOLOCAUST

Get ready to mix it up in the streets of Hollywood. This crash tour gives you some basic tools so that you can embark on your own exploration with a measure of confidence. The crash tour shows you how to do the following:

- 💣 Start the game.
- 💣 Get acquainted with basic movements and shooting.
- 💣 Gather weapons, ammo, and power-ups.
- 💣 Blow away a few aliens.

## STARTING THE GAME

You can only start *Duke Nukem 3D: Atomic Edition* from the DOS prompt. So, either be sure your computer is running in DOS or open an MS-DOS window in Windows 95 (or Windows 3.1*x*). Then make the game directory active. (For example, enter the command

**cd\duke3d** to change the current directory to Duke3d.) Then follow these steps to start the *Atomic Edition:*

1. With the game directory active, at the DOS prompt type **duke3d** and press Enter. In a few seconds, the program loads and the main menu appears (see Figure 1.1).

2. Use the arrow keys to move the spinning selection cursors next to the New Game option and press Enter. Now you must choose an episode to play, as shown in Figure 1.2.

3. Choose The Birth. Next you get to choose the skill level at which you want to play, as shown in Figure 1.3.

4. Choose Let's Rock.

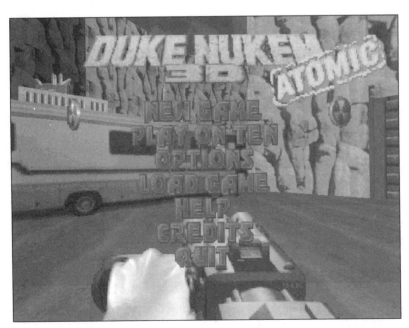

**FIGURE 1.1:** The *Duke Nukem 3D: Atomic Edition* main menu lets you start a new game, set game options, or load a saved game.

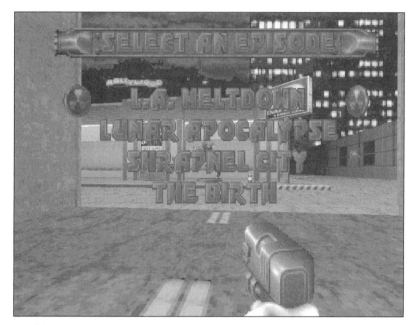

FIGURE 1.2: Select an episode to play on this screen.

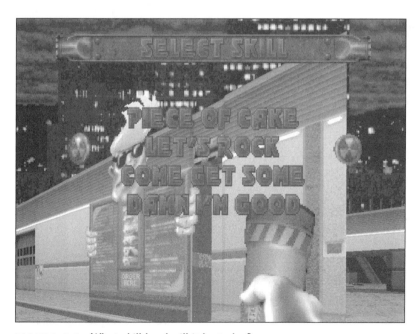

FIGURE 1.3: What skill level will it be today?

After a few seconds, you find yourself at the top of a downtown building, watching your ruined vessel plummeting to the ground and leaving a trail of smoke. You also see your hands loading a hand pistol with a clip. Rock on, Duke!

## IT'S TIME FOR ACTION

Take advantage of the relative calm on the rooftop to get acquainted with Duke's basic moves and controls. Because most people find the mouse/keyboard combination ideal, the discussions of play techniques will assume that you too are using this same setup.

### Looking Around and Picking Stuff Up

The first thing you should notice is that you are viewing everything through Duke's eyes. You have, for all practical purposes, become Nukem himself. Press ↑ to walk forward a few steps. Notice how your hand and your entire perspective weave slightly, just as if you're really walking.

Walk backwards by pressing ↓. You will probably bump against a small wooden crate. Turn on your axis by pressing either ← or →. You can also execute a swift 180-degree turn by pressing the Backspace key. Go ahead, try it.

Standing in front of the crate, press A and ↑ simultaneously to jump up onto it. Press Pg Dn to look for a pistol clip behind the crate. Move forward to drop behind the crate and pick up the clip. To pick up any item on the floor, you simply walk over it. To pick up items on higher surfaces, like tables or compartments, you simply get as close to them as you can.

> **TIP**
> Press F1 twice anytime for a list of movement options and other keystroke controls.

Now sidestep around the crate by pressing Alt and either ← or → at the same time. Use the direction keys to walk around the roof's central structure. Look up into the L.A. skyline by pressing Pg Up. Be sure you stand at a safe distance from those C-9 canisters over in the corner. It's time to blow them up and hit the streets.

### Blowing Stuff Up

Any time you have a weapon in your hands, you are aiming in the general direction in which you are moving. To obtain a higher accuracy rate, you have a crosshair at your reach any time you need it. Press the I key to activate (display) a small and unobtrusive crosshair. Press the I key a second time when you want to turn the crosshair off.

Aim at the C-9 canisters, and shoot at them by pressing either Ctrl key. To use the mouse to shoot, click the left mouse button. If you changed the defaults with the Setup program, then use the mouse button you assigned to this function. Brace yourself for the explosions. Notice that the metal fan near the canisters is also blown to bits, leaving a gaping opening.

## Running and Aiming

Run to the gaping hole where the metal fan used to be. To inject speed into your movements, press the Shift key in combination with the desired direction key. After a while, it becomes natural to run or execute your movements with extra speed in this manner. But in certain situations, it is best to move slowly and deliberately with sudden bursts of speed.

> **TIP**
> The 180-degree spin move (press the Backspace key) is extremely useful when you're being chased or attacked from the rear.

Drop into the metallic air duct, and fall down to the street level. You will probably suffer a few bruises from the fall. If your status bar's display is turned on, a quick look at it might show a slight decrease in health. You won't have a whole lot of time to rub your sore spots, though, before an assault trooper notices you from his spot on top of a large crate across the street.

Press Shift and ↑ to run toward the shameless invader, aiming your weapon slightly upward to catch him before he can reach ground level or use his jetpack to escape. To aim upward, press the Home key. In situations where you need to aim downward, press the End key. Pressing these keys is like pointing your head and your sight in the desired direction and keeping it there. To return to a normal viewing position, press the 5 key on the numeric keypad.

With the immediate danger gone, take a look around and assess the situation. You are at what appears to be the famous Hollywood "Walk of Fame," but the name seems hardly fitting when your fifteen minutes could be suddenly cut short. Your only friend right now is the gun in your hand. If you are to have a fighting chance, you must secure some heavier firepower.

### Jumping and Uncovering Secrets

Looking around, you can't help but notice the "Innocent" billboard at the end of the street. Somehow you sense there's something not so innocent about the sign. So you decide to get up there and investigate for yourself. But how can you get up there? The large wooden crate gives you an idea.

Take a short running start toward the large crate (press Shift and ↑ together). As you pick up speed, punch the A key at the proper moment to let the inertia carry your jump forward as you land on the top of the crate. Once on top, take a second hop onto the slanted surface of the nearby building. It's a bit slippery, but you can hold on. Aiming higher, turn toward the ledge where the "Innocent" sign sits, and hop up a third time.

> **TIP**
>
> To push or pull a door open, activate a switch, turn on a monitor, or open a compartment, all you have to do is get near the device and press the spacebar.

If you fall off on your first attempt, don't give up and try again.

When you finally land on the ledge, listen for the small hydraulic platform that lifts a rocket propelled grenade (RPG) launcher right below the sign. Walk over and grab it immediately. You now have a weapon of awesome destructive power hoisted on your shoulder. Before you hurt yourself with it, put it away by pressing the 2 key on the keyboard to change back to the pistol. (You can also use the keypad when Num Lock is enabled.)

### Operating a Monitor and Finding Another Secret

With the pistol in hand, jump back onto the building's slanted surface. Move parallel with the building along the slant to the second or third window and jump inside right through either one-way window. Notice the box of grenades on the platform in the middle of the room. As you walk over to get them, don't be caught with your guard down by the trooper who comes shooting at you from

> **TIP**
>
> If you want to turn off the messaging feature, press F8. See Chapter 3, "Duke's Enemies, Weapons, and Power-Ups," for a detailed discussion on changing game options.

the dark corner of the L-shaped room. Dispose of the trooper and grab the grenades. Notice that as you grab them a message at the top of the screen informs you that you picked up something useful.

While you're in the apartment, take a second to scope out the security monitoring system. Walk over to the monitor on the wall at the northwest end of the room and activate it with the spacebar. Press the spacebar again and notice how the scene on the monitor changes. You are in effect gaining access to multiple cameras installed throughout the level and can see what's going on in other areas of the Hollywood Holocaust level.

Pull back from the monitor using ↓. Now go back to the south end of the room, and notice the movie poster on the wall. Could it be hiding something? Press the spacebar. Sure enough, it lifts and reveals a bottle of steroid pills.

The steroids could come in handy later, so stow them away. In other words, just walk up to them to pick them up. Again, notice the message near the top of the screen informing you of your good find.

## Boosting Your Health and Learning the Sidestep

Jump out of the room through one of the windows. Land on the slanted surface, and follow it toward the south end of the street. Near the end of the street, you will see a glowing object on the inclined ledge—an atomic health unit. Take this precious power-up. It gives you a whopping 50 percent boost to your health indicator. Always keep a watchful eye on your health status; don't let it fall below 50 percent for very long, if you can help it.

By this time, you will have attracted the attention of some additional troopers. Run toward the small alley directly across the street. Take cover behind the wall and poke your head out, sidestepping enough to take pot shots at the troopers while avoiding their shots at you. To sidestep, simply press the Alt key in combination with either the ← or → keys. Sidestep moves are extremely important as they allow you to step out of the way of incoming projectiles. Of course, you can also try sidestepping very quickly by pressing the Shift key along with either of these combinations.

When the troopers are no longer a factor, run back toward the movie theater's box office. Switch to the RPG launcher by pressing the 5 key on top of the keyboard.

At a prudent distance, aim directly at the box office. Ideally, you want to annihilate the alien hiding there and also blow a big hole in the wall. With this objective accomplished, pull out your gun again and venture forth into the theater, where more enemies, weapons, and power-ups abound.

# Entering Duke's World

This chapter dispenses with the obligatory, but simple, mechanics for

operating the game and adjusting the environment. You know, stuff

like starting, saving, loading or quitting games. In addition, you also

learn the basics of moving Duke around his virtual environment.

Finally, learn how to keep an eye on your vitals and your arsenal

with Duke's status bar.

Your success—and survival—will depend on your skill to make Duke run, jump, crawl, walk, and change view perspective effectively and precisely. Perhaps most importantly, this chapter also covers how to select, aim, and shoot Duke's arsenal of weapons—and how to monitor Duke's status as you progress through the *Atomic Edition* episodes.

# OPERATING THE GAME

Operating *Duke Nukem 3D: Atomic Edition* is simple and straightforward. This section explains the mechanics for:

- 💣 Starting a new game.
- 💣 Saving a game.
- 💣 Loading a saved game.
- 💣 Quitting a game.

## STARTING A NEW GAME

Here's how to start the action. (Beware! You might not only be starting a new game; you might also be starting a new addiction.)

> **SEE**
>
> If you haven't installed the *Plutonium PAK* or *Duke Nukem 3D: Atomic Edition* on your system yet, see Appendix A, "Installation and Setup."

1. If the main menu isn't showing, press Esc.

2. At the main menu, use the arrow keys to move the rotating

> **NOTE**
>
> Presumably, *Duke Nukem 3D: Atomic Edition* is already loaded and running on your system. If it isn't, in DOS, access the game's directory (type **cd\duke3d**). Then, type **duke3d** and press Enter. The game loads in a few seconds.

radioactive signs (the screen cursors) to the New Game command, as shown in Figure 2.1, and press Enter.

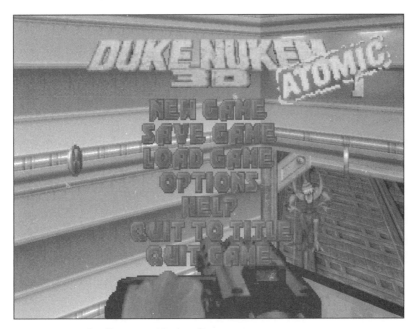

**FIGURE 2.1:** It all starts with that first game.

3. At the Select An Episode screen, move the cursor to the episode of your choice and press Enter. (See Figure 2.2.)

4. At the Select Skill screen, move the cursor to the skill level you feel you can handle and press Enter. (See Figure 2.3.)

Get a move on, Duke; it's bust heads or lose.

## SAVING A GAME (F2)

It's always a good idea to save a game in progress at regular intervals. That way, if you come to a premature demise, or you have to go outside to rescue your little brother from a mob, you can always pick up the game from where you left off. Otherwise you must start from the level's beginning.

To save a game in progress, do the following:

1. Press the F2 key. The game pauses and the Save Game screen appears, as shown in Figure 2.4.

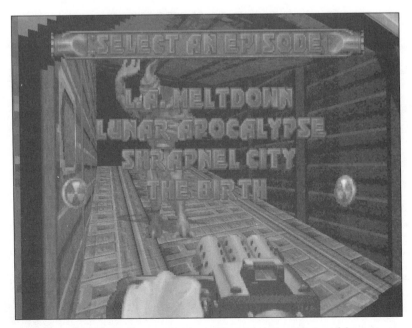

**FIGURE 2.2:** The Duke saga begins with your choice of any of four different episodes.

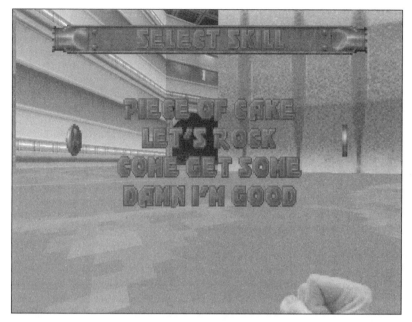

**FIGURE 2.3:** Just how much pain can you possibly enjoy? You get to decide on this screen.

**FIGURE 2.4:** Not to sound alarmist . . . but you'd better save your game before you die and lose your entire arsenal.

2. Move the cursor to the slot where you want to save the game, type a name in the space, and press Enter.

You can save a game under any name, phrase, or description you want, but it can be no longer than 19 characters. Also, you can type *over* names for games that have been saved previously. When you save over a game, the program asks you to confirm as the first game is lost from memory.

> **NOTE**
> Use Quick Save (F6) after you've already saved a game. As you make further progress through a level, you can update your saved game without having to type a name each time. Simply press the F6 key and then select Y (for Yes) to answer the "Save over last game?" prompt.

The frame on the left side of the screen captures the current scene and then returns you to the game. Now you can continue kicking butt, or protecting your *own*.

## LOADING A SAVED GAME (F3)

After you've saved one or more games, you can load any of them anytime and continue playing. This is how you do it:

1. If you are in the middle of a game, press the F3 key. (Otherwise, press Esc to display the main menu and then choose Load Game.)

2. At the Load Game screen (see Figure 2.5), move the cursor to the name of the game you wish to load.

> **NOTE**
> Use Quick Load (F9) after you've loaded a game once. You can reload the same game by pressing the F9 key during game play.

Notice that the frame on the left side of the screen shows the scene where the level will start.

**FIGURE 2.5:** Choose the game you want to relive all over again.

**3.** Press Enter.

The game picks up where it left off, and you're back in business.

## QUITTING A GAME

To quit a game in action:

**1.** Press the Esc key to display the main menu.

**2.** Move the cursor to the Quit command and press Enter.

**3.** When you're prompted whether to quit to DOS, type **Y** and press Enter.

Now you can go back to normal life.

# ADJUSTING THE GAME ENVIRONMENT

If you want to settle in for a productive and satisfying session of the *Atomic Edition*, you might as well tweak the game's environment options to set them up just the way you like 'em. Adjustable options for game play include the following:

- Picture adjustments

- Sound adjustments

- Mouse sensitivity

- Parental control (Adult Mode)

The remainder of this section shows you how to set things just right for your use.

## PICTURE ADJUSTMENTS

The picture adjustments you can control include the following:

- Resolution (the level of detail)

- Shadows (whether your enemies cast them)

- Screen tilting (useful if you're playing in your easy-chair)

- Screen size (good to change if you're playing the game under the blankets at night)

- Brightness (when you're playing the game on your pool deck)

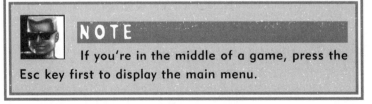

**NOTE**

If you're in the middle of a game, press the Esc key first to display the main menu.

You adjust all of these options from the same Options screen. To make your adjustments, do the following:

1.  At the main menu, move the cursor to the Options command and press Enter. The Options screen is displayed, as shown in Figure 2.6.

2.  Move the cursor to the option you wish to adjust, and make the desired adjustments, as described in Table 2.1.

| TABLE 2.1: *ATOMIC EDITION* GAME OPTIONS | | | |
| --- | --- | --- | --- |
| OPTION | DESCRIPTION | ADJUSTMENT | SHORTCUT |
| Detail | This option controls the level of resolution you will see on your screen. You have two choices: High and Low. With most systems, High is the only choice. Even machines as basic as 50 MHz 486s can still take advantage of the High detail level. | Press Enter to toggle between the High and Low levels. | Press F5 to toggle between the High and Low levels during game play. |

*(Continued on next page)*

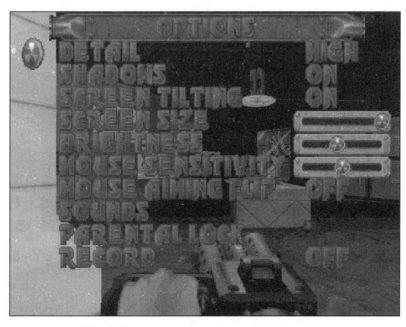

FIGURE 2.6: Tweak the game options to your heart's content.

*(Continued from previous page)*

| OPTION | DESCRIPTION | ADJUSTMENT | SHORTCUT |
|---|---|---|---|
| Shadows | This option controls whether your enemies will cast shadows. Characters that cast shadows require a little more computational power. | Press Enter to toggle between shadows and no shadows. | |
| Screen Tilting | When turned on (the default state), this option enhances the 3D effect by causing Duke to jerk his head (and thus, your view) whenever he is hit or dies. | Press Enter to toggle between screen tilting and no screen tilting. | |
| Screen Size | This option controls the size of the game play area on your screen. A larger game play area requires more cycles per second of computational power. Therefore, the larger the screen, the slower the game will run. Of course, with Pentium 90s or higher, the speed difference is barely noticeable. | Press ← or → to decrease or increase the screen size, respectively. | Press the − (hyphen or minus sign) or + (plus sign) key during game play to decrease or increase the screen size, respectively. |
| Brightness | This option controls how dark or light the picture appears. | Press ← or → to decrease or increase the level of brightness, respectively. | Press F11 to cycle through the eight levels of brightness during game play. When you reach the desired level, press the Esc key. |

3. When you're finished setting your adjustments, press the Esc key to go back to the main menu.

If you were in the midst of a game, you will return to the game with the new adjustments in place.

## SOUND ADJUSTMENTS

The sound adjustments at your command include the following:

- Music

🔥 Sound effects

🔥 Ambient noise

Like their picture counterparts, the sound adjustments can also all be made from the same screen. Here's how to set your own sound adjustments:

1.  At the main menu, move the cursor to the Options command and press Enter.

2.  At the Options screen, move the cursor to the Sound option and press Enter. The Sounds screen appears, as shown in Figure 2.7.

3.  Use the arrow keys to highlight the sound option you want to control and make your adjustments, as indicated in Table 2.2.

4.  When you've adjusted the sound levels to your desire, press Esc to get back to the main menu.

**FIGURE 2.7:** Tweak all the knobs you want to make sound adjustments.

### TABLE 2.2: *ATOMIC EDITION* SOUND OPTIONS

| OPTION | DESCRIPTION | ADJUSTMENT |
| --- | --- | --- |
| Sound | This option controls whether you hear anything at all. | Press Enter to toggle between sound on and sound off. |
| Music | This option controls whether you hear any music at all. (The music, sound effects, and ambient sound can be controlled independently.) | Press Enter to toggle between music on and music off. |
| Sound Volume | This option controls how loud the sound effects will sound. Sound effects include explosions, alien growls, and the normal sounds that happen naturally as you interact with the environment. | Press ← and → to decrease or increase the sound volume, respectively. |
| Music Volume | This option controls how loud the music will sound. | Press ← and → to decrease or increase the music volume, respectively. |
| Duke Talk | This option controls whether you hear Duke talk during game play. A man of few words, Duke is known to use a few colorful expressions from time to time. | Press Enter to toggle between talking and silent modes. |
| Ambiance | This option controls whether ambient sounds are present or absent. Ambient sounds are not necessarily produced by your interaction with the environment. They are simply the natural sounds of the environment you're visiting. | Press Enter to toggle ambient sounds on and off. |
| Flip Stereo | This option controls the sound signals going to the left and right channels. You can switch the direction of the signals so that the left channel becomes the right, and vice versa. | Press Enter to switch the stereo channel signals. |

## MOUSE SENSITIVITY

For most players, the mouse is a most useful interface device that allows you to move swiftly and deliberately (hmmm, just like a real rodent). In the aiming mode, the mouse gives you a great degree of control in choosing and isolating your targets. Set the sensitivity of your mouse to your liking (a little practice will tell), and improve your all-around scores. To set mouse sensitivity, do the following:

1. At the main menu, move the cursor to the Options command and press Enter.

2. At the Options screen, move the cursor to the Mouse Sensitivity option and press ← or → to

**N O T E**

With the Setup program, which is explained in Appendix A, "Installation and Setup," you can also assign actions to double-clicks. For example, you can assign the middle button (if your mouse has one) for jumping when it's double-clicked. The only double-click default is Open (as in open doors), and it's assigned to the secondary mouse button.

decrease or increase the sensitivity, respectively.

## PARENTAL CONTROLS

If you want to keep the more mature material from the prying eyes of youngsters and other, shall we say, prudish types, you can exercise the game's built-in parental controls. The procedure involves turning off Adult Mode and setting up a password. Without the password, the player is barred from viewing human flesh. However, you will still see plenty of blood, guts, and gore. To turn off Adult Mode:

1. At the main menu, move the cursor to the Options command and press Enter.

2. At the Options screen, move the cursor to the Parental Lock option and press Enter. The Adult Mode screen appears, as shown in Figure 2.8.

3. Press Enter to turn off the adult content of the game. The program will prompt you for a password, so you can turn the adult material back on when you wish.

4. Type a password of up to 12 characters and press Enter.

FIGURE 2.8: Keep prying eyes locked out. Exercise your parental controls.

From this point on, if you wish to view the adult content while playing the game, you'll have to access the Adult Mode screen, turn on adult content, and type the correct password.

# CONTROLLING DUKE'S MOVES

As you traverse the sinister, alien underworld, your success will hinge on your technique and execution. This section summarizes the keyboard controls for moving your Duke around. As you become a more experienced player, your moves will become second nature.

### WALKING, TURNING, AND RUNNING

Walking in *Duke Nukem 3D* is a no-brainer; it's almost like chewing gum. Just press the arrow key for the direction you want to go. To run, you simply press and hold down the Shift key in addition to the desired arrow key. If you like, you can leave Run mode on by pressing the Caps Lock key. Press (toggle) the Caps Lock key a second time to disengage Run mode.

Besides the arrow keys, you can also execute common turning maneuvers with other keys. For example, to execute a quick 180-degree turn, press the Backspace key. To take a quick glance to your left or right, without changing your direction, press the Insert and Delete keys, respectively. After you release either of these keys, your view returns to the forward position.

## LOOKING AND AIMING UP AND DOWN

To look up or down momentarily, press PgUp or PgDn, respectively. After releasing either of these keys, your view returns to the normal, level position.

Unlike looking up or down, aiming up or down changes your view until you change it back. To aim up, press the Home key until you reach the desired aiming position. Do the same thing with the End key to aim down. To go back to a level view, press 5 on the numeric keypad.

## MOVING AND AIMING WITH THE MOUSE

The more you learn to rely on the mouse/keyboard combination, the better a player you'll become. The mouse duplicates many of the keyboard controls, and it offers a single source to exercise multiple techniques. Three-button models are preferred over two-button models because they add an extra button for control.

The Setup program lets you assign functions to each mouse button, or you can use the default assignments as shown in Table 2.3.

### TABLE 2.3: THE DEFAULT MOUSE BUTTON FUNCTIONS

| MOUSE BUTTON | SINGLE-CLICK |
| --- | --- |
| Primary | Fire |
| Middle | Move forward |
| Secondary | Strafe |

In certain situations, particularly when you are stationary, you can turn on Aim mode for the mouse by pressing the U key. This simple action turns the mouse into a quite responsive aiming tool. While in Aim mode, you can perform all the aiming techniques described in Table 2.4.

### TABLE 2.4: MOUSE FUNCTIONS IN AIM MODE

| AIMING DIRECTION | MOUSE ACTION |
| --- | --- |
| Up | Pull mouse back. |
| Down | Push mouse forward. |
| Left | Push mouse to the left. |
| Right | Push mouse to the right. |

You can also combine motions so that you can aim upward as you turn to your left, or aim downward as you look to the right. To turn off Aim mode, press the U key a second time during game play.

## JUMPING AND DUCKING

Just as in previous incarnations of the original *Duke Nukem* and *Duke Nukem II*, the *Atomic Edition* provides you with extensive use of jumping and ducking maneuvers. Sometimes the only way to reach a platform, an air duct, or another elevated surface is to jump as high as you can. By the same token, other areas will remain undiscovered unless you get down to crawl on your hands and knees. Both of these operations are very simple. You jump by pressing the A key. You can also take running jumps by pressing Shift and ↑ together and then punching the A key (Shift + ↑ + A) at the right moment (that is, after you pick up some momentum to carry you forward). To duck, you simply press the Z key.

## SHOOTING AND CHANGING WEAPONS

You can fire the weapon you're currently holding by pressing either of the Ctrl keys. When you don't have any weapons, or if your mighty foot is the currently active weapon, you will see your right leg raise and snap a powerful kick when you press the Ctrl key.

To change weapons, all you have to do is press the number key associated with the weapon you want. Each weapon is always associated with the same number, as shown in Table 2.5.

| TABLE 2.5: WEAPONS AND CORRESPONDING NUMBER KEYS | |
|---|---|
| **WEAPON** | **NUMBER KEY** |
| Mighty foot | 1 |
| Handgun | 2 |
| Shotgun | 3 |
| Ripper chaingun | 4 |
| RPG launcher | 5 |
| Pipe bombs | 6 |
| Shrinker/Expander | 7 (Press it a second time to toggle between the shrinker and the expander) |
| Devastator | 8 |
| Laser trip bombs | 9 |
| Freezethrower | 0 |

# READING DUKE'S STATUS BAR

The status bar appears at the bottom of the screen during game play, and it's your feedback mechanism to find out how well (or poorly) you're doing. The status bar lets you monitor your health and the current percentage of your armor, as well as various other aspects of your arsenal. As you can see in Figure 2.9, the status bar's ergonomic design lets you appraise your conditions at a glance.

The status bar allows you to keep tabs on the following indicators:

1. The Health indicator displays your current health status. Under optimum conditions, and with enough atomic health units, your health can soar to 200 percent.

FIGURE 2.9: Keep abreast of your vitals with the status bar.

2. The Armor indicator displays the percentage of armor you have left. It can reach up to 100 percent with a fresh armor.

3. The Weapons indicator shows you the weapons you've got available, through their number designations (2 for the handgun, 3 for the shotgun, 4 for the ripper chaingun, 5 for the RPG launcher, and so on). This indicator also shows the number of rounds you've got, versus the maximum number of rounds you can carry.

4. The smaller Ammo indicator to the right shows you the number of rounds available for the weapon that's currently in your hands.

5. The Inventory indicator shows the power-up that is currently selected. You can change power-ups with either the [ or ] bracket key. To activate a selected power-up, simply press Enter.

6. The Keys indicator shows you the installation keycards you have in your possession, if any.

You can increase the screen size but still retain a minimized status bar, as shown in Figure 2.10.

> **TIP**
>
> The abbreviated status bar is available when you decrease the play screen area to one level below its maximum size.

FIGURE 2.10: The minimized status bar displays your most vital indicators: health and weapons.

# Duke's Enemies, Weapons, and Power-Ups

Before plunging head-first into a mission that could determine the fate

of life on Earth as we know it, why not get acquainted both with Duke's

adversaries and with the weapons and equipment that can be used to

defeat them? Newbies and veterans alike will benefit from the infor-

mation in this chapter. It will provide you with the solid foundation

you'll need to enter Duke's universe, so that you know what to expect

and how to handle yourself. In particular, this chapter delves into:

- Evaluating Duke's alien foes.
- Presenting Duke's arsenal.
- Reading the online maps.

## DUKE'S ALIEN FOES

However unsettling, it's time to talk about the unsavory company you'll keep when you play *Duke Nukem 3D: Atomic Edition*. The hostile and predatory cast of alien characters paying you a visit is quite motley. They've assembled with the common goal of subjugating our world. Their agenda also includes biogenetic experimentation with unwilling human females. If you're to fight and reach any level of success, you should definitely find out all you can about these uninvited guests. It's up to you to crash their party in a big way and find out the best trick to bounce them back to the void where they belong.

## ASSAULT TROOPERS (TROOPERS)

These reptilian-looking bipeds sport green vests, laser pistols, and jetpacks. The first wave to invade the Earth, the assault troopers form the grunt front-lines of the alien alliance. Because they're highly mobile and capable of hovering, assault troopers (sometimes called just troopers) are never easy to deal with. Although they can be killed with a few rounds from your handgun, assault troopers are seldom discouraged from their pursuit. As their designated prey, you should *never* let your guard down when a trooper lurks around. Each time a trooper's blast hits you directly, you'll experience as much as a 15 percent drain on your health.

## ASSAULT CAPTAINS (CAPTAINS)

Captains sport the higher-ranking red vests and make up the next-higher echelon in the alien hierarchy. Like their minion troopers, the assault captains also sport laser pistols and jetpacks. But, in addition, they wear phased-induced teleporter devices on their wrists. A captain can dematerialize at will—only to reappear when you least expect it, usually behind your back and firing at you point-blank. Don't let this happen to you, for each time you suffer a hit, you experience a commensurate health drain of up to 20 percent. Ouch! One way to avoid being caught from behind is to back up against a wall when a captain has gone invisible. He will have no choice but to reappear in front of you. Then your odds are a bit more even.

## PROTOZOID SLIMERS (SLIMERS)

Equipped with a very simple nervous system, these evolutionary throwbacks resemble giant, mutated amoebae. After sensing your presence, protozoid slimers emerge from their egg pods for the sole purpose of sucking your brain through your nose. What drives them to do this is a complete mystery, but it appears to be hard-coded in their genes. Slimers also like to crawl up your pant legs and work their way up to your nose. These creatures are quite elusive, as they're able to slime-crawl their way along walls and ceilings. They can also stretch their gelatinous bodies and bounce from ceiling to floor. The best way to dispose of slimers is by stomping on them or shooting them with your handgun. The ripper chaingun is also a good weapon to possess when you're surrounded by a colony of slimers.

## PIG COPS

At one point, these guys' motto was "to protect and to serve." But after undergoing advanced mutation, the L.A. police force has become a mindless army of slaves serving the aliens' beckoning. The dreaded pig cops are indeed faithful servants and ruthless killers. Toting shotguns and exhibiting absolutely no fear, pig cops are determined, unyielding opponents. Often announcing their presence by a growling snort, pig cops are really good shots. It isn't rare to see a pig cop drop to the ground to take careful aim before firing.

Your chances of overcoming an encounter with a pig cop get better if you're armed with a shotgun. But even so, and as if they weren't tough enough, many pig cops wear protective body armor. This can be a mixed blessing. Sometimes you can kill a pig cop and claim his weapon or body armor. If they're available, you will see these items fall next to a pig cop's bloated carcass. If you get shot by a pig cop, expect at least a 20 percent drain in your health. If you aren't wearing a body armor, the damage reaches a magnitude of 25 percent or even higher.

## RECON PATROL VEHICLES (RPVS)

Highly maneuverable and fast, RPVs are single-user, antigravity transports that allow pig cops to take to the air. Every RPV is equipped with powerful, side-mounted laser cannons. A well-trained pig cop can give chase and swoop down on you in his RPV. In addition, RPVs can hover indefinitely, allowing pig cops to get a fix on you and keep you in their line of fire. Get hit by the RPV's laser cannon and experience a major health loss of as much as 30 percent. Besides the laser cannon, each RPV also comes equipped with an automatic ejection seat. This means that even when you pluck one from the air, the pig cop will emerge from the wreckage and come chasing after you.

## PIG COP TANKS

Another form of transport for the fearless pig cop is the single-occupant pig cop tank. This is a solid piece of machinery, capable of withstanding impacts from most weapons. Pig cop tanks are somewhat slow, but they're highly maneuverable. In addition, a pig cop tank boasts double chainguns mounted on its front side. Avoid seeing a pig cop tank from the front side, or you stand a good chance of being turned into human Swiss cheese. If you have the devastator or RPG launcher, you can probably take on a pig cop tank, head on. Otherwise, you're best advised to avoid them altogether. Braver players, however, can run behind a pig cop tank and push the radioactive button. This causes the pig cop tank to blow up after a few seconds. If you're able to do this, you will want to clear out quickly, as the exploding tank can injure you seriously. But even after you blow up a pig cop tank, the pig cop inside can come chasing after you.

## ENFORCERS

Armed with blazing ripper chainguns, enforcers are charged with dispatching the remaining human opposition. Their powerful hind legs enable these reptilian-looking creatures to leap to great heights. Their toughness is partly due to the fact that many enforcers wear protective armor. Enforcers tend to run in packs, so when you see one, you can usually expect to see a few more. The shotgun is a good weapon to use against enforcers, when you're facing them at mid-ranges. Usually one or as many as three shotgun blasts are enough to put enforcers out of their miserable existence. Sometimes a dying enforcer will drop his ammo load, which you can use for your ripper chaingun, or will drop his armor plate, which you also can use for your own protection.

## OCTABRAINS

Resembling a giant octopus with three ferocious eyes, the octabrain has massive brain matter and trifocal vision, making him a mysterious and most heinous enemy. These unsightly creatures prefer to lurk in dark and moist places, and they're also known to take to the air as easily as they dominate the depths of bodies of water. Octabrains have a penchant for pouncing suddenly into view. Then, by focusing their immense mental energy into a concentrated "emanation," an octabrain can nearly paralyze you from a single shock, shaving your health by as much as 50 percent. At close quarters, an octabrain relies on razor-sharp, serrated teeth to saw you in half. Ow!

## BATTLELORD

Each episode has one or more bosses, and the Battlelord is the first boss you'll encounter in the level known as The Abyss. A true mastodon, the Battlelord is the deadliest of all the aliens you'll encounter in the L.A. Meltdown episode. The Battlelord's sheer size is enough to scare you silly. Once you feel the impact of his over-under ripper chaingun, which also doubles as a mortar launcher, you'll be praying for shelter and seeking it like mad. A sustained attack can decrease your health at the rate of 5 to 10 percent per second. In the midst of a flurry of hot lead, the Battlelord can switch modes and launch spherical explosives at your feet.

You'd better run. You'd better hide. In short, you'd better devise a strategy before confronting the Battlelord! If you can stay alive long enough to drive home about 30 to 35 rounds with your RPG launcher, you might enjoy the spectacle of watching the massive Battlelord crumble to the ground. But be cautioned that this giant menace does *not* believe in going gently into the night.

## BATTLELORD SENTRY

A smaller version of the original Battlelord, the battlelord sentry is not quite as ferocious as his taller cousin, and is easier to kill. Still, he packs a respectable amount of firepower and should never be underestimated.

## ASSAULT COMMANDER (COMMANDER)

A massive hovering torso on a free floating antigravity deck, the assault commander is a most formidable opponent, for three main reasons. For one, in spite of his stately port, the commander can levitate and dash through the air quite gracefully. Also, he can rip you to shreds in a matter of seconds. His antigravity deck is equipped with sharp blades, and it doubles as a food processor of sorts. One of the commander's favorite methods of killing involves dropping down on his victim with the blades at full spin. Finally, the commander is extremely dangerous even at long ranges. His posterior end, for lack of a more anatomically correct term, is capable of launching deadly projectiles. Get hit by one and lose as much as 50 to 75 percent of your health (as well as most of your appetite).

The best way to defend yourself and prevail over the assault commander is to keep him at bay, dodge his incoming projectiles, and hit him with one or two RPG rounds. If you're in close quarters, you can use the shrinker to bring him down to size and then simply stomp him flat. If you don't have the RPG, the freezethrower can also be extremely effective. Blast the commander until he turns blue, and then break him into shards with a simple bullet from your handgun—or even by kicking him with your mighty foot.

## SENTRY DRONE (DRONE)

This enemy is a mindless automaton with a simple program running through its silicon-based brain: "Seek Duke Nukem and destroy him." Sporting antigravity units, sentry drones are highly maneuverable and elusive. They can hover and dart through the air at lightning speeds. Once they trace you, drones will simply dive at you at full speed, delivering an explosive charge capable of reducing your health by up to 35 percent. Drones are a lot easier to deal with when they're at a distance, where you can pepper them with the ripper chaingun until they explode. If you hear the whining pitch of a sentry's antigravity unit engaging, you'd better seek quick shelter behind a thick door, wall, pillar, or whatever. A diving drone will often crash against an obstacle in its zeal to execute its endless loop program ("Kill Duke, kill Duke . . .").

## PROTECTOR DRONE

The vicious nature of the protector drone can only be seen and fully appreciated by users of the *Atomic Edition*. Making his first appearance in The Birth, the protector drone is a tall, leathery-skinned alien with razor-sharp teeth and claws. Protector drones are surprisingly agile and sport keen reflexes, moving at amazing speeds for creatures of their size. Another aspect of their powers that makes protector drones particularly dangerous is their ability to shoot shrink rays. If you get blasted by the pulsating green shrinking rays, you'll become the size of a cockroach. Should this happen, all you can try to do is crawl away and avoid getting stepped on.

If a protector drone doesn't gut you on your feet with his incisive claws or serrated teeth, he'll simply shrink you and stomp you out like a spent cigarette butt. Heavy weapons, though, like the RPG launcher or the devastator, are effective against protector drones. Also, if you can keep it pointed at him and firing, the ripper chaingun is particularly deadly. Steady streams of bullets tend to keep protector drones dancing in one place, unable to discharge their shrinking rays or claw the flesh from your bones. If you can hit the protector drone with three or four shotgun blasts, he'll most likely collapse in his own unsavory green fluids.

## MOON ASSAULT LEADER

Sporting dual-mounted rockets on his shoulders and a fast-speed chaingun in his underside, the Moon Assault Leader is one ferocious alien beast. The heavy harness around his reptilian body holds his weapons and also protects him from injury. His sharp eyesight, lightning-quick reflexes, and a self-contained arsenal are among the top predatory characteristics distinguishing this grotesque creature. Whenever you're forced to contend with the Moon Assault Leader, you'd do well to start out with as much health and armor as you can possibly amass. Then you might not have much of a choice *but* to play a deadly cat-and-mouse game, with you relegated to the role of the rodent. Take heart, though: a combined assault of all your heavy weaponry can eventually incapacitate the Moon Assault Leader.

## CYCLOID EMPEROR (EMPEROR)

A true abomination if there ever were one, the Cycloid Emperor is a deadly, walking nightmare. This one-eyed giant is dangerous for many reasons. First, there's his lethal breath, which is capable of emanating energy blasts in rapid succession. You can be overwhelmed and outmatched in a matter of seconds, if you sustain a full-breath assault. Then there's the Emperor's built-in devastators. Just as powerful as your own devastator, the Emperor can fire charges directly from the built-in ports in his mechanical, claw-like upper extremities.

## ALIEN QUEEN

For all the agony and humiliation that human females have had to endure at the hands of their alien captors and tormentors, you'd think that, no matter how differently she might have been brought up, any other female would feel sympathetic. But that's hardly the case with the Alien Queen. Aquatic by nature, the reclusive Queen spends her time doing little else besides procreating. Not one to engage in battle directly with commoners, the Queen fights her battles through her faithful minions—protector drones that she's able to lay on demand. When you first catch a glimpse of the Queen, you might not believe your eyes. Her armored, heavy, blue body contorts with a heavy electrical discharge every time she lays another drone. In other words, for every second the queen lives, your chances grow more and more slim. Before long, you could be swimming in a soup full of protector drones. When you confront the Queen, you'll have to hit her with everything you have—as there are no more battles to be fought. Overcome her, or die fighting.

# PRESENTING ARMS

Ask anyone who's ever saved the world and they'll tell you the same thing: the right hardware and firepower make all the difference. Although you'll face what seem like insurmountable odds, when you use your weaponry diligently, it'll see you through the worst. Naturally, knowledge and mastery of your weapons affect your success rate directly. And equally important is knowing the conditions when a specific weapon is most effective.

Every time you start a new *Duke Nukem 3D: Atomic Edition* game, you enter holding only a pistol. The first order of business is to find more weaponry and ammo so that you can defend yourself and prolong your own survival. This section details each weapon you can find, as you make your way through each level. Bear in mind that some levels may not contain all the weapons at your disposal in *Duke Nukem 3D: Atomic Edition*.

## THE MIGHTY FOOT

Ironically, your first arm is your foot. Even when completely unarmed, you can still kick like a mule, or rake an enemy with your feet and sharp toenails like a kangaroo. It's possible to stomp a pig cop to death, for instance, but it sure isn't pretty. Just hope that you're not often forced into such disagreeable situations. The mighty foot also comes in handy when you simply want to bash through an air duct grill, break a window, or deliver a coup de grâce to an agonizing opponent. Until the next-best weapon comes along, isn't it comforting to know that your foot can always carry you through?

## THE HANDGUN

The smooth, metallic grip of the semiautomatic handgun is certainly more reassuring than relying solely on your mighty foot. The least powerful of all your weapons, the handgun is nevertheless a godsend when no other weapon is in sight. The handgun lets you fire 12 rounds in succession before you have to reload it. That's when you leave yourself open for a second or two.

Whenever you find a handgun, it comes fully loaded, and you have enough clips to fire 48 rounds. The clips you find are good for 12 rounds each. The maximum number of bullets you can carry is 200. You can usually finish off assault troopers and assault captains with three to five shots. A pig cop requires at least five and maybe more. Taking on an octabrain with a handgun would be rather chancy, but you can do it if you can keep a safe distance and shield yourself from its mental energy blasts.

## THE SHOTGUN

Getting hold of a shotgun lets you assert yourself with a little more authority. Your first move in any level is to find a shotgun, if you don't already have one. A proverbial workhorse, the shotgun lets you make short work of most bipedal aliens, including the protector drones. Pig cops carry shotguns. Occasionally, you might be able to wrestle a pig cop's weapon. With a shotgun, you must pump to reload every time after firing. This takes about a second, leaving you open for an instant.

Any shotgun you find comes with 10 shells, unless you retrieve one from a pig cop you've just killed, and then the number of shells depends on how many shells the pig cop fired. Shotgun ammo also comes in boxes of 10 shells. The most shells you can carry at any time is 50. If your aim is exceedingly good, you can "off" most troopers and captains and even pig cops with a single blast. Protector drones require at least three shotgun blasts before succumbing. But because of its spread, the shotgun is most effective at medium or close distances. You can knock out an octabrain with three solid shots. Recon Patrol Vehicles also make suitable targets for the shotgun. You can plunk one from the sky with about two to four good shots. The shotgun, however, is not very effective against pig cop tanks.

## THE RIPPER CHAINGUN

An excellent weapon for sweeping down hostile crowds is the ripper chaingun. Accuracy, though good to have, is not mandatory for this weapon's effectiveness. The major drawback to the ripper chaingun is, of course, its voracious consumption of ammunition. Find a ripper chaingun and use it most effectively in crowded situations. Each ripper chaingun you find comes with 50 rounds, as do its ammo cases. You can carry up to 200 rounds at once.

Secure a ripper chaingun and shred through most troopers and captains with short, concentrated one- or two-second bursts. Pig cops might require a few more rounds. The ripper chaingun is particularly effective against octabrains. With it, you can stand your ground and square off. The sustained impact of its bullets on an octabrain's pulpy flesh will keep it from mustering one of its lethal mental energy blasts. Likewise, protector drones are vulnerable to the repetitious impacts of the chaingun. Keep a protector drone dancing under ripper chaingun fire, and watch him crumble in his own green stew after a few seconds.

## THE ROCKET PROPELLED GRENADE (RPG) LAUNCHER

You can almost afford to be cocky when you score the RPG launcher. In terms of sheer explosive power, no other weapon equals the impact of an RPG projectile. Not only can you blow opponents to bits from long distances, but you can also blow holes right through some building walls—and even dig tunnels into solid rock. But for all its sheer power, the RPG launcher is rather slow in sending off its load. Avoid drawing the launcher unless you're totally ready to use it. Should you happen to hit a nearby wall or another solid object, the impact could knock you off your feet and even kill you.

Every RPG launcher you find comes with five rounds, as does each case of ammo. A single projectile is capable of rendering a crowd of aliens into gruesome confetti. The octabrain is also highly susceptible to this weapon. When you face off any of the bosses, pray you

**WARNING**

If you accidentally discharge an RPG launcher near a wall, the blast could cause you serious damage or even kill you.

have a well-stocked RPG launcher. The most ammo you can carry for this weapon tops off at 50 rounds.

## PIPE BOMB

Crude, but extremely effective, pipe bombs are a guerrilla warfare type of weapon that you can fling and detonate remotely. Nearly matching the explosive power of the RPG launcher, pipe bombs are strategic weapons. The fact that you can deto-nate them from a distance lets you set up traps for your adversaries. Here is a likely scenario: you drop a bomb, make your enemy chase you, turn a bend, and then push the detonator at the right moment. After a power-ful KA-BOOM, you might hear an unpleasant splat as alien innards spray the walls.

Pipe bombs are also ideal when you can drop them into enclosed areas where ene-mies happen to be congregated. The main disadvantage of using pipe bombs is that after deploying one, you're basically unarmed until you detonate it or draw another weapon, which well could be another pipe bomb. In fact, in certain situations you'll *want* to carpet an area with pipe bombs and detonate them all at once. Explosions of this type are quite extraordinary and peculiarly satisfying.

 **WARNING**

If you detonate a pipe bomb while you're standing nearby, you can kill yourself accidentally—and that's never fun—or seriously maim yourself. The most pipe bombs you can amass and carry at any one time is 50.

## WALL-MOUNTED LASER TRIP BOMB (LTB)

This tactical, wall-mounted device is ideal for restricting your enemies' range of move-ment. Deploy a trip bomb on a wall, and it automatically projects a sensitive laser beam onto the opposing wall or surface. Any disturbance, however slight, to the beam triggers the trip bomb's plastic explosives. You can create explosive walls by lining up trip bombs at different heights. Perhaps some-thing to consider when deploying trip bombs is that, not only are you restricting your enemy's movements, but you're restricting your  own as well. So use them judiciously. At any one time, the most trip bombs you can carry is 20.

## THE SHRINKER/EXPANDER

The double-duty shrinker/expander is a most unusual and formidable weapon. When powered by glowing green shrinker crystals, this weapon has the effect of shrinking your opponents to the size of bugs you can flatten with your foot, or crunch between your teeth (if you're that weird). Be aware, though, that the shrinker's effects last only temporarily. So immediately after using it, you should rush your shrunk opponent and squash him like a grape. When you have expander ammo, however, which looks like a clip with a small dish-antenna attached, you can turn the shrinker into an expander instantly. To toggle between the shrinker and the expander, simply press the 7 key on the keyboard. You'll see a small microwave dish on the weapon when it's set to work as an expander. Aim and fire a sustained flow of superheated microwaves to cause your enemy to swell until he explodes like a ripe pumpkin. Again, shield yourself from these violent explosions, because you too could be damaged in the unsightly blast.

## THE DEVASTATOR

A double-barreled weapon of awesome destructive power, the devastator launches explosive charges with concentrated impact. After pulling the trigger, watch the barrels' pumping action as they dish out a flurry of charges. This weapon makes short work of most enemies, including assault commanders, enforcers, and protector drones. As when using the RPG, exercise caution when firing this weapon in close quarters. The explosive charges can harm you just as much as the enemy.

>
>
> **NOTE**
>
> If you switch to a weapon for which you don't currently have ammo, Duke Nukem will automatically switch to the next less-powerful weapon that has ammunition.

## THE FREEZETHROWER

Falling under the exotic category, a freezethrower could easily turn into a workhorse, provided you find enough ammo to keep it going. When you connect with the freezethrower and shoot it, your victim's molecular structure is radically changed to ice. Of course, the tougher the opponent, the more charges it takes to turn him into ice. (Think of certain politicians or radio shock jocks.) Once the opponent is in the catatonic ice state, you can simply kick him or shoot him to break the ice without uttering a word, so to speak. Be aware that the effect of the freezethrower lasts only a few seconds, and your opponents will thaw out and act as if nothing happened.

# DUKE'S POWER-UPS

In rounding out and complementing a well-stocked arsenal, the game's power-ups—useful equipment like jetpacks and beneficial devices like atomic health units—constitute another key element to victory. Not necessarily destructive, power-ups are items and equipment that bestow special abilities on you. For instance, a jetpack is a power-up that lets you hover over the landscape. Other power-ups can give you tremendous health boosts, let you see in the dark, or allow you to traverse underwater or safely negotiate canals of flowing toxic sludge. The details for each power-up follow; and remember, always use the right tool for the job.

## MEDKITS

These come in two sizes: small and large. In addition, portable medkits are also available. The small and large medkits increase your health by 10 and 30 percent, respectively. Whenever you grab either of these two medkits, your health is increased immediately (but never to go over 100 percent).

The portable medkit carries a full 100 percent of health, which you can use to restore your health level up to 100 percent. Unlike the two smaller medkits, this item is activated and used only when you press the M key. However, each time you use it, a corresponding percentage is deducted from it to replenish your health level up to 100 percent. For example, if your health is currently at 70 percent and you press M to activate a portable medkit, your health will go up to 100 percent. The portable medkit, on the other hand, will go down to 70 percent, which is available the next time you decide to use it.

## ATOMIC HEALTH UNITS

The atomic health units look like large, glowing, blue atoms, and they're truly lucky finds. A single atomic health unit will cause your health to soar by 50 percent, even above and beyond 100 percent. The upper limit to the health you can amass with atomic health units tops off at 200 percent. In a very real sense, atomic health units give you a new lease on life and help you even-up the often ridiculous odds against surviving.

## ARMOR

An armor can make the difference between mortal or merely flesh wounds. When you slide into an armor, you are suddenly better able to absorb punishment before it takes its toll on your health. Although armors are often found in secret places, sometimes you can strip them from the bodies of dead pig cops. Just like you shouldn't engage in chancy activities without proper protection, you should always strive to wear an armor when facing your opponents. A fresh armor gives you 100 percent of protection. Armors do, however, tend to wear out with every impact you sustain. When your armor percentage goes below 50 percent, you should definitely exercise more care, and pay more attention to your defensive techniques.

## KEYCARDS

Your keycards come in the primary colors red, yellow, and blue. Although used for nothing more than opening special doors or locks, keycards are often hidden or found in remote or seemingly inaccessible places. More often than not, your strategy for solving a level includes determining what cards you need—and in what order you must have them. Without the proper card or card-combinations, many level areas will remain a mystery and completely beyond limits. To use a keycard, you simply walk up to the door in question and press the spacebar.

## STEROIDS

Like keycards, steroids are often well out of view. When you happen upon these unassuming little brown flasks, you might not be too impressed. But the pills inside pack a hell of a kick, in more ways than one. After you activate this item, which you select by pressing the [ key (right or opening square bracket) and then pressing Enter, you'll learn to appreciate the sudden rush of energy and speed. Your kick will become at least twice as powerful, and your movements will be greatly accelerated. A flask of steroids is good for about 30 seconds. So use them judiciously, and try not to abuse them. You might consider limiting their usage to fighting situations in close quarters with multiple enemies. Also, if you wish to traverse long distances in a hurry without stopping to admire the scenery or engaging many enemies, learn to rely on the power of the steroid.

## HOLODUKE

Is it real or is it holoduke? This holographic likeness of yourself is of great value as a strategic device. Like steroids and keycards, holodukes are often found in unexpected or hard-to-reach places. When you deploy the holoduke (by pressing the H key), an image of yourself is left at the spot where you stand. The holoduke has a limited life span of about 35 seconds. You can disengage it by pressing the H key a second time. After deploying it, you can hide and wait for your enemies to go after the fake Duke, thus leaving themselves open for your retaliation from the rear. You can also plant a pipe bomb at the feet of the holoduke and detonate it when your unsuspecting adversaries get near it. This is perhaps a bit sly, but after all, this war is to the death—and you didn't start it in the first place.

## JETPACK

This is perhaps the single most useful power-up anybody can ask for. With one of these babies safely strapped to your back, you can take to the air. The steel-gray jetpack gives you a most significant strategic advantage. No longer earthbound, you'll find that your options suddenly multiply. Once you find a jetpack, you can activate it by pressing the J key. Then you can ascend or descend with the A and Z keys, respectively. To turn the jetpack off, you simply press J a second time.

A new jetpack is fueled up to 100 percent, but goes down to 0 percent in about 45 seconds of continued use. With a jetpack, you can reach high places and uncover secrets that would otherwise remain a mystery. A jetpack also allows you to plot direct, short routes to certain destinations. In many cases, a jetpack can allow you to blaze

**NOTE**

Always try to reach a landing spot when your jetpack reaches the 20 percent mark.

through a level by letting you circumvent all manner of obstacles in the Earth-bound terrain.

### NIGHT VISION GOGGLES (NVG)

With a pair of these, you gain the ability to see in the dark. While your view won't be as good as in daylight, you will certainly gain a clear advantage over opponents and aliens lurking in the darkness. After scoring the NVG, you can turn them on by pressing the N key. The 100 percent mark goes down to 0 percent in about 35 seconds. Save the NVG by pressing the N key a second time.

### SCUBA GEAR

There's simply no way you can get through some levels without going under-water—and sometimes for extended periods. Once you obtain the scuba gear, it becomes active whenever you submerge. Like other power-ups, the scuba gear's 100 percent load decreases as you use it. A fresh set of tanks is good for about 45 seconds.

### PROTECTIVE BOOTS

Although not exactly fashionable footwear, a pair of protective boots are a lot more than mere galoshes. They can keep you from coming into direct contact with the toxic liquids and chemicals that circulate through many game levels, as if through the poisoned veins of a hopeless junky. Like the scuba gear, your pro-tective boots are smart. They know when to turn on and off.

# READING THE ONLINE MAPS

As you begin to navigate in ever more complex levels of *Duke Nukem 3D: Atomic Edition*, you'll find the online maps to be quite handy in showing you around a given installation or area. The online maps are available in two modes: first, as overhead line maps that you can superimpose over the actual area where you're moving; and, second, as textured maps that completely block the view of your immediate surroundings. The line map only shows the dividing lines between the installation's various rooms and areas. The textured map shows additional installation details, such as the surface qualities of rocky terrain, liquid expanses, and concrete or metallic areas. Here's how the map modes work:

- To view the overhead line map, simply press the Tab key once.

- To view the textured map, press the Tab key a second time.

- To get back to the normal view, press the Tab key a third time.

Once you're displaying an online map, you can size it to your needs by pressing the - (hyphen or minus sign) key or the + (plus sign) key on the keyboard.

While you're viewing the textured map, you can choose to continue moving, and the map will show your movement and progress. However, if you're moving while viewing the textured map, you won't be able to view your enemies and counter their vicious onslaughts. If you wish to explore the map on screen and be able to scroll around and blow up different sections without moving physically in the level, you can turn off the Follow mode. Just press the F key while watching the map on screen. Use the arrow keys and - and + to scroll and zoom in and out of map sections. Press the F key a second time to turn Follow mode back on.

# Mapping Out Strategy and Winning

Just how does one become a winner? There's always the self-help book route . . . or the lottery. And then there's true discipline plus a fiery passion for what you do. Duke falls in with the latter group, and his motivations are not solely for personal gain. This time Duke is looking further than the self. He is contemplating the delicate and perilous balance by which humanity's fate can be decided—one way or another. The two sections in this chapter cover:

- Fighting solo
- Using the level maps

Fighting Solo describes a few skills and techniques that any serious player should master. Using the Level Maps shows you how easy and intuitive a process it is to read the level maps you'll see for each level in Part II of this book.

## FIGHTING SOLO

Most players will experience single-player fighting before playing in DukeMatch or Co-Op modes, and there's a good reason for this. You'll want to hone your skills before duking it out with the big boys. To be not just a good, but a superior solo player, you must master:

- Moving with agility
- Fighting with grace
- Exploring with intelligence

## MOVING WITH AGILITY

Your chances for overcoming your opponents are directly related to how well you can move in your virtual environment. Naturally, being fleet of foot and light on your toes will allow you to elude your attackers and retaliate with impunity. After learning the basics of getting from point A to point B, you should inject speed into your movements by pressing Shift in conjunction with the other keys.

### Side Stepping and Strafing

You side step and strafe to dole out punishment and then take shelter quickly behind a wall or other inanimate object. Side stepping is also very important when you come around corners or sudden turns. When you side step around a corner, you'll be in a better position to fire your weapon accurately. The *last* thing you want to happen is to be blindsided by an incoming projectile. Recall that you use the Alt key and either ← or → to side step.

### Strategic Movement

Good gaming strategy dictates that you learn to take advantage of your full range of motion. You can look up and down with the PgUp and PgDn keys, and you can look to either side with the Insert and Delete keys, no matter where you are in any level. Use the A and Z keys to jump and duck, respectively. There'll be many opportunities to duck behind a counter, only to jump up and surprise your enemies.

Be aware that you're not the only one who can duck. Pig cops will routinely drop to the ground and aim up at you. When this happens, you too should drop to the ground and beat the pig cop to the trigger.

As for jumping, in certain situations, especially if you don't have a jetpack, you'll have to hop onto crates, elevated surfaces, and even wall indentations to reach high places. Put all your movements together, and soon they'll become second nature.

The 180-degree turn is also a very useful technique to master. For example, you can use it as an offensive strategy against an opponent who is chasing you. As you are running away, hit the Backspace key to execute a smooth 180-degree turn, and you'll suddenly be staring at your pursuer down the barrel of your weapon.

## FIGHTING WITH GRACE

Fighting gracefully is never easy. It takes skill and hours of practice. But it can be done. Just what is involved in fighting with grace? It turns out that the most graceful and effective fighters are those who are intimately acquainted with their arsenal, know their opponents as they know themselves, and can master the rudiments and elements of their environment.

### Get the Heavy Weapons

Whenever you start a new game, your first concern should be to find a respectable weapon. This doesn't mean the pistol is inconsequential. In fact, it's an extremely useful weapon when shooting at mid-range or long-range targets. But your pistol will seem ineffective when you're confronting enemies in close range—especially enemies who can fire rapidly, like enforcers and the Battlelord.

You'll fare much better against these kinds of enemies when you are able to score a shotgun. Make the shotgun your workhorse. Of course, be aware that after firing a shot, you must take a second to reload. Seek shelter when loading your shotgun. Once you obtain a Devastator, a shrinker/expander, or the exotic freezethrower, you can become quite formidable. But, all the same, don't get overly dependent on these weapons because they are not very common and their ammo does not come quite so readily. Also, they are most useful in specific situations. For example, don't pull out your RPG launcher in a long, narrow hallway; more than likely, its explosive power will injure you severely or kill you on the spot.

## Know Your Enemy

Every opponent you face has strengths and weaknesses. Learn to minimize the former and exploit the latter:

- Assault troopers, for instance, aren't exactly very bright or quick. Their hovering ability gives them a clear advantage, but if your aim is good and you're quick on the trigger, they're as good as sitting ducks.

- Assault captains have a device that lets them teleport at will. When in their presence (or absence), back into a corner or against a wall so that they're forced to appear within your field of vision.

- Pig cops know only one way of fighting, and that's going forward. Learn to use a tough pig cop's own single-minded quality against him. The strafing technique pays handsome dividends. Lure the pig cop. Turn a quick corner, or hide behind a wall or an object, and then take a side step and shoot. Two or three shotgun blasts usually do the trick.

- Recon patrol vehicles (RPVs), the pig cops' preferred mode of hovering transportation, are cause for concern because the highly maneuverable crafts can hover and dart about with great agility. The shotgun and particularly the chaingun work well in bringing RPVs to the ground. Then you can get back to your side stepping and strafing for dealing with any pig cop who survives.

- Enforcers are a different beast altogether. Their rapid-fire ripper chainguns are nothing you want to step in front of for very long. Their heavy armors also make them quite hardy. Couple that with their leaping ability, and you can see why you don't want to engage enforcers in the open. Whenever you find yourself in their unpleasant company, look for objects that you can use as shields (walls, panels, crates, rocks, or anything else). Then strafe and deliver your response. The shotgun is the weapon de rigueur when it comes to enforcers.

- Octabrains are very dangerous indeed. With their hovering ability and debilitating mental energy blasts, they can inflict great harm even from a distance. However, you're faster and more supple of movement. By far the quickest way to dispose of them is to use the RPG launcher or the Devastator, but you can also save the exotic weapons for more critical moments. If you're good at strafing, you can take on an octabrain at mid-range with nothing more than your shotgun. Side step out of the way of their mental energy blasts, deliver three solid shotgun blasts, and the octabrain will collapse like a deflated hot-air balloon.

- Sentry drones are susceptible when you first spot them at a distance and their servo motors haven't homed in on you yet. The relative rapid fire and wide range of the Devastator will come in quite handy when dealing with these mechanical simpletons whose tiny silicon brains are programmed for self-sacrifice in the interest of your early demise.

- Protector drones can really test your reflexes. Speed is your best ally when confronting the leaping, leathery figure of the protector drone. Avoid his sharp claws, and don't let him hit you with shrink rays or you're as good as a bug on a windshield. You can overcome protector drones with rapid-fire weapons like the Devastator and the less powerful ripper chaingun. The freezethrower and the shrinker/expander are also made to order for protector drones—*if* you can catch them from a reasonable distance.

The ripper chaingun is another choice weapon for dealing with many a cantankerous octabrain. Keep the octabrain squarely in your sights, and squeeze the ripper chaingun's trigger until the beast is riddled with hot lead. A sustained ripper chaingun attack will keep the octabrain from working up its thunderous mental blasts. The freezethrower is also quite effective against octabrains. Once an octabrain becomes an ice statue, switch to the handgun and shatter the beast out of existence with a single coup de grâce.

If you're suddenly overcome by several octabrains in close quarters, then look to the shrinker to save the day. You'll probably sustain some injuries, but if you were to rely on other weapons at close range, you might be damaged even more severely. Use the shrinker to reduce your opponents to size, and then stomp them with your mighty foot. When using the shrinker, you want to rush your opponent as you unload a charge. As though it had a mind of its own, your mighty foot knows what to do and will instinctively stomp the little devils into nasty stains on the floor.

The bosses for each episode, however, are not overcome so simply. Because this book covers only The Birth, our focus is on the ultimate boss: the alien queen. The finer points of strategy are almost completely wasted on the alien queen. You can only overcome the queen to the extent that you can keep her in your sights and hit her with every available weapon before she procreates as if there's no tomorrow. And procreate she will, laying fetal protector drones that spring into action after only a second or two.

## Master the Rudiments of the Environment

The other aspect of the formula for fighting with grace involves a natural feel for the assortment of terrain you'll be traversing. Every level in The Birth offers a wide variety of architectures—from the whimsical Babe Land theme park, to the arid outdoor scenes in Area 51, or the tight corridors of Shop-N-Bag. The more familiar you are with the particular trappings of the terrain, the better you can deal with the alien menace. Throughout many levels, you'll run into passive explosive devices, such as fire extinguishers or C-9 canisters. When a group of aliens is unlucky enough to be standing next to such devices, shoot the canisters and then take cover from the flying alien viscera.

Often, even a simple elevator can help you overcome serious adversity. Whenever you board an elevator, you don't know what could be waiting for you at the end of the ride. If it's something unpleasant—and often it is—you'll want to stay in the elevator and reach for a pipe bomb. As soon as the elevator door opens, throw the pipe bomb outside and close the door immediately. As the elevator takes you back to your starting point, feel free to detonate the bomb. A variation on this technique is to open an elevator and drop a pipe bomb or two. Then activate the elevator to make it go up or down (whichever way it happens to go). When the elevator reaches its destination, detonate the pipe bombs to clear the way for you before you actually get on and ride it, with a big fat smile on your face.

Your biggest allies, by far, are the walls, rocks, and other surfaces that surround you. There are times when you should face nasty situations head on, but the line between bravery and insanity gets ever so fine so very quickly, particularly when your ego's as big as Duke's. Just remember that there's more at stake here than your own pride. Use walls, rocks, and other surfaces as shields. Use the time to plot a path or strategize a course of action. Sometimes retreating is *not* totally dishonorable. Regroup, and then come back with a vengeance.

## EXPLORING WITH INTELLIGENCE

Given the diversity and the types of ground you'll be covering, you must make the most of every sense and take in as much information about your whereabouts as possible. Learn to identify switches, and look for areas that might be obvious (and not so obvious) hiding places. Many compartments and secret doors can be found throughout almost every level. Often, a locked gate or a force field is linked to a switch in a remote part of the installation. Begin to see and anticipate what the mechanical and electronic devices do in each level. Frequently, monitors are placed next to important switches. Look at the monitor before and after pressing a switch to find out if you were successful in removing a barrier.

When you spot visible cracks on walls, rocks, and other surfaces, it usually means that you can blow a hole through them with a pipe bomb or the RPG launcher. The Devastator is also capable of punching holes through certain surfaces. You can count on finding useful items in holes or tunnels you happen to unearth when you blow up these surfaces.

Use the security monitoring systems for your cause. Prying eyes watch you at almost every step. Most levels are wired with a network of cameras and monitors. Whenever you see a monitor, it's always a good idea to walk up to it and press the spacebar. This way, you'll gain access to cameras spread throughout the level. Look for power-ups and weapons, as well as for possible enemies. Also try to look for signs that might identify where the particular chamber you are looking at is found. Ask yourself: Is it a big or small chamber? Are there any keycards visible? What aliens might lurk there?

Be sure to activate your overhead map when necessary. (Just press Tab once.) Switch to the textured map by pressing Tab a second time. Identify the areas where you've already been, and try to determine where you should go next. If a certain area is barred by a security latch requiring a keycard, notice what color the keycard should be. And then attempt to find it.

# USING THE LEVEL MAPS

With only a few exceptions, every level description in Part II, "Duking It Out," has two maps to help guide you along the way. The first map is a textured representation of the level's layout or floor plan, showing you the main areas of interest as well as a prominent route to follow. The marked route closely follows the recommended route that's described in detail in each *Blazing through . . .* section. The second map is a wire frame, or line map, of the level's layout that also shows the locations of significant weapons, ammo, power-ups, and keycards. When you put together the information from each level's set of maps, you should have a very good idea of what you must do to get where you need to go.

## THE ROUTE MAPS

The textured route maps provide you with essentially three types of information for each level: its different types of terrain, a recommended route from its starting point to its exit, and the locations of key switches that open up or unlock certain areas. As you can see in Figure 4.1, the map's textures reflect the types of terrain you'll be traveling as you make your way through the level. For instance, rocky terrain, smooth surfaces,

**FIGURE 4.1:** Use the textured maps to identify prominent level features and to find out the route to follow.

air ducts, and even toxic canals and water pools can be readily made out on the textured maps.

The recommended route to follow appears as a *solid line* when you're traveling along a more or less level surface. A *dashed line* along the path indicates areas you must climb, whether it's along a slope, up a stairway, or by riding an elevator or a moving platform. A *dotted line* along the path, by contrast, indicates areas you must descend, as when you're going downstairs or jumping from a high place to a lower area.

To make the map as easy to read as possible, significant locations and items are identified liberally with descriptive labels. In particular, the locations of security locks that can only be opened with the keycards are each identified by the keycard's color initial—B for blue, R for red, or Y for yellow—within a triangle. This tells you which keycard you'll need to use to open a latch for a door or gate, giving you access to areas otherwise out of reach.

## THE LINE MAPS

The second map in each level's set represents a wire frame, or line drawing, of the level's overall layout. The main purpose of this map is to point out the general locations of the more significant weapons, ammunition, and power-ups that you can get hold of as you battle your way to the level's exit. Each item is identified with a label, as you can see in Figure 4.2. These maps also reveal the locations of the often-crucial keycards that are necessary to access areas vital to your successfully completing the level.

SEE

For more details on playing DukeMatch or Co-Op modes, see Appendix B, "Multiplayer Tips and Online Resources."

**FIGURE 4.2:** Use the line maps to identify weapons, ammo, and power-ups.

PART II

# Duking It Out

It doesn't take a certified psychic friend to guess you know and appreciate a good action game. Especially if that game also engages your mind and dazzles your eye. Perhaps that's why you choose to play *Duke Nukem 3D: Atomic Edition*. (Perhaps there's other—maybe deeper—reasons.) Whatever the case, this part of the book lays out the information you need to confront all four of the Atomic Edition episodes:

- Chapter 5: L.A. Meltdown
- Chapter 6: Lunar Apocalypse
- Chapter 7: Shrapnel City
- Chapter 8: The Birth

# L.A. Meltdown

L.A. Meltdown is the introductory episode in Duke Nukem's latest and most demanding adventure. At the conclusion of *Duke Nukem II*, our hero had beaten the Rigelatins and deflated their dreams to enslave humanity. Against all odds, Duke had managed to destroy the invaders' interstellar ship and get away in a stolen vessel. Expecting a hero's welcome, Duke is instead nearly blown out of the sky as he enters L.A. airspace.

Apparently, during the time Duke was kidnapped, another wave of malevolent aliens arrived, storming the town and terrorizing the citizenry. Once again, it's up to Duke to save the day (or at least his own skin) and maybe learn more about the aliens' questionable motives, which clearly involve scores of young human females, who are turning up all over town in strange cocoons. They are still alive, but understandably, they are not very cheery.

There are six levels in L.A. Meltdown. (One of these is a secret level, accessible only if you can find the special secret exit within one of the other levels.) With levels built in and around Los Angeles, L.A. Meltdown places you in a wide assortment of backdrops and terrain. Early on, you'll find yourself in the midst of urban and moral decay as you traverse Hollywood Holocaust and penetrate deep inside The Red Light District. Later on, just minutes away, you'll be doing time in the prison island of Death

Row. Your reward for escaping Death Row? How about a tour of the Toxic Dump's drum processing plant and its perilous canyons and underwater passages. And then there's the Launching Facility, complete with a rocket to the moon. Near the end of the episode, you'll be in the desert, hiking along tenuous mountainside trails, overlooking deep canyons, or crawling in long, dark, and moist caverns as you seek to uncover the buried secret of The Abyss.

# HOLLYWOOD HOLOCAUST

The word in the streets is that the streets aren't safe for anyone anymore. Sure, things weren't exactly peachy before the aliens' arrival. After all, this is L.A. in the mid twenty-first century. But since the aliens landed and began encasing human females in sticky cocoons and murdering anyone who stood in their way, the situation has degenerated considerably.

A wise woman once said, "Before you can walk, you must crawl." Hollywood Holocaust gives you every opportunity to crawl until you find your footing and introduces you to Duke Nukem's interactive, futuristic, and perilous 3D environment. Use this level to get acquainted with many of the architectural constructs you will find later. Also, if you can find one or both RPG launchers, the jetpack, and the pipe bombs, you'll be eternally grateful in the next level.

## MAPS AND ROUTE

In spite of being the first *Atomic Edition* level, Hollywood Holocaust's design is deceivingly simple, as shown in Figure 5.1. But as you are about to experience, solving this level is anything but simple. However, if you prevail, you can collect a sizable cache of goodies to fortify yourself for The Red Light District, as you can see in Figure 5.2.

**FIGURE 5.1**: Welcome to Hollywood Holocaust with its promise of infamy and misfortune.

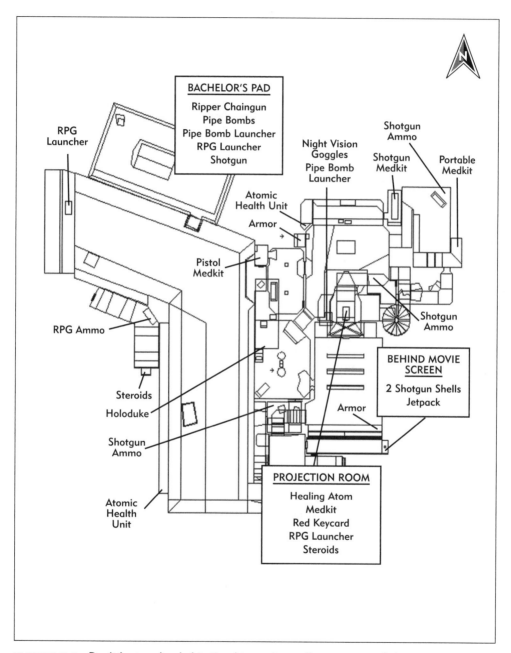

**FIGURE 5.2:** Don't be too dazzled in tinsel-town, just collect as many of these items as you can to build up your arsenal.

## THE GOODS

Table 5.1 shows a rundown of the items you might be able to collect in Hollywood Holocaust. A jetpack can help you get to a nice cache of weapons in this level.

| TABLE 5.1: THE GOODS IN HOLLYWOOD HOLOCAUST | | |
|---|---|---|
| **WEAPONS** | **AMMO** | **POWER-UPS** |
| 2 shotguns | 7 cases | 1 portable medkit |
| 1 ripper chaingun | 0 case | 3 atomic health units |
| 3 RPG launchers | 1 case | 2 armors |
| 2 pipe bomb cases | | 2 steroid flasks |
| | | 1 jetpack |
| | | 1 NVG |
| | | 1 holoduke |

## BLAZING THROUGH HOLLYWOOD HOLOCAUST

Here's how you can complete this level as soon as superhumanly possible and experience a definite adrenaline rush. (Do not attempt the following if you are on any medication.) Start the *Atomic Edition*; select New Game, the L.A. Meltdown episode, and the Let's Rock skill level; and get ready to rumble.

### On Top of the Skyscraper

♣ **Grab some ammo and hit the street.** Take the ammo behind the crate. Shoot the C-9 canisters from a safe distance, and drop down the metal chute to reach the street level.

### On the Street

1. **Get the RPG launcher.** First, jump on top of the large crate near the northwest side. From the crate, jump onto the slanted surface of the building. From the slanted surface, jump onto the small ledge on the perpendicular wall (with the "Innocent" sign). Walk on the ledge toward the sign, and an RPG launcher emerges from a secret compartment below.

2.  **Raid the secret apartment.** Jump back onto the slanted ledge, and walk over to the second window. Jump through the window, and you will be inside an apartment. Take the RPG ammo and the steroids from behind the "Biker Bimbos" poster.

3.  **Take the atomic health unit.** Exit the apartment through its southern-most window, and follow the slanted ledge of the building southward toward the atomic health.

4.  **Blast into the movie theater.** Jump back to the street and run north toward the street corner to get in position across from the movie the-ater's box office. Switch to your RPG launcher and launch a rocket into the theater's box office. Then run inside through the demolished box office wall.

Watch out for trooper snipers in the apartment at the southeast end of the street. Also, the movie theater's foyer and lobby are congregating grounds for troopers and captains. Expect to see a pig cop or two there as well.

## Inside the Theater

1.  **Score a shotgun and another atomic health unit.** Swing the lobby's doors open and raid the snack bar. Take the shotgun from the small adjacent locker room on the east side of the snack bar. Then run out to the snack bar's west side, and take the atomic health unit from behind the secret door, which should now be open.

2.  **Stop by the bathroom.** Enter the bathroom, climb over the stalls, and tear through the air duct grill. Crawl in and follow the bend 90 degrees to the right.

3.  **Make your way to the projection room.** Drop into a small, dark metallic chamber and dispose of the troopers guarding their cocooned victim. Then, feel for the secret door along the west side of the room that leads to the projection room.

4. **Storm the projection room and start a movie.** Shoot your way inside and grab the red keycard. Find and push the switch to the right of the projection window to start the evening's feature attraction.

5. **Shoot the screen.** As the curtains open and the action begins, shoot another RPG into the middle of the screen. You will blow a hole big enough to crawl through and for a very good reason, as you will soon see.

6. **Score a jetpack and some shells.** Descend into the movie room via the spiral staircase, and crawl behind the screen. Take the jetpack and the shotgun shells. Then exit through the window at the west end.

7. **Get out of Hollywood Holocaust.** Activate the jetpack and levitate onto the red-glowing corridor. Get to the exit switch and punch it.

## ADDED ATTRACTIONS IN HOLLYWOOD HOLOCAUST

You haven't seen much in Hollywood Holocaust if you haven't experienced:

- Fun and games at the theater's arcade
- A swank bachelor's apartment

### Fun and Games at the Arcade

Besides the obvious reason for entering the arcade—and you can guess what that is—there is one other compelling factor: the holoduke. This likeness of yourself can be deployed to fool your opponents into thinking it's really you. Also, if you weren't able to secure the jetpack, your only way out of Hollywood Holocaust is to go through the arcade.

Inside the theater's lobby, approach the southwest corridor toward the neon "Arcade" sign. Activate the metal elevator and surprise any enemy that could be riding in it. Usually a shell in the face does the job. Climb inside and ride the elevator to the top level. Again, be ready to unload a few rounds on the awaiting pig cop (or pig cops, depending on the skill level you chose). Before venturing forth, notice the C-9 canisters in the southeast corner of the room. Hit any of them with a bullet, and take shield as best you can. Flying guts are likely to redecorate the walls.

When the commotion dies down, enter the arcade. Walk up to the *Duke Nukem II* video-game machine and press the spacebar. A secret compartment raises to show the slightly translucent holoduke (see Figure 5.3). Take it quickly because the compartment remains open but a second or two. Then march toward the security door, and use the red keycard to open it. Have your shotgun handy. You will meet a trio of pig cops in succession.

As you climb the ramp of the small metallic room, the wall behind the wooden crate blows up, and you might find yourself nose-to-

> **TIP**
> Avoid a nose-to-snout confrontation with a most unfriendly pig cop as you leave the arcade. Duck behind the crate and stand up only to unload the shotgun.

snout with a most unfriendly pig cop. You might want to duck behind the crate and stand up only to shoot your weapon. With the pig cop out of the way, proceed into the narrow dark corridor. Shoot directly at the red, beady eyes shining in the far corner. It's another pig cop. If you hit the fire extinguisher behind him, you will make short work of him.

**FIGURE 5.3:** Move quickly if you want to grab the holoduke before the compartment closes.

Now all you have to do is open one more latch, walk onto the metal bridge, and face off any other pig cops, assault troopers, or assault captains that are still alive. Then you can choose to check out the swank apartment next, or simply run straight for the level's exit.

### The Swank Apartment over the Movie Theater

There is a cushy third-floor apartment above and to the right of the movie theater's marquee. While you don't have to visit this cool bachelor pad to solve this level, there are some compelling reasons to consider dropping in. For one thing, there is some impressive booty in there: one ripper chaingun, an RPG launcher, a case of ammo for it, and some pipe bombs. Besides that, you can kick back on the soft couch, enjoy a dry martini, and even take in a titillating clip on the television. You can access the apartment in one of two ways:

- With the jetpack
- Through deft footwork and precise jumping

**USING THE JETPACK** The simplest way to reach the secret apartment involves using the jetpack. This means that you must first get it if you don't already have it. (The jetpack is hidden behind the movie screen. You have to blow a hole in it to reach the other side.) Once you have it, simply get near the tall palm tree to the right of the theater and activate it. Ascend to the third story, by the marquee, and go in right through the window. Enjoy the amenities.

**USING DEFT FOOTWORK AND PRECISE JUMPING** To reach the apartment in this manner, you have no choice but to visit the arcade first. (See *Fun and Games at the Arcade*, on page 64.) If you haven't been able to get the jetpack, this is, in fact, the only way to reach the cozy cove. But you must also possess the red keycard to be able to unlock a special latch in the arcade. The red keycard is inside the projection room. After taking care of business in the arcade, and exiting via the door with the red key latch, be prepared to trade shotgun blasts with a few pig cops.

As you emerge onto the bridge leading directly to the level's exit, drop carefully onto the narrow ledge that skirts the building and ends right by the theater's marquee. Hug the wall and follow it as it turns 90 degrees to the west and then makes another 90 degree turn to the north. Stop in front of the palm tree. Then aim your sights up, and jump so that you land right on top of the tree. Turn to face the building, and jump straight through the window. (Figure 5.4 shows you these locations.) Once inside, relax for a few seconds, check out the goods, and don't forget to collect the weapons.

## COVERT DETAILS

Table 5.2 lists a complete rundown of the secrets in Hollywood Holocaust.

| TABLE 5.2: THE SECRETS IN HOLLYWOOD HOLOCAUST | | |
|---|---|---|
| AREA IN LEVEL | SECRET ITEM | HOW TO GET IT |
| The Walk of Fame | RPG launcher | A secret compartment below the "Innocent" graffiti emerges as you approach it. |
| | steroids | These are behind the poster in the second-story, west side apartment. |
| | shotgun ripper chaingun RPG launcher pipe bombs | A swank bachelor's apartment above and to the right of the theater's marquee is where you will find this weapons bonanza. |

*(Continued on next page)*

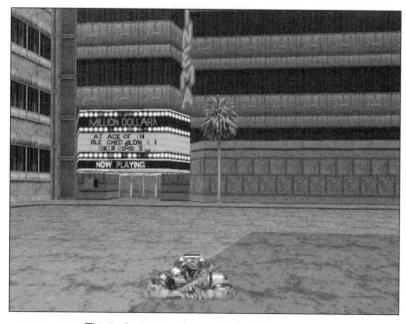

**FIGURE 5.4:** This is the way to the swank apartment.

*(Continued from previous page)*

| AREA IN LEVEL | SECRET ITEM | HOW TO GET IT |
|---|---|---|
| The movie theater | pipe bombs | These are in a secret compartment above the trash can by the elevator to the arcade. |
| | armor | This item is in a hidden elevated chamber on the west side of the main lobby. Open the chamber by activating the cash register behind the snack bar. Then stand on a receding (unseen) pillar below and slightly to the right of the chamber and press the spacebar to activate it. |
| | RPG launcher | Behind a secret wall on the west side of the projection room is where you will find it. This wall raises when you jump on top of the projector to grab an atomic health unit. |
| | a secret wall that opens | The secret wall is at the southwest corner of the projection room. The adjoining room is a dark metallic chamber with a female in a cocoon. The chamber is also accessible through an air duct on the east side that connects it to the theater's bathroom. |
| | jetpack shotgun shells | These are behind the movie screen. |

# THE RED LIGHT DISTRICT

As with all major cities in the world, L.A., too, has its seedy side. And you are about to witness it in some graphic detail. Complete with an adult bookstore and peep-shows, The Red Light District offers many attractions for the seeker of fleshly delights. But beware of everyone you meet, for many pack a trick or two up their skirt. (By the way, you might want to get some cash before entering the district. Tipping is heavily encouraged.) This level introduces a new addition to your enemies' arsenal, the recon patrol vehicle (RPV).

With its many side attractions and surplus of temptations, it would be easy to lose one's head in The Red Light District. Definitely more physically demanding than Hollywood Holocaust, this level will surely test your stamina. Your chances to make it through The Red Light District are high as long as you move swiftly in the open spaces and very carefully when there isn't as much leg room. To solve this level, you must acquire all the keycards in a specific order: blue, yellow, and red. To get the yellow keycard, you must first demolish the condemned building on which it sits. A final word or two—if you don't have a jetpack when you reach the area behind the curtain in the gentleman's club, you will have to draw open the curtains and endure a good ol' fashion barroom brawl.

## MAPS AND ROUTE

The Red Light District offers many distractions indeed. But don't get too distracted because your enemies will die trying to prevent you from getting to the floor show. On the route map shown in Figure 5.5, notice the locations of the special latches that require the blue, yellow, and red keycards to unlock them. The keycards' locations are shown on the map in Figure 5.6. The blue keycard gives you access to a detonation switch, and the yellow and red keycards provide you access to the bar and floor show areas.

## THE GOODS

Table 5.3 shows a rundown of the items you might score in The Red Light District.

| TABLE 5.3: THE GOODS IN THE RED LIGHT DISTRICT | | |
| --- | --- | --- |
| WEAPONS | AMMO | POWER-UPS |
| 2 shotguns | 3 cases | 1 portable medkit |
| 2 ripper chainguns | 1 case | 4 atomic health units |
| 1 RPG launcher | 3 cases | 2 armors |
| 3 pipe bomb cases | | 2 steroid flasks<br>1 jetpack<br>3 NVGs<br>2 holodukes |

## BLAZING THROUGH THE RED LIGHT DISTRICT

Ready for some fast action? You've come to right place. Can you handle the hard and fast lane ahead? Do your best to keep up. Of course, nothing prevents you from exercising your freedom of choice. Feel free to wander, explore, and take a few risks.

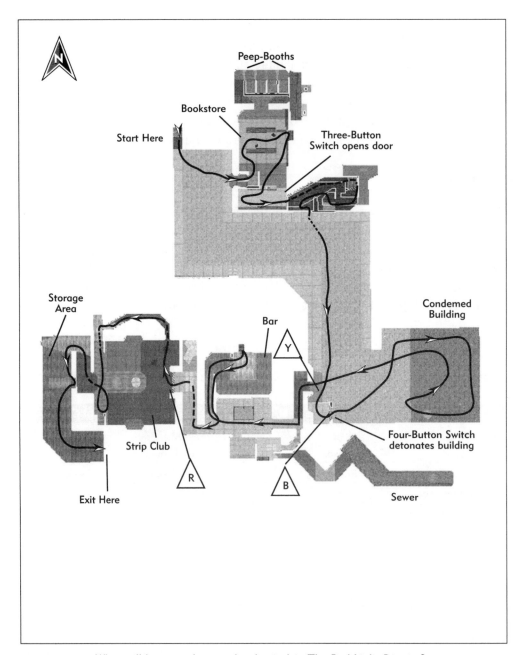

**FIGURE 5.5:** What will be your pleasure (or demise) in The Red Light District?

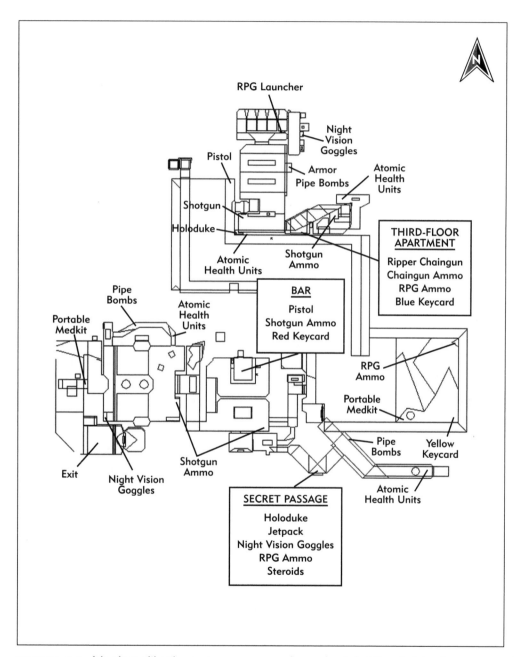

**FIGURE 5.6:** It's places like these your mom warned you about, but there's lots of weapons and power-ups to gather.

## In the Bookstore

1. **Head for the bookstore.** The second you come out of the elevator, run straight for the bookstore's entrance to your left. Do not waste time engaging the pig cop on the hovering recon patrol vehicle (RPV). It's almost always a loosing battle. Also, beware that standing on the other side of the steel door is another pig cop. Pour lead into his countenance the second you see the red of his eyes.

2. **Search for good material.** After looking over the good material, open the secret door behind the magazine rack, and take the armor and pipe bombs. Also raid the area behind the counter for a shotgun (by the monitor) and the atomic health unit on top of the magazine racks. While you're reaching for the atomic health unit, push against the corner where the magazine racks converge and uncover the holoduke behind the secret compartment.

3. **Access the upstairs alcove.** Activate the two outside switches on the east wall to unlock the red door, and proceed into the dark, sloping corridor. Guarding off the troopers creeping in the dark, run to the elevator at the end of the hall, and ride it to the alcove upstairs.

4. **Get more goods and go.** Take the RPG ammo on top of the mattress and look behind the small compartment in the wall for the blue keycard. Chop down the troopers in the adjacent room, and take the ripper chaingun rounds. From the window in this room, take pot shots at the RPVs and the troopers outside and across the street. When you've softened them up a bit, jump out the window and onto the wide avenue below.

## On the Main Avenue

1. **Access the 3D Realms Demolition quarters.** Run toward the south end and enter the small partition along the building labeled "3D Realms Demolition." Shoot your way in, right through the awaiting pig cop.

2. **Uncover the combination switches.** Activate the blue keycard reader to reveal two circular switches on each of its sides.

3. **Use the right combination.** Activate the two inside switches to uncover a detonator switch. Push it and watch the condemned building across the street crumble to the ground.

> **TIP**
> The bookstore is another known hangout for alien troopers, pig cops, and captains. Use doors and video shelves for protection. Often, you can surprise your opponents by jumping on top of the shelves and shooting down at them.

4. **Collect the yellow keycard, ammo, and a portable medkit.** Run out into the rubble and collect more RPG ammo, the yellow keycard, and a portable medkit.

5. **Enter 3D Realms Demolition's headquarters.** Use your newly acquired yellow keycard to open the latch that unlocks the metal door to 3D Realms Demolition's headquarters.

> **TIP**
> Don't be too hasty to run over to the rubble in search of the yellow keycard. It could be your undoing. Wait until the explosive charges go off completely before rushing out.

## Inside the 3D Realms Demolition Building

1. **Check out the bar.** Go up the ramp, past the pool table, and take a right into the bar.

2. **Duck for the red keycard.** Open the secret door behind the bar, and crawl inside to grab the red keycard.

3. **Head for the floor show and into the duct.** With the red keycard in hand, enter the floor show area. Find the air duct near the northeast corner, blow it open, and jump inside by climbing a nearby table (see

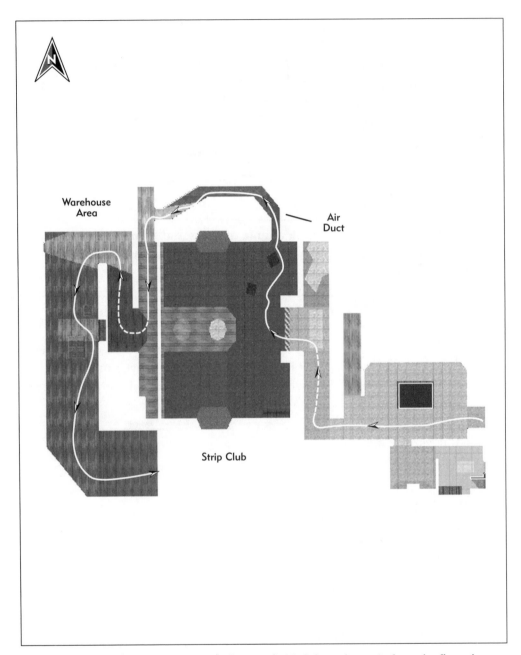

**FIGURE 5.7**: Use the air duct to reach the area behind the red curtain from the floor show.

Figure 5.7). Drop into the narrow corridor below to reach the area behind a large red curtain.

4. **Elevate to freedom?** Activate the jetpack to reach the platform above. Go around to the south into a warehouse-like space with an angular ceiling and a few wooden crates. Battle a few obstinate pig cops around the crates. Then run around the bend to locate the exit switch. Now get ready to do a little bit of time as you await your turn on death row.

## ADDED ATTRACTIONS IN THE RED LIGHT DISTRICT

For all the cheap thrills one might experience in The Red Light District, it goes without saying that there's a heavy price to pay. This section highlights some of the tough encounters you might have. It also describes areas you might want to visit if you just can't get enough. Get ready to:

- Take in a peep show or two.

- Square off in the bar and take the red keycard.

- Cause a serious commotion in the floor show.

### Catching a Sneak Peek at the Peep Show

If you never as much as walked into an adult bookstore before because you felt self-conscious or embarrassed, don't worry. Besides stocking a wide variety of magazines and videos, the bookstore also has a discreet row of peep stalls in the back, where you might enjoy a few private screenings. Not only that, but you will be able to lay your hands on a choice piece of hardware, a loaded RPG launcher.

After taking the armor and pipe bombs behind the secret magazine rack, head toward the north end of the bookstore. Turn quickly to the right side as you cross the threshold and dispense with the awaiting pig cop. Then turn your attention to the west side of the hallway. As you come around the corner, pounce on the pig cop. Turning eastward now, clear the way of assault troopers and captains lingering about. Then run to the end of the hallway, and open the door to the stall at the very end. Open the small screen and grab the RPG. If you are not easily offended by erotic sights, visit the other stalls. But beware of the occupants inside. Pig cops are known to like movies too. The best technique for emptying the stalls is to open the door, stand aside, and catch the enemy as he pokes his head out to look.

## Squaring Off at the Bar

The second you enter the bar inside the 3D Realms Demolition building, it might seem like everyone knows your name and wants you dead. Yet, you have no choice but to go in search of the red keycard. When you reach the top of the ramp, avoid stepping inside the bar right away. Instead, stand just outside, pepper the aliens with your shotgun, and then take refuge behind the wall.

After thinning out the gnarly bar crowd, throw a pipe bomb down the ramp and then rush in behind the counter. As you enter this area, you will cross a trigger that causes a few pigcops to materialize. In a few seconds, the gang of bad pig cops, hot after your trail, will make its way up the ramp. Crouch under the bottle rack and open the secret compartment. Crawl inside to grab the keycard. In the process, push the thumb-activated detonator. That should take care of at least one pig cop and damage the rest. Switch to the shotgun and hold your ground inside the little crawl space (see Figure 5.8). From this cubbyhole, shower with bullets anything that moves outside.

> **TIP**
>
> If you need a respite to gather your wits, you can close the small door to the tiny compartment. Just press the spacebar again.

Once the noise dies down, crawl out and be sure to check out the TV monitor. Remember the now infamous slow-speed chase of a particular white bronco?

## A Final Show Down in the Bloody Floor Show

The floor show in The Red Light District is nothing short of extraordinary. The instant you step in through the heavy metal door, you will see three separate stages appear. The main stage emerges from the floor and dominates the center of the room. Two side stages descend from the ceiling. As with many other danger areas, it's always best to proceed cautiously. Rather than running in and risking an ambush, open the door and pick off as many troopers and pig cops as you can from the outside.

Once it's safer to venture in, find the air duct in the northeast corner of the room, blow it open, and jump inside. Follow the duct to the end. You will run into another

**FIGURE 5.8:** Crawl into the small compartment below the bar for protection and to grab the red keycard.

grill. Tear through it, and then drop a pipe bomb into the narrow space below and detonate it. Repeat the procedure if necessary. You want to blow up the vicious pig cops in the confined space before you jump down from the duct. When you do jump down, switch to the RPG launcher and aim up at the pig cop on top of the large platform. If you have the jetpack, you'll be able to avoid a nasty scene. Simply activate it, reach the top of

> **TIP**
>
> Anytime you can confront your opponents indirectly, such as from behind walls or to one side of an entrance to a room, you stand a better chance of dodging enemy fire. Strafing across, you can also unload your own offensive.

the platform, and proceed around the corner into a darkened warehouse. After a final turn, you'll be facing what appears to be the exit switch.

However, if you don't have the jetpack, you'll have to draw the curtains open. The only problem with that is that the floor show area will be repopulated with scores of pig cops. With that in mind, approach the switch at the south end of the corridor and

> ## WARNING
>
> Be warned against getting too physical with the dancers. Tipping is encouraged and accepted, but if you dare to shoot a dancer—accidentally or not—you will pay dire consequences. Every time a dancer dies, a captain and a trooper materialize on the scene.

activate it. As the curtains begin to draw open, engage the RPG launcher and slaughter as many pig cops as you can. You can also run to the north side of the corridor (it's best to avoid the main floor, for as long as you can) and throw pipe bombs into the moshing pig cops.

Eventually, climb the main stage, face the west side, and take a flying jump onto the elevated platform. Then simply follow the path to the exit. But don't be terribly disappointed when you find yourself captive at the end of this level.

## COVERT DETAILS

The secrets of The Red Light District are exposed for all to see in Table 5.4.

| TABLE 5.4: THE SECRETS IN THE RED LIGHT DISTRICT | | |
|---|---|---|
| **AREA IN LEVEL** | **SECRET ITEM** | **HOW TO GET IT** |
| The bookstore | holoduke | This item can be found in the secret compartment behind the counter and above the magazine racks, at the southwest corner. |
| | armor and pipe bombs | These items are behind the middle bookshelf on the east side. |
| The demolished building | atomic health | This healthy find is in the sewer, underneath the manhole cover. |
| The strip bar | ripper chaingun | This handy weapon is behind the north side stage. |
| | pipe bombs | You will find these in the air duct at the northeast corner. |
| | NVG | These are on top of a metallic box at the southwest end of the main floor and behind the massive curtain. |
| The crate area | portable medkit | This item is behind the secret compartment along the east wall, right by the wooden crates. |

| AREA IN LEVEL | SECRET ITEM | HOW TO GET IT |
|---|---|---|
| Bathroom near bar | steroids holoduke jetpack | Push against the secret door behind the toilet. It opens into a ramp that descends into a toxic sewer. The goods rest near some pipes on the right side. |

# DEATH ROW

You open your eyes in Death Row only to be momentarily blinded by a sudden and painful electrical jolt. Collecting your wits and taking stock of your surroundings, you notice you're the center piece in an execution room. The rigid chair you're on is anything but inviting. (The last thing you recall is when the aliens took you prisoner at the conclusion of your Red Light District tour of duty.) Before enduring another blast, you jump off the chair and realize you are completely unarmed. It appears as though your seconds in Death Row are numbered. Indeed, you are trapped in a correctional facility where good behavior means absolutely nothing.

The only way out of Death Row is via an aquatic escape. You must endure a rough ride to the area known as Cell Block 2. There is said to be a tunnel there that might lead either to an awaiting submarine or a horrific death in the clutches of fierce octabrains and their alien allies. Your path through Death Row will send you on a search for all three keycards (in the order blue, yellow, and red). If you can survive the first few seconds in Death Row, you might yet have a fighting chance.

## MAPS AND ROUTE

Look over Figures 5.9 and 5.10 to help you plot your imminent jailbreak. You're at liberty to choose your own path, but the recommended route leads straight to a chance for freedom.

**FIGURE 5.9:** They say that breaking out of Death Row is hard to do.

FIGURE 5.10: Because you must start this level with nothing in your arsenal, better look for the first weapon you can find.

## THE GOODS

Don't waste your time while doing time. You can actually amass a good deal of loot, even while you are behind bars. Check out Table 5.5 for a complete list.

| TABLE 5.5: THE GOODS IN DEATH ROW | | |
|---|---|---|
| **WEAPONS** | **AMMO** | **POWER-UPS** |
| 1 shotgun | 1 case | 2 portable medkits |
| 2 ripper chainguns | 4 cases | 7 atomic health units |
| 2 RPG launchers | 2 cases | 2 armors |
| 3 pipe bombs | 1 case | 2 steroid flasks<br>1 scuba gear<br>2 NVGs<br>1 holoduke<br>1 pair of boots |

## BLAZING THROUGH DEATH ROW

All claustrophobia aside, Duke Nukem was made to roam with unbridled abandon. Dark, squalid corridors and walls, steel bars, a completely restrictive life style, and Duke simply don't mix. However, you can greatly minimize your time in the big house. Follow these steps to blaze through the Death Row level. As always, you're free to roam, but don't get caught.

### In the Execution Area

1. **Get a pistol.** Jump off the hot chair. Walk around the small control room to the east, open the door, and rush for the small compartment to get a handgun and a clip. Turn around and pelt the pig cop.

2. **Get a shotgun.** Throw the switch on the left side of the window. Jump through the window as the chair lowers to the ground. Duck inside and grab the shotgun and ammo behind the chair.

3. **Make your way out of the execution chambers.** After taking the shotgun, get back in the control room and throw the switch on the right side of the window. Then position yourself so you can aim at the awaiting

(and naturally disappointed) crowd as the curtains draw open. When everyone is dead or dying, jump over the half wall and find a narrow hallway. Run to the end of the hallway, and grab the medkit at the end.

> **TIP**
>
> You start out this level completely unarmed. And what else would you expect? You're in the big house, after all. But even worse, you start out sitting on the electric chair. If your health is failing from the beating you may have taken in The Red Light District, you might not be able to withstand more than a single charge at the chair. So get off the hot chair as quickly as you can, and not an instant too soon.

## Inside the Room with Killer Cogs

1. **Grab the atomic health and night vision goggles.** Enter the gap left by the exploding wall. Approach the smaller rotating cog. Jump, aiming for its center. Then synchronize your turning rate so you can time a second jump and reach the narrow ledge along the west wall. Take the atomic health. Crawl south along the ledge, and open a secret compartment at the very corner to bag the NVG.

2. **Collect the blue keycard and an RPG.** Jump directly onto the larger cog. Then execute a second jump onto the southeast corner. Landing on a control area, grab the RPG and the blue keycard behind the wall compartment.

3. **Get out of the cog room.** Execute a series of well-timed jumps, first onto the large cog and then onto the smaller one. Finally, at the right moment, jump back into the room's entrance and exit.

## In the Central Room and Jailhouse Courtyard

1. **Take the yellow keycard.** Enter the small circular room on the north side of the central control room. As you reach for the keycard, the side

mounted light panels slide open to reveal trip bombs. Duck under the light beams and leave the room.

2.  **Go after the red keycard.** Enter the large control room, and head for the yellow latch at the north end. Unlock the gates to the jailhouse courtyard and turn westward. You will find the red keycard at the southwest corner. Unfortunately, you will be under fire from roving pig cops in their RPVs. And if that isn't enough, you're a wide open target to the turrets strategically mounted along the north end of the courtyard.

3.  **Unlock Cell Block 2.** Back in the main control room, climb the ramp and unlock the red latch on the southeast corner. Push a second switch and gain access to the hologram room. Grab the ripper chaingun on the central platform. Then push either of the switches on the circular rotating walls of the room. When the room stops spinning, enter the small opening along the southwest side. Ascend a small ramp and enter the small room containing the switch that deactivates the force field to Cell Block 2.

### At the Northeast End

1.  **Find the tunnel in Cell Block 2.** Take the Control West exit, ascend the ramp, and find the entrance to Cell Block 2 (northeast of the room that once held the yellow keycard). Standing at the entrance to Cell Block 2, push the switch panel until the last cell opens. Rush to the cell and look behind the poster in the corner. Be careful not to fall in; you've just found the secret tunnel.

2.  **Reach the sewage line.** It turns out the tunnel is only partially excavated. You will have to drop a couple of pipe bombs to finish the job. Eventually, you will reach a toxic sewage line. Follow it northwest to an open area where you will see a submarine.

3.  **Board the sub.** You will have to dive and board it from below, so score the scuba gear before diving. It's around the south stone wall of the open area. After entering the sub, throw the periscope switch and then activate the exit switch.

## ADDED ATTRACTIONS IN DEATH ROW

They say time in the slammer hardens a person. Perhaps. You decide for yourself after experiencing:

- A moment of reflection in the prison chapel
- A bruising battle in the courtyard

### Praying Is for the Weak

Even if *pious* or *spiritual* are not words anyone would use to describe you, you might consider stopping to reflect for a minute in the jailhouse's chapel. You might not become blessed or sanctified, but you are sure to uncover some unholy secrets. If you're not totally overcome with religious fervor, you could well leave the chapel with a ripper chaingun, a few pipe bombs, and an atomic health unit.

Don't let the SILENCE, DISCIPLINE, REMORSE sign at the entrance keep you from entering. Catch the kneeling troopers and captains from behind while they are facing the altar. It helps to have an RPG launcher to better your chances, but even with a shotgun, you should be able to dispose of the few faithful in there. Approach the main altar and look above you at the tall, pointed ceiling. Shoot the hanging monk and absorb the atomic health that comes out of his body as he hits the floor.

Standing at the floor of the altar, press against the podium to activate a secret door behind the stained glass. Walk to the southernmost window, and kick it in. Go into the narrow passage, and do your very best to plant three solid shotgun blasts at the floating octabrain. Then proceed to the end of the red-lit corridor where you will find a ghastly sight—nothing less than the mangled torso of a former *DOOM* marine. Put the poor soul out of his misery, and collect the ripper chaingun behind him. Do it quickly because anything you touch here is harmful. Get back to the altar, bust the window on the right side, and grab the steroids.

The next maneuver requires impeccable timing and execution. Your goal is to reach a confined space above the chapel's entry. Notice the switch high above the altar. Stand near the middle of the room, maybe even behind the pew. Aim for the switch, and shoot it with your pistol. Then turn immediately around (or run backwards if you prefer) to stand on the narrow ascending pillar. Once at the top, crouch to reach the case of pipe bombs. Jump down and be on your way. Figure 5.11 shows the chapel's layout and your route in more detail.

### Showdown at the Courtyard

A visit to the north courtyard is inevitable. There lies the red keycard that you need to unlock Cell Block 2. However, because it is so close to the only way out, the courtyard is heavily guarded. Several pig cops patrol the area in their RPVs. A network of turrets atop an elevated area flanks the north side of the courtyard. You are also the prime target of troopers

and captains inhabiting the cell blocks that look over the courtyard along its south wall. Beside the fact that you must have the red keycard, there are other good reasons to storm the courtyard. You could build a surplus of health if you can manage to reach the secret area housing four atomic health units.

When you first open the door to the courtyard, avoid rushing out. You would only serve as a target to a mob of murderers. You will have to take the courtyard in stages. First nail the pig cops by the door. Then, adjust your aim to about 45 degrees and face the west side as you sidestep to launch a grenade at the first visible firing turret. Slide back near the door and go back inside if necessary. (Do your best to avoid engaging the RPVs.) Adjust your aim and repeat the process, sliding out of the door to hit the next turret. Turn your attention to the turrets along the east side and start again.

Without the constant threat of the turrets, you will be better able to deal with the RPVs. A useful technique against an RPV in the courtyard is to simply run away from it. Then, make a sudden 180 degree turn and fire off an RPG projectile.

If you can't wipe out every RPV, don't sweat it too much. Climb the elevated north side area. Do it by first jumping onto the slanted surface beside the closed north gate.

**TIP**

The Backspace key is a great way to turn quickly and swiftly.

Then take another short jump onto the elevated area. Again, climb the slanted surface of the central structure in the elevated area, and you will run into a secret area. Go right through the wall to find a long corridor with a line of atomic health units and take them. Get back near the entrance to the corridor, and bombard the cell occupants with the RPG, a handgun, or the shotgun from your relatively safe position. Get back on the elevated surface, and run its length to either side, collecting additional ammo and weaponry.

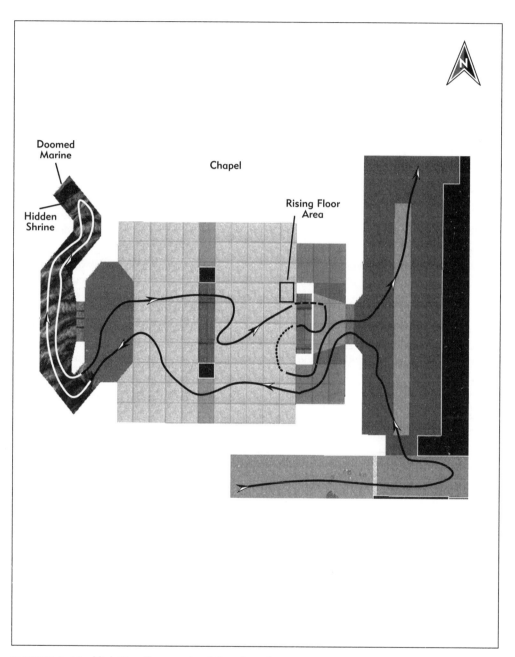

**FIGURE 5.11:** Violating the secrets of the chapel.

## COVERT DETAILS

Check out Table 5.6 for a list of the stuff you might otherwise miss on Death Row.

**TABLE 5.6: THE SECRETS IN DEATH ROW**

| AREA IN LEVEL | SECRET ITEM | HOW TO GET IT |
| --- | --- | --- |
| Execution chamber | shotgun | This item is in the secret area behind and below the electric chair. The switch on the left side of the window lowers the electric chair's platform. |
| Prison chapel | ripper chaingun | This baby is in the secret shrine behind the altar. The shrine is accessible through the stained glass window to the left of the main altar. |
| | pipe bombs atomic health unit | You'll find these in the loft area on the east side. To access this area, you must first flip a switch above the altar, so a pillar rises out of the floor near the loft. Then run and jump on top of the pillar to reach the loft. |
| The small holding cell | RPG ammo | It's in the secret tunnel behind the cot. |
| The central control area | atomic health unit pipe bombs | These are in the small chambers to the right and left (respectively) of the central totem-like structure. |
| The cell blocks | secret tunnel | This is behind the pin-up poster in the easternmost cell. |
| | exploding wall | This is at the westernmost wall of Cell Block 1, which connects to the prison courtyard. |
| The prison courtyard | multiple atomic health units | These are found inside the central structure, above the north side gate. |
| Near get-away submarine | NVG | Find the large gate behind the south wall. Climb onto the slant on the pillar on the right side. Push against the pillars surface and crawl inside the small secret space to grab the NVG. |
| Spinning chamber south of Central Control | armor | Look for the duct in the wall of the circular room after you cause it to spin. Bust through the grill and grab the armor. |

# TOXIC DUMP

The small cargo submarine you hoped would carry you out of Death Row and into free-dom took a nose dive. Needless to say, it was booby-trapped. It now resembles a giant cigarette butt sticking straight up from a sand ashtray. This is a fitting entrance to the Toxic Dump, an austere rock, concrete, and metal installation for the disposal of dangerous chemicals and radioactive substances. The Toxic Dump dominates over a large expanse of territory with interconnected bodies of water and small canyons. Structures like the multi-level treatment plant, at the north end, foreshadow the increasing sophistication of later levels. The Toxic Dump is also the gateway to the secret level, The Launching Facility.

There are basically two ways to clean up the Toxic Dump. One is significantly more efficient, circumventing the treatment plant and the sewage lines. To solve this level the second way, you must slip on those protective boots. You will be knee-deep in toxic sludge sooner or later. The key to surviving in a dump like the Toxic Dump is to boost your immune system. Cherish and seek atomic health. They are bountiful in this level. And one last thing: In this level you have to literally become small to reach key switches and passages. How do you get small? You simply stand in front of the flashing lens and look at the birdie. Get the red keycard and then learn to crawl.

## MAPS AND ROUTE

Try not to be overwhelmed when you look at Figures 5.12 and 5.13. The Toxic Dump is a sprawling structure of varied and complex architecture.

**FIGURE 5.12:** The general surgeon wants you to know that entering the Toxic Dump is hazardous to your health. Proceed at your own risk.

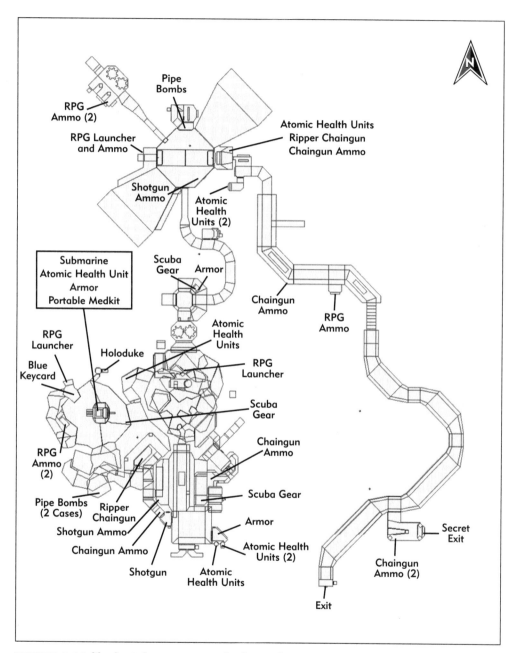

**FIGURE 5.13:** You best don your protective boots, for you are about to make a splash in the Toxic Dump.

## THE GOODS

Toxic materials, notwithstanding, not everything stinks in the Toxic Dump. Check out the goods you can collect and covet on this level in Table 5.7.

| TABLE 5.7: THE GOODS IN THE TOXIC DUMP | | |
|---|---|---|
| **WEAPONS** | **AMMO** | **POWER-UPS** |
| 2 shotguns | 9 cases | 4 portable medkits |
| 2 ripper chainguns | 11 cases | 9 atomic health units |
| 3 RPG launchers | 7 cases | 3 armors |
| 3 pipe bomb cases | | 1 steroid flask |
| | | 4 scuba gear sets |
| | | 1 NVG |
| | | 1 holoduke |
| | | 1 pair of boots |

## BLAZING THROUGH THE TOXIC DUMP

Do you want to avoid heartache? Are most of your limbs valuable to you? Any third-rate genius will agree that your chances of survival in the Toxic Dump will rocket if you can cut your stay there in half.

### In the Southwest Canyon

1. **Get out of the sub.** Submerge in the water-logged sub and find the vertical row of switches. Activate the top and bottom ones. Then turn around and go out of the sliding doors.

2. **Snatch an RPG and the blue keycard.** Emerge to the surface level along the rocky shore on the southwest side. Run up the rocky incline and take possession of the RPG launcher. Then grab the blue keycard and dive into the water hole, heading for the far shore.

3. **Wrestle a ripper chaingun.** Enter the Toxic Dump through the red door. A step or two after the first turn, push the wall on the right side to access a secret passage. Push a dark metallic wall to enter the narrow room that overlooks the canyon from the southeast corner. The ripper chaingun is in there, but so are a few troopers who are packed like sardines.

### In the Drum Processing Plant

1. **Take the red keycard.** Make your way to the small platform at the end of the conveyor belt near the southeast corner. Let the mechanical crane pick you up and drop you at the opposite end. Climb a second platform, and let another crane take you back to the south end. As soon as you are dropped, look for a glass door on the right side and bust in. The red keycard is inside the small compartment on the south wall, next to the computer panel. (See Figure 5.14.)

**NOTE**
Speaking of rocketing, to blaze through and live to tell, you must have a jetpack strapped on. As there are none to be had in the Toxic Dump, hopefully you secured one back in Death Row.

2. **Get small and open the way to the north section.** Use the red keycard on the panel at the northeastern room. Wait for the shrinkage device to blast you. Then run under the small opening on the right side. Make a right and a hard left into a metallic room equipped with its own shrinkage device. Activate the switch on the far side of the room. (It unlocks the red latch in the previous room, thus granting you access to the rest of the level.) Take another shrinkage dose, and leave the same way you crawled in.

### In the Central Canyon

1. **Reach the central canyon.** Leave the drum processing plant through the red gate, heading northeast. Go underwater and veer to your left to reach a submerged control room in ruins.

2. **Raise the water level.** Brave the octabrains while eluding the mines to reach the sunken chamber across and to the north. Find the small switch near the computer console and activate it. The water level will raise several feet.

3. **Reach higher ground.** Swim up and out of the waters into a rocky plane at the east side of the canyon. Climb the ascending plane to come out

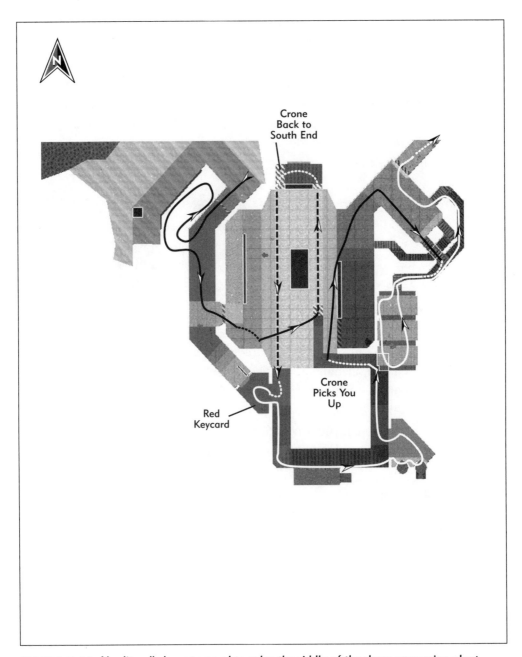

**FIGURE 5.14:** You literally have to crawl to solve the riddle of the drum processing plant.

overlooking the canyon over a large rock that splits into two runway-like outcroppings.

4. **Bridge the gap.** Take a running start up the outcropping on the left side and leap over and onto the more or less flat surface of the boulder across to the northwest.

5. **Find the invisible crack.** Stand as close, without falling over into the water, to the edge of the rock where you can look eastward at a similar landing in the other side of the canyon. In a defiant act of faith, leap high and directly into the wall between the landings. This is the spot where the otherwise flat wall forms a sharp angle. You will be stepping into a teleporter and come out a few paces away from the exit switch, clear at the south end of the toxic sludge tunnel.

## ADDED ATTRACTIONS IN THE TOXIC DUMP

There are plenty of reasons why you would want to check out the added attractions the Toxic Dump has to offer. Perhaps your craving for adventure leads you to want to know what it's like to be:

- Northbound and determined
- Mistreated at the treatment plant

### Head North, Young Duke

As you emerge into the sunken office in the central canyon, you notice the heavy metal door labeled "Gate 2." It bars you from reaching the treatment plant and any chance of escaping. Opening gate 2 requires a series of orchestrated maneuvers and techniques. With a bevy of octabrains swimming and hovering around the canyon, it's nothing short of risky.

Press the switch at the corner of the window to raise the canyon's water level. Stand your ground in the sunken office for a few seconds, and meet the circling octabrains with the rapid fire from your ripper chaingun. Use the floating mines as targets when an octabrain is near one.

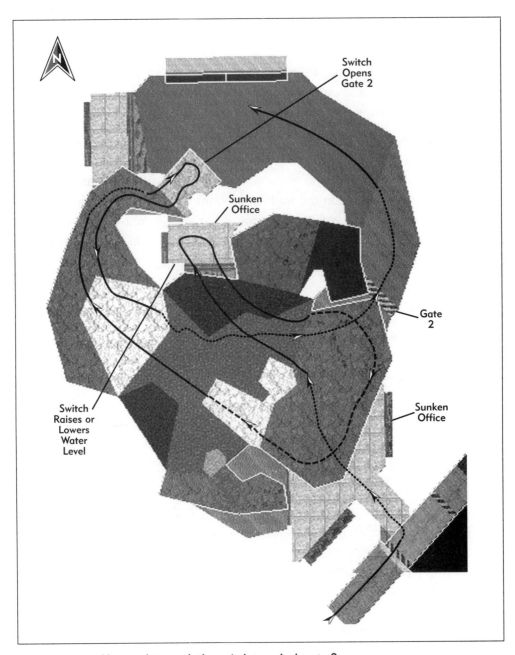

Switch
Opens
Gate 2

Sunken
Office

Gate
2

Switch
Raises or
Lowers
Water
Level

Sunken
Office

**FIGURE 5.15:** You need to reach the switch to unlock gate 2.

Swim out of the sunken office, hugging the wall on your left side. Surface by the rocky shore near the northeast part of the canyon, and climb the sloping rocks around the curve. Make short work of floating octabrains with well-guided rocket propelled rounds. When the action lessens somewhat, take a running start from the bottom of the rock outcropping on the left side, and jump across to the nearly level ground on the northwest side. Follow the curving, sloping terrain to reach a small control room tucked away in a fold of the rock at the very top. Spray the troopers with a generous dousing of lead. Then step in, grab an RPG launcher, and, most importantly, press the switch by the monitor. In fact, look at the monitor after throwing the switch. Gate 2 will yield. Run back to the water and dive down. Pass right through the gate. Figure 5.15 summarizes the route graphically.

You'll emerge in a yet another confined underwater area. Reach yet another sunken office and throw the switch found in there. The next heavy gate will clear the way to the north. However, upon reaching the gate, you might be initially discouraged by the sight of two massive cogs, churning and spinning steadily. To clear this next obstacle, you must time your movement forward with a section of the cogs that appears metallic gray. Wait for the cogs to turn a few times. When you think you have the timing down, venture forth slowly but with determination. If you fall in right in time, the cogs will simply deposit you into the next underwater chamber. Say hello and good-bye to a couple of octabrains. And get ready for a showdown with aliens who have deplorable manners at the treatment plant.

## Blooming Violence at the Treatment Plant

The treatment plant is an impressively large, funnel-like structure with high currents of slopping waterways. It is also a veritable octabrain nesting ground. Besides wrestling with their wrath, you must also solve the riddle of the plant to reach the toxic sludge canals, which lead to one of two exits. Stepping into the fast moving sludge, you are pushed forward by the sheer mass and quantity of the thick goo. Land a shot with your RPG launcher near the visible crack along the wall on the right side. Then fight the current to reach the small room behind the blown-up wall. Mount the teleporter and materialize in the remote enclosure at the northwest side of the plant. Slide out of the teleporter booth carefully, and pelt any captains and their troopers. Then grab the cases of RPG ammo. With your RPG aiming forward, slide down into the narrow canal to reach the plant's center.

As you enter its spacious dimensions, aim and fire with precision. Chances are that some octabrains will chase you to the bottom of the plant's main tank. Work your way to the small control area at the north end of the main pool. Climb around the ramp and press the switch in front of you. Watch above and to the right as a small wall opens to reveal an elevated chamber on the south end.

Get back in the water, and climb the southwest ramp against the current. Jump onto the small ledge near the top, on the right side, and follow it to the front, once again overlooking the pool below. Climb over the separate and narrow floor section. Then aim your weapon and fire to hit the switch due south of your position. The column you stand on will move toward the center of the pool. A similar column will approach from the opposite end. Board the approaching column, and ride it back to the east side. Go around the dividing wall with the ripper chaingun handy. Pour it on the implacable octabrain, and push on into the toxic sewage network. It leads to the secret exit and the more obvious level exit.

## COVERT DETAILS

It might be a dump, and a toxic one at that; but, as shown in Table 5.8, it certainly has no shortage of interesting secrets.

| TABLE 5.8: THE SECRETS IN THE TOXIC DUMP | | |
| --- | --- | --- |
| **AREA IN LEVEL** | **SECRET ITEM** | **HOW TO GET IT** |
| The western canyon | two RPG ammo cases | The ammo is in the secret compartment behind the turret recess in the elevated rock wall, directly east of the sunken submarine. |
| | holoduke | This item is in a similar chamber behind the turret recess on the opposing rock formation. |
| | hidden cave | Swim into the gaping hole on the south wall of the canyon. Blow up the cracked rock at the end of the tunnel. Then continue swimming up the slanted floor and picking up pipe bombs as you go. Surface when you reach a roughly circular area. Drop a pipe bomb near the barrels and blow it up to open a hole near the building at the south end of the canyon. |

| AREA IN LEVEL | SECRET ITEM | HOW TO GET IT |
|---|---|---|
| The western canyon | atomic health unit<br>armor<br>portable medkit | Stand on top of the submarine and step over the small fires to activate a secret compartment inside the sub. Swim back inside and reach the top of the sub to cash in. |
| The drum processing plant | ripper chaingun | This weapon is in the chamber behind a secret door along the right wall (found a few steps into the hallway leading to the plant). |
| | ripper chaingun ammo | This is in the secret compartment at the south end, which you can access by catching a ride on the mechanical crane. |
| | atomic health units | These are inside the cylinders in the small chamber at the southeast corner. |
| The central canyon | a series of exploding walls | These dig a tunnel connecting the two canyons. |
| | shotgun<br>portable medkit | Reach the large rock with the runway outcroppings. Leap from the runway on the right side to reach the landing at the northeast. Activate your NVG (if you have them). Otherwise feel around in the darkness for the goods. |
| The treatment plant | teleporter | This is hidden behind an exploding wall in a descending canal to the south of the plant. The teleporter leads to a chamber located just northwest of the main treatment plant, where two RPG ammo cases can be found. |
| | atomic health units | Two of these are in the elevated toxic duct in a chamber just east of the plant. |
| | exploding wall | This is near the south end of the sinewy canal. It leads to the exit switch that will transport you to the secret level, The Launching Facility. |

# THE ABYSS

Was it Nietzsche who said he stood defiantly staring at the abyss, and the abyss stared back? If you feel compelled to say "gesundheit" when you hear "Nietschze" and philosophy is at best an amateurish pursuit, you might still share Nietzsche's awe when you confront your own abyss. Welcome to The Abyss and to the end of L.A. Meltdown, the first *Atomic Edition* episode. (There is of course the secret level, The Launching Facility, provided you found it back in the Toxic Dump.)

The Abyss will tax not just your strength and ability but also your character and mental fortitude. Among the jagged cliffs, rocky roads, mountain sides, lava lakes and waterfalls, and fast running, toxic sludge canals, you'll find just how far the alien infiltrators have gone in their quest to possess the Earth. After exploring their bizarre temples, carved into the flanks of hanging peaks, you will be forced to conclude that the aliens' mythology combines mysticism and technology in equal measures. But you aren't here for an anthropological assessment. You're here to put an end to whatever the hell is going on. Your entire mission in The Abyss is to find the giant alien ship lying dormant in the stinking bowels of the Earth. You must then descend into a veritable inferno and face off against the gigantic Battlelord.

Bridging The Abyss requires you to blow key sections of mountain sides. The only route to the alien ship is through a net of cavernous tunnels running like veins encased in rock. Set out to find the San Andreas Fault marker, an unassuming slab of concrete. Then penetrate the mountains' temples and uncover their secrets. In the major and larger of the temples, set off a key trigger and blow open an entrance into the solid burrow where the alien craft is nestled. Gain entry to the ship and best of luck. Humanity is counting on you.

## MAPS AND ROUTE

No, you're not looking at the latest mutation of the virus of the week. Figures 5.16 and 5.17 show you maps of the best route out and all the goodies, respectively, in The Abyss and all its glory.

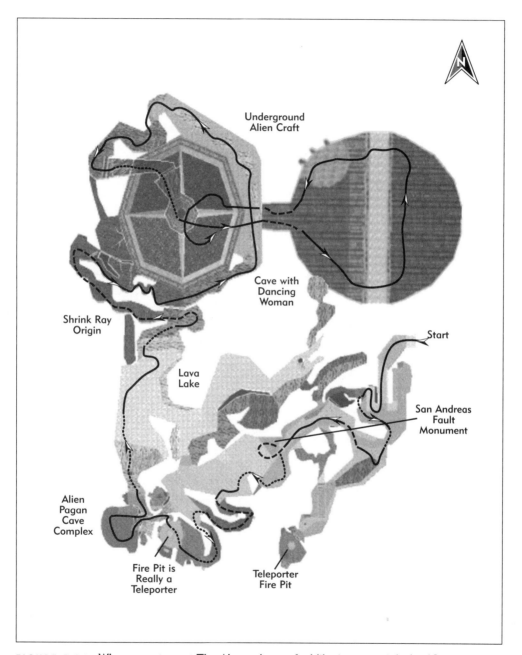

FIGURE 5.16: When you stare at The Abyss, do you feel like it stares right back?

**FIGURE 5.17:** The Abyss brings your experience in L.A. Meltdown to a cliff-hanging consummation.

## THE GOODS

Considering the caliber of the opposition—after all this is the level in which you will find the Battlelord, the episode's boss—The Abyss is well stocked in the goods department. Table 5.9 shows the entire cache.

### TABLE 5.9: THE GOODS IN THE ABYSS

| WEAPONS | AMMO | POWER-UPS |
| --- | --- | --- |
| 2 shotguns | 11 cases | 5 portable medkits |
| 3 ripper chainguns | 17 cases | 14 atomic health units |
| 4 RPG launchers | 10 cases | 2 armors |
| 3 pipe bomb cases | | 1 steroid flask<br>1 jetpack<br>3 NVGs<br>1 holoduke<br>5 pairs of boots |

## BLAZING THROUGH THE ABYSS

*Blazing* might actually be an inaccurate verb for getting through The Abyss. Even the shortest of routes puts you at serious peril and forces you to overheat your thinking cap. Find the blue keycard before you can reach the San Andreas Fault marker.

### Along the Sludge Drain and Surrounding Mountain Paths

1. **Get the boots and RPG launcher.** Run out of the narrow toxic sludge tunnel and turn a quick right. Open the door on the rock side, and grab the protective boots. Jump into the floor below by the blue keycard door and take the RPG launcher.

2. **Go with the flow.** Let the current carry you to the point where the sludge canal bends at a sharp angle. Jump off to the left so you set foot on a slanted rock serving as landing.

3. **Follow the narrow path to the blue keycard.** Hug the wall on the left side and follow the narrow zigzag path. Go under the dilapidated bridge and past the cactus to a spot where the blue keycard rests on a short

pillar. Take the card, the shells and trace your steps back to the door with the blue security lock.

## Reaching the San Andrea's Fault

1. **Use the blue keycard and score the NVG.** Stepping into a dark cavernous enclosure, battle of the pig cops and grope for the NVG. Find the small exit at the end leading to daylight and to a narrow pathway along the side of the rocks.

2. **Step out and leap across.** Taking a few steps onto the narrow ledge, do your best to contend with the troopers and captains. Then, jump over the sludge canal to land on the cave across and to the south. Collect the chaingun ammo and follow the path as it curves and ascends, leading you to a spot where you can reach the monument.

3. **Jump across and cause a big shock.** At the top of the path, lunge yourself back over the sludge canal below to land near the San Andrea's Fault monument. Walk towards it and steady your footing as tectonic plates rearrange to change the scenery somewhat.

4. **Collect two atomic health units.** Jump onto the newly accessible slanted surface. Take the first atomic health. Hopscotch onto the next surface, and take the second atomic health before heading toward the caverns.

## In the Eerie Alien Caverns

1. **Enter at your own risk.** Jump back over the canal, and run around the rock formation to reach another area fallen by the quake. From here, work your way down until you reach the level ground with the canal, which is now the size of a gurgling brook. Cross over the canal again, and reach the gaping entrance to the network of alien caverns.

2. **Reach the pit of rituals.** Crawl up the steep, rocky ground to reach a level opening where the path divides. Turn a hairpin left onto yet another tunnel that ascends all the way to the pit of rituals. Drop into the pit and

activate the alien hand print on the south wall to uncover a hidden area where you can get another RPG launcher.

3. **Uncover a hidden tunnel.** Touch the alien hand print on the north side of the pit. When the nearby rock slab slides, go into the connecting tunnel.

4. **Drop into the largest of the alien caves.** Fight off the octabrains as you take in the layout of this room. There is no apparent way out. But, wait. There is. You must trigger certain events before you can leave.

5. **Activate the hidden stairs.** Activate the hand print switch along the north wall. Then climb the stairs as they circle around the periphery of the alien pit.

6. **Trigger another quake.** Reaching the platform at the end of the stairs, you will set off a tremendous explosion. Looking through the cross opening on the wall, you will see an entire mountain side crumble to dust.

7. **Produce a pillar and get small.** To get out of the pit, you must get shrunk. Jump to the narrow ledge on the east wall, where you can press another hand print switch. Get off the landing and jump back into the pit to get on top of an ascending pillar. At its top point, turn to face the emanation from the shrinking ray across the distance. Get shrunk and jump back down into the pit. Then just crawl out the small opening at the base of the north wall. Coming out by a sunken fountain, take the westward path.

8. **Score the boots and take a plunge.** Heading north out of the caves, grab the boots and plunge into the noxious chemicals below. Dust off whatever octabrains come at you. The RPG is most dependable in this situation. Continue northward until you reach a safe landing by the demolished boulders.

## In and about the Alien Ship

1. **Find the entrance.** Begin a long and perilous ascent inside a red glowing tunnel. Follow the hairpin turn into a space where the ground is marred by major cracks. (Through a small opening in the wall, you should be

able to catch sight of the alien ship.) Continue the downward path around the lower circumference of the octagonal vessel. Leap-frog the series of narrow rocks to reach a very steep series of rocks serving as steps. These give you access to the north side of the ship. Straighten your tie and knock on the door.

2. **Drop in for a short visit.** Open the massive door to the alien ship and walk inside. At the end of the walkway, enter through a second, even larger door. Turn to the right immediately, and activate the alien hand switch on the wall. Slide down into the funnel-like floor. You're now on the main floor of the alien craft.

3. **Exchange pleasantries with the boss.** Open the door on the east side. Enter through the green metallic tunnel. Collect all the RPG ammo you can hold before the Battlelord makes his presence known. When he emerges from an underground holding tank, manage to hit him 25 times with your RPG launcher and claim a righteous victory.

## ADDED ATTRACTIONS IN THE ABYSS

If you're just wild about go-go caves or want a few tips on how to make the right impression on the alien boss, consider the following added attractions:

- Going to a go-go cave
- Facing off with the boss

### Going to a Go-Go Cave

After wrecking large boulders and rock outcroppings in the northern lava region of The Abyss (by setting off a trigger in the larger alien cave), you can go for a final showdown with the ever-so-jealous-of-his-job Battlelord. Or, you could take the low moral road to visit a not-so-nearby cave for a bit of, shall we say, licentious amusement? Here, we opt for the latter.

Make sure your protective boots are adequate before visiting the northern hemisphere. The Abyss is an eroded land with flowing lava lakes, scorching waterfalls, and perilous cliffs. The setting couldn't be more appropriate for octabrain spawning grounds. They swim freely all around the lava. They can also hide behind rock outcroppings and burrow within large crevices. Watch out.

Jump into the lava hoisting your RPG launcher and aiming slightly above the lake's horizon. The second you spot three eyes in a giant gelatinous head, pull the trigger. While they are at a safe distance, you should be able to pick your targets. At the same time, you want to become an elusive target yourself, darting left and right, while struggling against the current to keep a safe distance.

Find the passage flowing eastward. Head northeast, staying near the wall on your right side. What will seem like legions of octabrains swimming upstream to spawn will do their damnedest to stop your progress. Persevere undeterred. Find the small platform with the alien hand print and activate it. Then climb over the opening above the flowing lava. Fight upstream until the ground levels and then suddenly drops into a small circular cave. Enter the cave, grab the atomic health, and don't attempt small talk with the dancing woman. She's apparently entranced by the deep beat of a primeval alien rave.

## Facing Off with the Boss

This is the moment of truth. You've demolished mountains to reach the alien ship, which is encrusted deep in California mountain rock like a metallic seed of unreal proportions. Now, standing on its imposing bridge, you're suddenly aware you've entered truly alien territory. The ship's controls, engineering, and architecture were never meant for human occupants. The atmosphere is still and eerie, and you can't stop feeling imminent danger and dread. You've come very far, but not far enough. You have an appointment to keep with the Battlelord, and he hates to wait.

Armed with all the RPG ammo you can hold, walk toward the only door on the east side of the bridge. Activate the alien hand print switch to look behind the green door. Start into the room and begin running. Just before an overhead beam crosses the hallway, jump as high as you can to propel yourself forward. You want to avoid running over trigger 1, near the chamber's entrance. This trigger causes the door at the start of the hallway to shut permanently.

The idea is to leave yourself an out if the idea of standing toe-to-toe with the Battlelord is not even halfway appealing. Hover onto the circular platform on the northwest side. Don't let the ghastly sight of the women in cocoons distract you from your task. Take the jetpack and the additional RPG ammo. By this time, the Battlelord should be emerging from his slumber. Seize this moment when he's vulnerable, and pound him with all the rocket propelled grenades you can possibly launch. If you've got the temperament for it, you can attempt to fight the Battlelord on his grounds. The first thing you must do is maintain a safe distance while you make him chase you from one half of the chamber to the other, over the elevated lava canal. You will have a few precious seconds to act as he starts to cross the canal, leaving the top of his ferocious face exposed. You stand to sustain some damage, so make it a point to pick up the two atomic health units in this room.

If you can maintain a sustained attack before you're really hurt, you're a better Duke than most. But even so, remember that you can get back to the bridge area—if you remember not to cross over trigger 1. Bet as sure as daylight the Battlelord will follow. Unfortunately for him, his corpulent frame might prove too much for the door frame. This is your perfect opportunity to punish him with impunity.

## COVERT DETAILS

Labyrinthine and enormous in its sheer proportions, The Abyss cradles many a secret, as shown in Table 5.10.

| TABLE 5.10: THE SECRETS IN THE ABYSS | | |
|---|---|---|
| **AREA IN LEVEL** | **SECRET ITEM** | **HOW TO GET IT** |
| The alien caverns | fire pit that is really a teleporter | This device sends you to the otherwise inaccessible circular chamber, due directly east of the cavern complex. Loot abounds in this area, including RPG ammo, atomic health units, and armor. |
| | ripper chaingun | Jump into the water fountain. Inside you will find the ripper chaingun. |

| AREA IN LEVEL | SECRET ITEM | HOW TO GET IT |
|---|---|---|
| The rocky outcroppings | atomic health units | These vital items can be found in the northeastern chamber, the home of the dancing cavewoman. |
| | shotgun and ripper chaingun ammo | The ammo can be found in the rocky tunnel that looks like an appendage near the eastern end. The tunnel is only accessible through an exploding wall on its north side, across from an alien hand print. |

# THE LAUNCHING FACILITY

Why are you here? Don't look for really deep answers. Either you stumbled upon the secret exit back in the Toxic Dump, or you purposely sought it out. But all that's irrelevant now. Your mission here, if you can accomplish it, is nothing less than to sabotage a rocket to the Moon. The rocket carries helpless female specimens wrapped in leathery green cocoons. (God only knows for what purpose.)

Destroying the rocket is a two-stage proposition. First you must get onboard to activate the self-destruct mechanism with the aid of the red keycard. Next, you have to find and push the remote detonation switch. But this seemingly straightforward task is anything but that. To begin, the rocket might as well be invisible until you cause it to surface from its underground silo. To do that, you must first secure a blue keycard, without which the security switch will not work. And just as important, you also must find a way to open gate 2 to access the northern half of The Launching Facility.

## MAPS AND ROUTE

The Launching Facility's layout, as shown in Figures 5.18 and 5.19, consists of medium-sized chambers connected by a network of corridors and passages at right angles. And as the route makes it painfully obvious, you have to run its entire length to accomplish your goal.

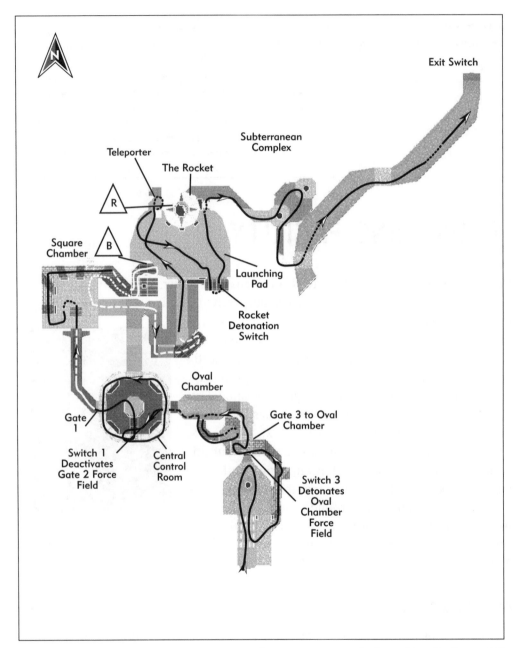

**FIGURE 5.18:** Ten, nine, eight, seven, six . . . Can you penetrate the Launching Facility and blow up the rocket before it's too late?

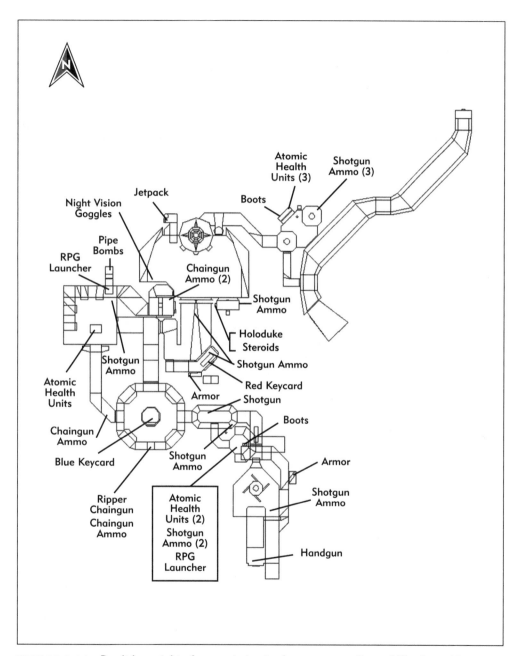

**FIGURE 5.19:** Don't lose sight of your mission in the narrow confines of The Launching Facility; but above all, don't lose your head.

## THE GOODS

While not particularly overflowing with goods, The Launching Facility has a respectable number of atomic health units—and you know you can never be too healthy (see Table 5.11).

| TABLE 5.11: THE GOODS IN THE LAUNCHING FACILITY | | |
|---|---|---|
| **WEAPONS** | **AMMO** | **POWER-UPS** |
| 1 shotgun | 1 case | 1 portable medkit |
| 1 ripper chaingun | 12 cases | 6 atomic health units |
| 1 RPG launcher | | 2 armors |
| 3 pipe bomb cases | | 1 steroid flask |
| | | 1 jetpack |
| | | 1 NVG |
| | | 1 holoduke |
| | | 2 pairs of boots |

## BLAZING THROUGH THE LAUNCHING FACILITY

How do you cause a rocket to rise from its out-of-reach silo, board it, get out of it, and then cause it to blow up? You're about to find out (but maybe not in one breath).

### Before Entering the Central Control Room

1. **Gain access to the middle, oval chamber.** Reach the north side of the toxic pit on the opposite side of the churning blades. Activate switch 3 to deactivate the force field barring access to the oval chamber. Run back to the ramp, and cross over the elevated ooze canal into a green corridor. Grab the protective boots from the compartment next to the monitor. Then follow the corridor as it turns westward into the oval chamber.

2. **Dive for pearls.** Dive right into the ooze and grab a shotgun. (The ooze in this pool is completely harmless.) Find the circular openings to a connecting underground tunnel to access a smaller sunken chamber. Then surface to claim two atomic health units and two cases of shotgun ammo.

3. **Go kick butt in the central control room.** Beaming with health and more ammo, get back to the oval chamber.

## In the Central Control Room

1.  **Reach the top level.** As you enter the room, run toward the southwest corner. Run up the platform that circles the entire area until you reach a row of four circular switches.

2.  **Gain entry to the control column.** Activate the first, second, and fourth switches (starting on the left side). Cross the metal bridge to the central column. Grab the blue keycard and activate the switch labeled "1." It deactivates the force field in gate 1, so you can reach the next chamber.

## In the Square Chamber

1.  **Get more health.** Run up the corridor leading to the largest chamber in The Launching Facility. With a short running start, land on the central pillar to claim an atomic health.

2.  **Reach the rocket control switch.** Climb along the ramp and over an irregular patch of ground to emerge in a small chamber with a few monitors and other control panels. Go into the small connecting division on the east side to use the blue keycard on switch 2, and then watch the rocket emerge from its underground storage base. This same switch also opens a door to the warehouse. The warehouse, of course, is adjacent to your target, the rocket.

## In and around The Launching Pad

1.  **Get the red keycard.** Go back to the large square chamber, and enter the hallway on the east side. Go straight through a raised door, and climb the steep walkway, heading south, to come upon a set of swinging doors. Open the doors, enter, and reach the top area to grab the red keycard. Also, throw the switch along the half wall to open the large metal doors.

2.  **Board the rocket and drop the card.** Get out onto the launching pad. Take the elevator on the west side to the very top. Emerging in a small and dark control room, grab the jetpack by the console before jumping into the teleporter. Open your eyes to see you are now inside the rocket.

Walk over to the key switch and drop the red keycard. As the lights turn red, get back on the teleporter and ride the elevator back to ground level.

3. **Detonate the rocket.** Crawl into the narrow opening east of the warehouse gates. Find a simple toggle switch and push it. Watch the once proudly erect structure come crashing down in a smoldering heap.

4. **Reach the underground.** Take the elevator on the east side of the fallen structure a good distance into a subterranean complex.

## In the Subterranean Complex

1. **Grab the boots and push the switch.** Follow the corridor eastward. Coming upon another computer console area, take the boots on the northwest panel. Then push the adjacent switch to open a wall at the end of the short southern corridor.

2. **Ride the ooze to victory.** Get out into the ooze and let it lead you to the exit switch.

3. **Give yourself any form of kudos you prefer for your conquest of the L.A. Meltdown episode.**

## COVERT DETAILS

As the secret level, it's only natural that the Launching Facility contains quite a few secrets. Witness them in Table 5.12.

### TABLE 5.12: THE SECRETS IN THE LAUNCHING FACILITY

| AREA IN LEVEL | SECRET ITEM | HOW TO GET IT |
|---|---|---|
| The toxic tank room (east of the central control area) | RPG launcher shell cases atomic health units | These items are in a sunken chamber, which you can get to by diving into the sludge and swimming through a narrow passage. |
| The cubic green chamber | pipe bomb case | This item is tucked away in a duct above the ceiling fan. |
| The hangar area | armor | This item can be found in a secret compartment in the elevated control area at the south end. |
| The underground chamber | atomic health unit | The item is behind the computer panel. |

# Lunar Apocalypse

At the conclusion of the L.A. Meltdown episode, you found an alien craft embedded in the Earth's rock mantle. Undaunted, you entered the strange vessel and faced off with a fearless Battlelord, pulling quite a job on his head. Using the ship's monitors, you also learned that the aliens were loading scores of women in cocoons into one of their huge interstellar ships. You vowed to not let this intergalactic kidnapping continue unabated.

Lunar Apocalypse, the nether region between L.A. Meltdown and Shrapnel City, marks the second episode in Duke's quest to undermine the alien's evil plot. As the level of the opposition rises, your arsenal also undergoes a considerable face-lift. In this level, you get to measure your might and wits against new adversaries, including the hovering sentry drone, the leaping enforcer, and the single-minded assault commander.

## SPACEPORT

You proved your mettle in L.A. Meltdown, and now you are back for more. Spaceport is your first stop along your tour of duty in Lunar Apocalypse. Spaceport sees you aboard a hovering, man-made station in lunar orbit. The place is obviously infested with aliens, and the blood trail flows ever so freely. Your job is to board the docked shuttle and reach The Incubator, the next station in the maddening Lunar Apocalypse episode. Commensurate with the higher level of the opposition, you will also find nifty new weapons of awesome destructive power. Witness the shrinker and the devastator, yours only for a few quarts of blood.

Reaching the elusive shuttle involves fighting through walls of enemies and working the installation's secrets to unlock the path. Be especially careful when confronting chaingun-wielding enforcers because this might be the first time you confront them. The shuttle you must board is behind a door that won't yield unless you have the red keycard. However, getting the red keycard involves first finding the blue keycard and then deactivating the force field around the central shaft; to do this you must use the right combination on a panel of switches.

## MAPS AND ROUTE

The layout of the Spaceport level, as you can see in Figures 6.1 and 6.2, is a no-frills, utilitarian docking station. Because there are two completely overlapping floors in the main central area, Figure 6.2 shows views for both the lower and the higher floors.

## THE GOODS

Table 6.1 displays the bountiful weapon and power-up cache to be had in Spaceport.

### TABLE 6.1: THE GOODS IN SPACEPORT

| WEAPONS | AMMO | POWER-UPS |
| --- | --- | --- |
| 1 shotgun | 3 cases | 1 portable medkit |
| 1 ripper chaingun | 2 cases | 5 atomic health units |
| 1 RPG launcher | 5 cases | 2 armors |
| 1 shrinker | | 1 steroid flask |
| 1 devastator | | 2 jetpacks |
| 2 pipe bomb cases | | 2 NVGs<br>1 holoduke |

## BLAZING THROUGH SPACEPORT

The steps in this section will help see you through the mayhem in Spaceport and, thus, limit your exposure to space madness.

**FIGURE 6.1:** Welcome aboard Spaceport, but don't expect a bag of salty peanuts.

**FIGURE 6.2:** Don't be afraid to wander around the Spaceport and take in the beautiful vistas, as you collect what you need.

### Around the Arrivals Docking Bay

1. **Get an RPG launcher.** Hop onto the teleporter behind you to board the inoperative docked shuttle. (This is not the shuttle you need to reach the next level.) Grab the RPG launcher and the steroids near one of the wings. Then, teleport back to the station.

2. **Take stock of the situation, and beef up your arsenal.** Reach the monitor behind the dividing wall at the northwest corner. As you turn the corner, listen for the hissing sound of the secret compartment behind you (directly facing the monitor). Turn around quickly and jump inside the slightly elevated compartment to grab a case of RPG ammo.

3. **Activate a switch to gain access to the central area.** Work your way to the southwest corner, disposing of the troopers and their captains along the way. Crouch in front of the computer panel as you take a shotgun, and push the broken computer monitor to enter a small secret area. Grab the atomic health unit and get out. Finally, throw the switch to the left of the computer panel to deactivate the force field that is barring entrance to the central area.

### On the Central Area's First Floor

1. **Get the blue keycard and a few other necessities.** Descend the long ramp, past an intermediate chamber, and make a hairpin turn into the wide open space of the central area's first floor. Although you will have a very nice view of the blue planet, you should be more interested in the blue keycard for now. (This is a good time to use the RPG launcher on the leaping enforcer.) Enter the storage compartment behind the door on the west wall. Climb on the crates to get the blue keycard, the scuba gear, and the armor.

2. **Access the second floor of the central area.** Get out to the main floor and find the narrow lift on the north side. Ride the lift to an elevated control area where you can use the blue keycard on the switch next to the opening. Activate the switch. It makes an elevator accessible at the

south end of the floor. This elevator is your only way of reaching the second floor. Go get on it.

### On the Central Area's Second Floor

1.  **Uncover the panel of combination switches.** When properly configured, these switches deactivate the shield around the central shaft. (The red keycard lies at the bottom of this shaft.) Switch 2 is inside the out-of-order elevator at the north end of the floor. Blow up the C-9 canisters next to the elevator to create a gaping opening you can walk through. Step in and push switch 2.

2.  **Push the right combination of switches.** Run out of the elevator and climb the short ramp to the green metallic chamber. Walk up to the panel of switches, and push them in the same configuration as shown in Figure 6.3.

3.  **Take a dive down the shaft.** With the shield no longer barring you from the main shaft, dive right in and touch bottom. Grab the red keycard, and, while there, open the small compartment to take a jetpack and an atomic health unit. Climb out of the shaft and head back to the metallic chamber.

4.  **Board the shuttle and wave good-bye.** With red keycard in hand, cross over the heavy blue door and enter a chamber connecting the central area to the docked shuttle. Walk right up to the switch, and use your red keycard to open the circular door. Fend off the sentry drone, walk in, activate the exit switch, and catch a ride to The Incubator.

## ADDED ATTRACTIONS IN SPACEPORT

Although you can get through Spaceport expeditiously, why not prolong your stay and claim two awesome weapons? Once you try them, you will agree that the devastator and the freezethrower are worth the extra time.

**FIGURE 6.3**: Activate the correct combination of switches to gain access to the main shaft.

### In Search of the Devastator

The only way to get the devastator is to reach an elevated hallway through the central shaft. If you haven't scored a jetpack yet, that should be your first priority. There are two jetpacks in this level. One is at the bottom of the central shaft; the second is on top of a small platform along the west wall of the second floor in the central area.

After deactivating the force field around the central shaft, simply step in it and activate the jetpack. Fly straight up until you come upon a hallway that runs north and south. Take the hallway south, and grab the devastator at the very end of the hallway. Then turn around and get back in the shaft. If you like, you can continue climbing all the way to a small top dome where you can also collect a pair of NVG.

### Scoring the Freezethrower

As you take the final straightaway toward the awaiting shuttle, notice a roughly oval area along the middle of the floor. It is in reality a platform that lowers automatically as you enter the anti-chamber to the shuttle. If you jump into the open pit, you will come upon an octagonal chamber where the freezethrower is hibernating. Grab it quickly and then make your way out of the sunken chamber by crawling into the narrow duct on the northwest wall. The duct starts a steep ascent and lets you come out through a one-way secret wall in the green metallic chamber.

## COVERT DETAILS

Table 6.2 airs out every secret in the Spaceport level.

| TABLE 6.2: THE SECRETS IN SPACEPORT | | |
| --- | --- | --- |
| **AREA IN LEVEL** | **SECRET ITEM** | **HOW TO GET IT** |
| The arrivals docking bay | atomic health unit | You'll find it in a secret compartment at the southeast corner. Crouch and press the broken monitor to access the secret area. |
| | RPG ammo | It's inside the elevated compartment at the northeast corner, directly across from the monitor. A sensor near the monitor triggers the compartment open. |
| Central area, first floor | pipe bombs | These are tucked away inside a duct. The duct is accessible in one of two ways: through the duct opening inside the small storage chamber at the west side or by jumping through a secret place from the small chamber that leads into the central area. Take a running start and jump directly at the sign that reads "Authorized Personnel Only." |
| Central area, second floor | devastator | This item is at the south end of an elevated tunnel. Once you have deactivated the shield, access the central shaft and hover to the tunnel's opening. Head southward to take the devastator. |
| Anti-chamber to the shuttle | freezethrower | This is at the bottom of a chamber that connects the central area to the exiting shuttle. |

# THE INCUBATOR

Why this installation is called The Incubator will become painfully obvious very soon. Another station orbiting the moon, The Incubator is literally infested with alien folk and their ghastly young. Organic, web-like formations grow wildly along metallic walls and computer panels. The basic layout of The Incubator consists of two chambers joined by a single doorway. The southern half of The Incubator is littered with dozens of eggs ready to spew a new member of the alien race—a crawling, bouncing, formless protozoid slimer with vicious serrated teeth in its underside. Could these eggs be the next progression along some aberrant evolutionary path crafted by alien intelligence? Is this what's become of human females? You shudder to think.

Your main concern in The Incubator is to reach the southern chamber, where the exit door is found. But the southern half will remain inaccessible unless you can deactivate the force field blocking the entrance. Once you make it to the southern chamber, you need only get past a few formidable adversaries and a barrier of hatching eggs to grab the yellow keycard. With this keycard, you will be able to access another chamber where a special switch opens the alien egg nest. After experiencing The Incubator, you will never think of poached eggs in quite the same way.

## MAPS AND ROUTE

As you can see in Figures 6.4 and 6.5, The Incubator is basically composed of two sections joined by a single doorway.

## THE GOODS

Table 6.3 lists the booty you can amass in The Incubator.

| TABLE 6.3: THE GOODS IN THE INCUBATOR | | |
| --- | --- | --- |
| **WEAPONS** | **AMMO** | **POWER-UPS** |
| 1 shotgun | 5 cases | 3 portable medkits |
| 1 ripper chaingun | 3 cases | 3 atomic health units |
| 1 RPG launcher | 1 case | 1 armor |
| 1 devastator | 1 case | 2 steroid flasks |
| 1 shrinker | 4 crystals | 1 NVG |
| 3 laser trip bombs | | 1 holoduke |
| 1 freezethrower | 2 charges | 1 jetpack |
| 3 pipe bomb cases | | |

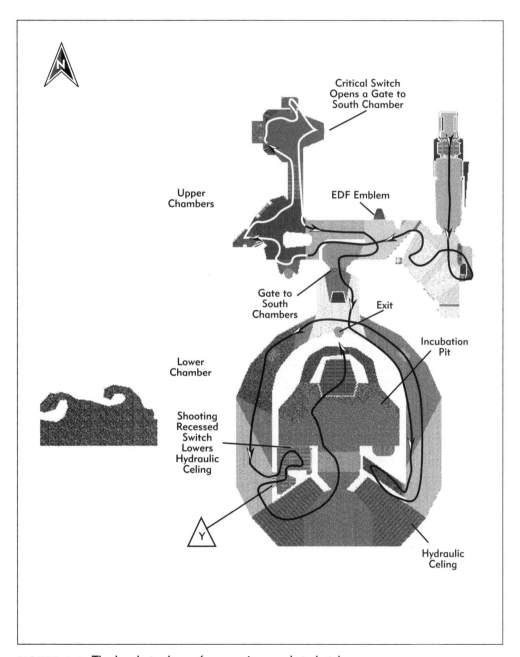

FIGURE 6.4: The Incubator has a few surprises ready to hatch.

**FIGURE 6.5**: Do you like your eggs scrambled? You will fry in The Incubator, and not necessarily from the excess cholesterol.

## BLAZING THROUGH THE INCUBATOR

Alien eggs by the dozens, sentry drones, and a few vicious enforcers are only a few of the reasons why you might want to blaze right through The Incubator. Stick to the plan below, and you will live to earn bragging rights.

### In the Northern Chamber's East Wing

1. **Reach the computer room at the southeast corner.** Open the door in front of you and enter a small chamber. Take the shotgun from a hidden compartment to your left, before opening the door into the rectangular room to the south. You will become the target for a couple of sentry drones. Knock off the sentry drones, and enter the dark computer chamber to the south.

> **TIP**
> The moment you spot a sentry drone, back off to put some distance between you and the enemy and then begin firing. Once a sentry drone gets too close to you, you can count on suffering a hard concussion, at the very least, from the sentry drone's diving attack and ensuing explosion.

2. **Reap the secret booty from a computer room.** Step into the computer room and grab the case of shotgun shells from the computer panel on the left. Then push the square metallic panel to the right of the computer terminals to open a secret compartment. Grab the pipe bomb case and hop inside. Then push a second secret panel to access a narrow room behind the terminals. Take the case of shotgun shells and the armor before you jump back inside the room through the one-way wall.

3. **Get healthy quickly.** Cross the room and throw the switch in the middle of the wall on the southwest side. Two large metal panels open to reveal a view of the southern chamber. At the same time, an elevated compartment on the east side gives way to unleash a couple of sentry drones, and a secret door gives way to the remainder of the northern chamber.

### In the North Chamber's Middle Section

1.  **Get a large medkit.** Run right into the Earth Defense Forces emblem on the north side wall, and take the medkit in the small space behind the wall.

2.  **Get the freezethrower.** Continue up the ramp to a double door that appears to be locked. Your presence will trip a sensor, and the doors will lower as the computer room is being automatically assembled inside. Enter the dark computer chamber and head for a set of tall panels at the west side. The one on the right yields to let you inside a small enclosure where a holoduke and a freezethrower are your rewards (see Figure 6.6).

### In the Small Northwest Computer Room

1.  **Take more loot.** Follow the short ramp up to a small, dark computer room in the northwest corner. The sunken floor in this chamber will rise

**FIGURE 6.6:** The lovely sight of two of your favorite items.

as the sensors detect your presence. This is a good time to drop a pipe bomb onto the rising floor and wipe out the troopers before they reach the ground level. Along the west wall, you can grab a ripper chaingun and two atomic health units. The panel on the north wall hides a case of chaingun ammo.

2. **Throw the force field switch.** Walk to the wall on the east side and throw the switch that deactivates the force field connecting the northern and southern chambers.

## Near the Southern Chamber's Entrance

1. **Take the RPG before going too far.** Standing at the threshold of the southern chamber, dart into the weapons armory and grab the RPG and the two ammo cases before retreating.

2. **Bust in and get the yellow keycard.** Open yourself a path into the east wing (on your left). Enter the small door at the end of the half-circular hallway. Grab the yellow keycard near the bottom of the ramp, and run back out.

3. **Proceed to the right wing.** Once you have scored the yellow keycard, circle all the way around the southern chamber to reach a small chamber on the west side. Use the keycard to enter the chamber. Look for a small indented switch along the metallic wall, and fire a single bullet to activate it. This switch lowers the entire southern wall, thus granting you access to The Incubator's egg nest.

> **TIP**
>
> You don't want to stand inside the southern chamber for very long. Hatching eggs to the left and right and a meandering octabrain can easily overwhelm you. It is best to drop pipe bombs or pick off the protozoid slimers that come after you. After thinning out their numbers, run straight for the left wing of the southern chamber and pluck off the octabrain in mid air with a single shot from the RPG launcher.

## In the Egg Nest

1. **Penetrate the egg nest.** Hop onto the lowered southern wall, and dive into the racing water to reach the circular egg nest. You will come to rest on a solid platform overlooking a ghastly sight indeed. Before you risk more injury to yourself, walk over to the small compartment on the west side and take the large medkit.

2. **Unlock the exit and get away.** Hop into the uninviting water, and swim quickly across to the mess of organic matter that carpets the entire northern half of the chamber.

3. **Throw the organic switch.** Find a circular, organic switch along the middle part of the organic mess, and stand back as the middle section of the organic formation is lifted to reveal the exit switch. If your devastator is up to the task, pop any remaining eggs and throw yourself toward the switch.

## ADDED ATTRACTIONS IN THE INCUBATOR

By the time you reach the southern chamber and its gruesome alien egg nest, you might be ready to get out screaming. However, on a more rational level, consider checking out the sizable loot to be had there. It can only make you stronger over the long haul.

> **TIP**
>
> You can detonate multiple pipe bombs at once. Throw your first pipe bomb. The detonator button appears in your hand. Press **6** on the keyboard to put away the detonator and grab another pipe bomb. Throw the second bomb as well. Again, press **6** to grab a third pipe bomb. Repeat this process as many times as you like, so long as your supply of bombs doesn't run out. After throwing the last bomb, stand a good distance away and punch the detonator switch for an explosion equal in proportion to the number of pipe bombs you deposited.

### Padding Your Arsenal in the Egg Nest

After unlocking the entrance to the nest egg, you can potentially score a devastator and a shrinker and even ammo for these formidable weapons, in addition to a jetpack. The devastator and its ammo are found underwater. Because octabrains and protozoid slimers swim freely in the water pit, drop four or five pipe bombs in succession into the water; then detonate them all at once.

Feeling a bit more confident, jump into the tepid waters and look for an indentation along the submerged organic wall on the north side. The indentation on the right side takes you directly to three devastator ammo cases. The indentation on the left side leads to an actual devastator.

Ascend from the depths and reach the east side of the organic formation. Climb along the series of rocks along the west side until you come upon the entrance to a tunnel that burrows right through the organic structure. Near the eastern side of the tunnel you will find a jetpack behind a slightly translucent area in the wall.

## COVERT DETAILS

Secrets abound in The Incubator, and Table 6.4 summarizes them for you.

### TABLE 6.4: THE SECRETS IN THE INCUBATOR

| AREA IN LEVEL | SECRET ITEM | HOW TO GET IT |
| --- | --- | --- |
| North chamber, east wing | pipe bomb case<br>armor<br>shotgun shells | The pipe bombs are hidden behind a small metallic plate next to a small bank of computers. Stepping inside the enclosure, a second secret panel gives way into a hidden chamber lined with electronic circuitry. The chamber hides the armor and a case of shells. |
| North chamber, west wing | freezethrower<br>holoduke | These are tucked away behind a small closet-like enclosure. |
| Computer room, northwest end | ripper chaingun ammo | This item is behind the panel on the north wall. |
| Hallway in the upper chambers | portable medkit · | Jump right through the EDF emblem on the north wall and collect the portable medkit. |

# WARP FACTOR

Appearing more like a spaceship than a sedentary orbital station, Warp Factor is light years more complex than the previous two levels in this episode. Expect the unexpected in Warp Factor. Opportunity and danger lurk around every nook and cranny. This level also introduces yet another menacing figure, the rocket-spewing assault commander. And if that isn't enough, how about an appearance by the smaller, but still deadly version of the Battlelord, the battlelord sentry.

A multilevel structure, Warp Factor is characterized by long, wide hallways and a wide variety of utilitarian chambers. Near the main observation deck at the north end, you will see some telling clues as to the aliens' plan to crack Earth like a walnut by targeting California's San Andreas Fault. In a humorous way, Warp Factor is also a tribute of sorts to a staple American science-fiction television show. If you persevere, you might be able to pay a visit to not just a famous captain's ready room but to a "really ready room."

Making it in Warp Factor is all about picking your battles and being completely aware of your surroundings. You must traverse the totality of this installation before you get rightful access to the level's exit. The path to the exit is barred by a deflecting shield. The critical switch is in a secret area at the north end of Warp Factor. But to get to that area, you must first find both the blue and then the yellow keycards, and in just that order.

## MAPS AND ROUTE

If the general shape of Warp Factor reminds you of anything, your imagination is definitely engaged. Your number one priority is to get familiar with every aspect of Warp Factor. Logically, Figures 6.7 and 6.8 are good places to start.

## THE GOODS

It's only fair that such a complex structure as Warp Factor delivers on the goods too, and Table 6.5 proves that it does.

| TABLE 6.5: THE GOODS IN WARP FACTOR | | |
|---|---|---|
| WEAPONS | AMMO | POWER-UPS |
| 1 shotgun | 3 cases | 4 portable medkits |
| 2 ripper chainguns | 2 cases | 7 atomic health units |
| 3 RPG launchers | 1 case | 1 armor |
| 2 devastators | 2 cases | 1 steroid flask |
| 1 shrinker | 2 crystals | 1 NVG |

| WEAPONS | AMMO | POWER-UPS |
|---|---|---|
| 2 freezethrowers | 1 charge | 1 holoduke |
| 1 laser trip bomb | | |
| 2 pipe bomb cases | | |

## BLAZING THROUGH WARP FACTOR

The pace in Warp Factor is nothing short of frantic. Even if you wish to blaze through this level, you will still have to cover the entire length of this installation.

### In the Southern Chambers

1. **Get a ripper chaingun.** Make a hard right stepping out of the elevator to claim the ripper chaingun on the floor.

2. **Lay your hands on a devastator.** Proceed into the chamber to the north, dashing across to the armory closet on the left side of the green metallic chamber. Open the semicircular door and nab the devastator. Turn around as soon as possible, and use

> **TIP**
> Before stepping out of the small elevator, be aware that a sentry drone flanks you on each side. Therefore, when you step out, be ready to fire on a sentry drone or to back up into the safety of the elevator enclosure. Of course, you can also run to a far corner of the room to get a bit more breathing room so you are able to aim squarely at them.

> **TIP**
> To better your odds of making it to the bottom floor, try going down once and shooting the enforcers from the dubious safety of the elevator. Then, with the enforcers out for good, drop one or two pipe bombs and activate the elevator to get out of harm's way. As the elevator begins ascending, detonate the switch. Now you are clear to go down again and proceed into the hallway, with the laser trip bombs safely exploded.

Ready Room

Bridge

Really Ready Room

Observation Deck

Switch Opens Access to Secret Bridge and Really Ready Room

Conveyor Escalator

Y

Core Reactor

West Wing

East Wing

Central Region

Exit

B

Southern Chambers

Entry

Ride shuttle to West Wing    Ride shuttle back to East Wing

**FIGURE 6.7:** This is Warp Factor, where no Duke has gone before.

**FIGURE 6.8:** Don't look for anyone to beam you out of Warp Factor.

your new weapon on the enforcer and the sentry drones that were auto-matically released from the dark chamber on the right side.

3. **Get down and claim the blue keycard.** Step on the platform to the left side of the chamber. It will immediately collapse to a lower level area where the blue keycard is found. Search along the rubble, sticking to the left side, and crouch along the northwest corner to reach the blue keycard.

4. **Reach the lower floor on the east side.** Having obtained the blue keycard, get back to level ground and then head toward the platform on the oppo-site side. The platform will lower into a wide hallway, but further progress will seem unlikely because, not only are you dealing with a couple of enforcers, but the threshold of the hallway is lined with laser trip bombs.

## In the East and West Wings

1. **Access the east wing.** Having cleared the laser trip bombs, head north and take a quick right into a small door where you will need to use the blue keycard. Step inside the small enclosure, and activate the elevator to reach the long and narrow east wing. Deal with the sentry drones, and travel southward along the east wing.

2. **Ride the shuttle to the west wing.** When you reach the southern end of the east wing, activate the switch near the observation deck. Notice how the shuttle travels across from the west wing to where you are (see Figure 6.9). When the shuttle arrives, hop on it and activate the trans-port switch.

## In the West Wing

1. **Go for the yellow keycard.** Forge northward along the west wing. Near its middle section, you will see the yellow keycard locked behind a seem-ingly impenetrable barrier. Throw the middle switch in a nearby switch panel, and the barriers blocking the yellow keycard will yield.

**FIGURE 6.9:** The shuttle is your ticket to the west wing and the yellow keycard.

2. **Ride the shuttle again.** Get back to the southern end of the wing, and push the button to beckon the shuttle. Get on it and get back to the east wing.

### Toward the Critical Switch

1. **Meet an old acquaintance.** Stepping down back into the main level, you will run into the Battlelord. Remember him? If

> **TIP**
>
> Because you won't gain much by engaging the Battlelord, you might also just run past him and head directly for the door leading to the north section of Warp Factor. You might sustain some damage in the process, but as soon as you step inside, you can claim an atomic health unit from the secret door behind the first computer control panel on the left side.

your health, armor, and weaponry allow it, you might be able to pepper the Battlelord with a combination of your devastator and RPG launcher.

You can also retreat into the small elevator, and close the door in front of you.

2. **Probe beyond the yellow door.** Run all the way to the north end, where a massive metal barrier cuts you off from reaching the very large, semi-circular observation chamber at the north end of Warp Factor.

3. **Reach the observation deck, and get the freezethrower.** Use the yellow keycard to gain access and press past the yellow door, and ride the conveyor escalator to the observation deck's entrance. At once, run directly across to the cylindrical enclosure and push the door open. Step inside and grab the freezethrower; you have earned it.

## On the Observation Deck

1. **Reach the circular control chamber.** Run to the very north end of the observation deck, and notice that there really isn't much to observe yet. Ascend the short ramp into the circular control chamber, and activate the switch behind the 3D model of the Earth. The shields around the observation deck will raise to reveal a breathtaking view of our home planet.

2. **Access the secret area.** Walk directly to the large map depicting the point of impact along the North American continent, and open a secret door behind the map. Step inside and claim the RPG launcher along the elevated ledge. Also, the middle section of the computer banks has a holoduke behind a small secret compartment.

3. **Activate the critical switch.** Look for the switch near a monitor on the west side. Turn on the switch to lower a shield barring access to the core reactor.

> **TIP**
>
> As you head for the yellow door, you might engage the curiosity of the assault commander. If he comes after you, keep a safe distance between you and him, leaving yourself the ability to find shelter from the rapid-fire rockets he is so fond of expelling in your general direction. Then retaliate with sustained fire from the devastator, or score one direct hit with the RPG launcher.

### Back in Warp Factor's Central Region

1.  **Retrace your steps.** Get back to the middle area, just south of the yellow door.

2.  **Find the back door to the core reactor.** Proceed to the large cubic chamber located right smack in the center of Warp Factor. Open the large metallic door, and race across the empty, but highly harmful, chamber. Radiation contamination in this chamber is quite high.

3.  **Time your move and go for it.** Wait for the moment when the rotating, incandescent shields leave a gap through which you can actually see a clear path to the central core, and then rush in. (See Figure 6.10.)

4.  **Ride up and away.** Activate the core (it acts like an elevator), and you will come upon an elevated circular enclosure, with the exit switch prominently displayed on the east side. Push the switch and you're gone.

Count your blessings; not everyone makes it this far and stays sane.

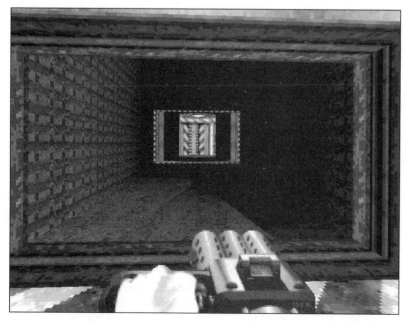

**FIGURE 6.10:** Make your move at the right moment, and get in through the back door.

## ADDED ATTRACTIONS IN WARP FACTOR

Space, the final frontier, can also be highly stressful and maddening. For that reason, if no other, most mortals might need a special place to find solace and renew their energy. For the captain of the Enterprise, this place is the "ready" room. For Duke Nukem, such a place might be the "really" ready room. Here is how you can find it and take a little time to kick off your shoes.

### Getting Some R&R

Should you decide to take a breather—and you really ought to—then the really ready room is the place to be. But reaching the really ready room is not completely an effortless proposition. Timing and execution are critical.

Near the southeastern end of the observation chamber, you will notice a wall panel with small green LEDs. This panel is in reality a secret wall. Open it and aim up to fire your gun at an elevated switch inside. Without loosing a second, run around the southern end of the observation deck to reach a lowered area along the outside west wall of the circular control chamber. Step inside and ride the elevator to reach a secret area above the circular control chamber.

Notice that the secret area, too, is circular and very reminiscent of the bridge of a once maiden starship. Access the chamber with the "Ready Room" sign on its door. Walk behind the desk and activate the desktop computer. Then step into the festive, lounging atmosphere of the really ready room, and let your hair down—for awhile, anyway.

## COVERT DETAILS

Table 6.6 summarizes the secrets in Warp Factor.

| TABLE 6.6: THE SECRETS IN WARP FACTOR | | |
|---|---|---|
| **AREA IN LEVEL** | **SECRET ITEM** | **HOW TO GET IT** |
| Northern observation deck | starship bridge | This area is accessible only after you activate the switch along the southeast wall (behind the computer panel with illuminated green LEDs). The switch lowers a panel on the west side of the central structure. |
| | really ready room | This area becomes available after you enter the "ready room" and activate the computer on the desktop. |

# FUSION STATION

Essentially, the Fusion Station is nothing more than an oversized instrument for spewing forth massive power loads to juice up all the lunar stations. Circular in shape and strictly utilitarian, the Fusion Station is an impressive structure of gargantuan proportions. Standing erect and dominating its central area, a very wide cylindrical column reaches up to the black heavens. This central core reactor houses three floor levels inside, each one posing a clever puzzle.

The north and west side periphery of the Fusion Station is crowned by another series of chambers and a long tunnel. Orgiastic in its unbridled decor, the Fusion Station is far from *Home & Gardens* fare. Your mission in the Fusion Station is to reach the head of the reactive column and blow it completely off.

To reach the head of the reactor, you will need to traverse the four corners of the Fusion Station and confront more sentry drones, enforcers, and assault commanders than ever before. If your current arsenal includes a devastator, an RPG launcher, or a more exotic weapon like a shrinker or a freezethrower, things might not be as dire.

The Fusion Station paces your progress because, as you reach a major area, you have to solve a puzzle before moving onto the next place of interest. This means you should pay particular attention to secret passages, switch-controlled doors, and other installation features. You would be surprised what you can find and where you can find it in the Fusion Station.

## MAPS AND ROUTE

The seemingly straightforward layout of the Fusion Station belies the fact that its multiple levels and secret passages make it a very hard level to crack open. Study Figures 6.11 and 6.12, and refer to them as often as necessary.

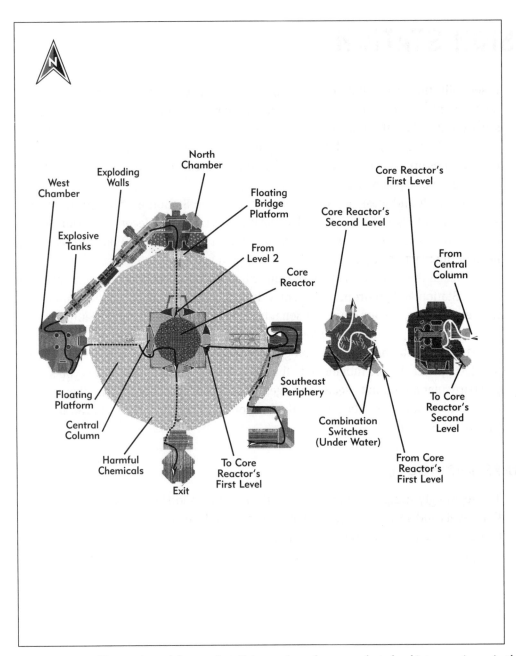

**FIGURE 6.11:** You are bound for an electrifying and maybe somewhat shocking experience in the Fusion Station.

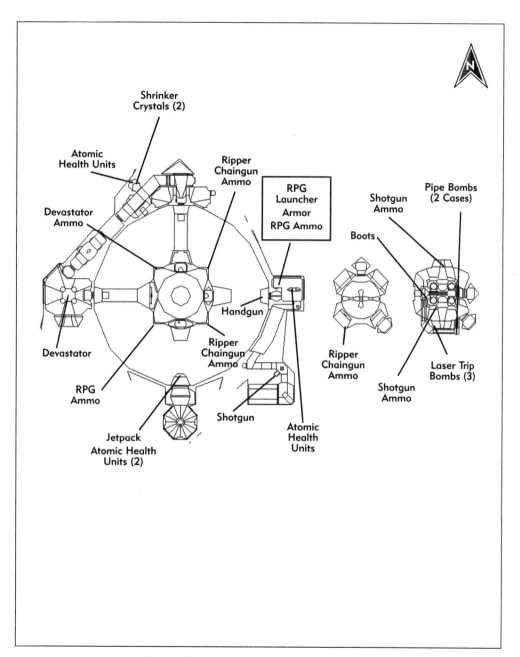

**FIGURE 6.12:** As you solve the Fusion Station's puzzles, you can collect from its sizable cache of weaponry and power-ups.

## THE GOODS

As you can see in Table 6.7, the goods in the Fusion Station are commensurate with its physical proportions.

### TABLE 6.7: THE GOODS IN FUSION STATION

| WEAPONS | AMMO | POWER-UPS |
| --- | --- | --- |
| 2 shotguns | 2 cases | 2 portable medkits |
| 2 ripper chainguns | 1 case | 7 atomic health units |
| 1 RPG launcher | 1 case | 2 armors |
| 1 shrinker | 2 crystals | 2 steroid flasks |
| 1 freezethrower | 1 charge | 4 NVGs |
| 5 laser trip bombs | | 1 jetpack |
| 4 pipe bomb cases | | 1 pair of boots |

## BLAZING THROUGH FUSION STATION

Getting from point A to point B in the Fusion Station level is never as simple as it might seem. Let this section be your pocket guide along the way.

### In the Southeastern Periphery

1. **Pick up a shotgun.** As you come around the second turn, take the shotgun behind the female in a cocoon.

2. **Take out the turrets.** Proceed up the long hallway, and duck to avoid direct turret hits. Stand up with the RPG launcher at the ready, and take out one of the turrets. Still ducking, move a few feet, stand up, and repeat the process with the second turret.

3. **Reap the goods in the eastern chamber.** Take the RPG and armor at the northwest corner of the chamber, by the Earth Defense Forces (EDF) monitor. Then claim the atomic health unit below the rising pillar. (A sensor near the monitor triggers the pillar.)

4. **Reach the central column.** Throw the switch near the door to open a small chamber leading to the exit. Throw the second door open, and be

ready to back up and pound the diving sentry drone. Cross the hand rail bridge to reach the central column.

## On the Core Reactor's First Level

1. **Pick up a few shotgun shells.** Enter the chamber and follow the path to the north side. Hop onto the elevated platform, and grab the case of shotgun shells.

2. **Activate the switched door.** Hop down from the platform and onto the first pumping pillar. Crouch and scoot southward into the small space between the two pillars. Then look the length of the glowing tunnel, and aim directly at the alien hand switch (see Figure 6.13). It causes the switched door on the southeast corner of the chamber to give way.

3. **Reach the second-level floor.** From your precarious position between the pumping pillars, sneak into the second pillar's hole. Then immediately

**FIGURE 6.13:** The switch at the end of this tunnel opens up access to higher floors and many more possibilities.

jump out onto the main floor of the chamber, and race for the door at the southeast corner. Get on the elevator and ride it up to the next floor.

### On the Core Reactor's Second Level

1. **Activate the combination switches.** There are two switches that activate a door in this chamber that opens in stages. You can only access the door after you activate both of the switches. Each switch is located inside the pool at the east and west ends, and each raises a portion of the door on the north end. You must time your movement in and out of the pool to avoid the heavy, churning arms of the central mill-like asps.

> **TIP**
>
> Jumping into a pillar hole is extremely dangerous. If your timing is anything but perfect, you could be the thickness of a silver coin in two or three seconds flat. Therefore, getting into the hole should be a two-stage procedure. First, jump up right next to the pumping column. Then, as soon as it reaches bottom and starts its upward motion, slip right through. Immediately crouch and move into the cubbyhole just south of the first pillar.

2. **Reach the third floor.** When the door is fully open, step out to view a wide chasm and the north end of the station.

### On the Core Reactor's Third Level

1. **Cross the chasm.** Activate the switch at the end of the observation deck to beckon the floating platform from the north side. Get on top of the platform, aim your gun at the alien hand print switch, and fire. The floating platform will take you across the chasm and deliver you to the entrance of the north chamber.

> **TIP**
>
> It's always a good idea to save a game before you attempt to do something that could damage you seriously or kill you. That way, if the worst should happen, you can pick up the game from the place where you last saved it.

### In the North Chamber

1. **Get more stuff.** Grab the pipe bomb cases and any other weaponry strewn about.

2. **Head southwest.** Proceed along the west side to find a door yielding into a long tunnel that connects you to the west side chamber.

### In the West Side Chamber

1. **Collect the devastator.** Quell the opposition in the square side chamber on your left and then take the devastator weapon from the oscillating floor in the middle of the room. If your shrinker has been under used, feel free to pour its frigid might onto the assault commander guarding the devastator.

2. **Reach the central column's west side.** Find the hand print switch behind a dividing wall on the south

> **TIP**
>
> As you reach the mid point of the first section of the tunnel, sensors will cause the wall on the right side to explode violently. To avoid needless harm, consider throwing a pipe bomb or firing an RPG at the wall before you venture inside the tunnel. When you reach the second tunnel section, look for the C-9 canisters and detonate them from a safe distance. You have come too far to be blown away by a careless mistake.

side of the chamber and activate it. Without skipping a single beat, turn around and race for the door on the east side before it is shut down automatically. Standing on the deck, beckon another flying platform as before and reach the central core reactor.

### Back in the Core Reactor

1. **Blow up the reactor's head.** You are now at the top level of the core reactor, and the massive pillar in the middle of the room will descend shortly to reveal a claw-like head buzzing with energy. Run around the

four corners of this floor, collecting all the ammo to be had. Then stand near the point where you entered, fire an RPG round or two, and seek protection behind the dividing wall. You will need it. The reactor will blow in a big way.

2. **Ride the floating platform.** The otherwise impenetrable door at the south end of the core reactor should now be cracked open. Go through the hole. Now you must bridge another chasm to reach the southern chamber. If you have a jetpack, you are set; if not, don't despair. If you look down, you will see a small platform below the entrance to the southern chamber. Take a running jump and land on the platform. Replenish your health with the atomic health units while you are there. Notice also that there is a jetpack waiting for you. Strap on the jetpack and rise straight up.

3. **Defeat the assault commander and adios amigo.** Go through the final gate. Sensors will cause the exit switch to rise from the floor. But, unfortunately, a sentry drone will be released at the same time. If you have some devastator charges left, this is the time to put them to use.

## ADDED ATTRACTIONS IN FUSION STATION

Although mostly utilitarian, the Fusion Station is not totally without its charm and beguiling surprises. Don't expect creature comforts, but you owe it to yourself and future generations to investigate a couple of the Fusion Station's elusive secrets.

### Life at the End of the Tunnel

The first floor of the core reactor is an interesting structure in more ways than one, and there are nice perks to be had on the side. To begin, the core's heavy, industrial quality is reinforced by the lattice of wiring and pipe work lining the walls. Four pumping pillars dominate the main area of the chamber, pounding away incessantly like well-tuned high performance pistons.

The poor lighting of this chamber makes you slightly more vulnerable if you don't have a pair of NVGs. Upon entering you are beset by overzealous enforcers. Choose your favorite weapon to put down the reptilian menace. Jump right next to the pillar, and drop into the gaping hole as the pillar begins its upward motion. Crouch and move into the small cubbyhole so you're actually sitting right between the two opposing pillars. Look eastward for a long but narrow crimson tunnel. Aim a bullet directly at the hand print switch to unlock the exit to the chamber. Notice the atomic health units at the end of the tunnel. You will make them yours very soon.

Time your next jump into the hole for the second pillar and, just as quickly as possible, jump out onto the main floor of the chamber. Take care of the enforcer and trooper parade, and jump onto the elevated platform on the south wall. Pick up the laser trip bombs in the corner. Then look for a slightly brighter panel along the south wall and push it open. You have reached a secret duct. Follow it as it turns westward to pick up two cases of pipe bombs. Retrace your steps, follow the duct to the west, and then go on a very steep incline as the duct turns northward. You will come upon those precious glowing objects otherwise known as atomic health units.

## COVERT DETAILS

The Fusion Station's secrets are listed in Table 6.8. Your job is to find them all.

| TABLE 6.8: THE SECRETS IN FUSION STATION | | |
|---|---|---|
| **AREA IN LEVEL** | **SECRET ITEM** | **HOW TO GET IT** |
| Central core reactor, first floor | atomic health units | You'll find these at the end of a long crimson tunnel nestled between two pumping pillars. Because the tunnel is too narrow, you must find the secret duct leading to the end of the tunnel. The duct's entrance is through a metal panel on the southern wall, on top of the large platform. |
| | pipe bomb cases (2) | These are at the eastern end of the secret duct. |
| | ripper chaingun | This weapon is in the cubbyhole between the two pillars on the east side of the chamber. You must time your jump inside the hole of either pillar and then rapidly scoot into the narrow space between the pillars to claim the ripper chaingun. |

*(Continued on next page)*

*(Continued from previous page)*

| AREA IN LEVEL | SECRET ITEM | HOW TO GET IT |
|---|---|---|
| Along the northeastern bridge | atomic health unit shrinker crystals (2) | These items are in a secret area above the air ducts. The exploding wall in this segment serves as a guide post to tell you where you should look up. In fact, use the rubble on the wall to climb onto the overhead duct. Go through a secret passage on the inside wall and follow it around as it comes out over the other duct. At the end of this duct, you will find a female held captive by a strange alien vine. Grab the crystals, waste the unfortunate soul, and claim the atomic health unit. |

# OCCUPIED TERRITORY

Making serious headway into Lunar Apocalypse, you are about to confront what is arguably the toughest level. If for nothing else, Occupied Territory is daunting by the sheer number and the viciousness of your co-occupants. It's as though a fearsome force of fiendish foes has come together to cause your fall and evict you permanently from Occupied Territory. Occupied Territory is also the entry point to Spin Cycle, the first secret level in this episode.

Returning to a slick and pleasantly simple geometric level design, Occupied Territory spreads from an immense central observation chamber with huge translucent panes to three extensions of various lengths and shapes. To the east, the dark Battlelord's quarters house the blue keycard. But don't count on the Battlelord handing it to you when you get there. The west wing is dominated by a wide and large open skyway, which ends right where you start your foray into Occupied Territory.

Circumventing the many perils of Occupied Territory is just impossible. So brace yourself for serious bare-knuckle action. But for the raw brutality that awaits you, there are still some important pieces of strategy you should keep in mind. First, your ultimate destination is to penetrate the tightly guarded central cage in the observation mall. That is where the exit switch is. But knowing it's there means nothing, if you can't penetrate the cage. The aforementioned blue keycard will let you in, but there is another problem. The Battlelords' chamber is beyond reach unless you have the red keycard to begin with. No problem. You can get the red keycard with your trusted ripper chaingun. This weapon excels at cleaning a path over the vicious protozoid slimers as you work your way up the ramps into the southernmost cavernous chamber. You will find the red keycard deposited at the tip, as it were.

## MAPS AND ROUTE

Figures 6.14 and 6.15 show Occupied Territory to be a simple, sleek, but quite perilous construction.

## THE GOODS

This level isn't necessarily overflowing with goods, but sometimes the work should be its own reward. Table 6.9 shows you the goods to be had.

### TABLE 6.9: THE GOODS IN OCCUPIED TERRITORY

| WEAPONS | AMMO | POWER-UPS |
| --- | --- | --- |
| 1 shotgun | 4 cases | 2 portable medkits |
| 1 ripper chaingun | 4 cases | 3 atomic health units |
| 1 RPG launcher | 3 cases | 2 armors |
| 1 devastator | 3 cases | 1 steroid flask |
| 2 laser trip bombs | | 3 NVGs |
| 2 pipe bomb cases | 2 shrinker crystals | 1 holoduke |

## BLAZING THROUGH OCCUPIED TERRITORY

Getting through Occupied Territory requires you to cover a large amount of ground and endure many fierce battles. Only your sharp skills and the wise use of your weaponry will see you through.

### In the Entryway and on the Skyway

1. **Open the door and boost your health.** Grab the shotgun and the shells before using the switch to open the circular door. Clear the path of crawly protozoid slimers with a few pipe bombs before proceeding into the chamber behind the Earth Defense Forces emblem. Take the ripper chaingun from behind the emblem, and spray bullets at the troopers

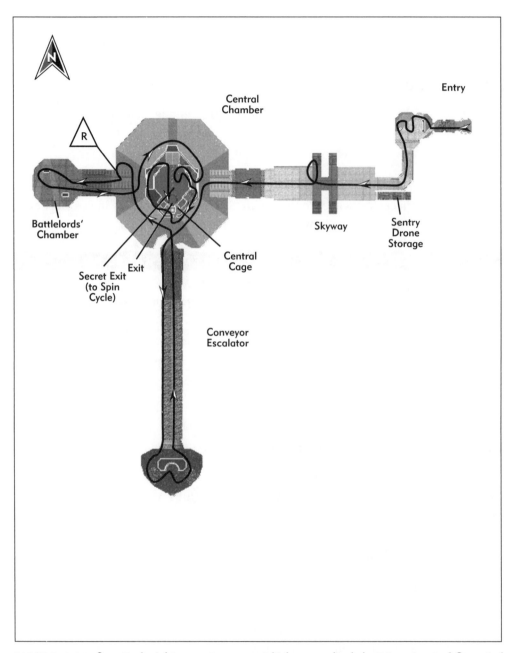

**FIGURE 6.14**: Squatter's rights or not, you must kick every alien's butt to get out of Occupied Territory.

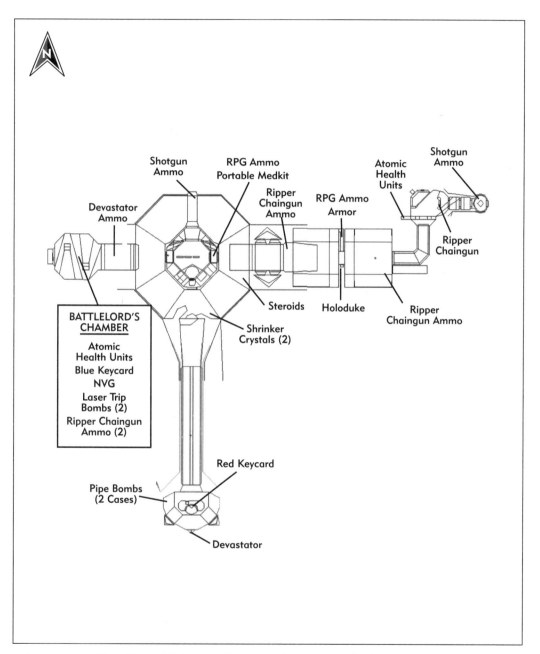

FIGURE 6.15: That this level is lean on the goods demonstrates further just how tough this level can be.

behind the diagonal partition. Enter the partition through the side door, and flick the switch on the wall to open the large door to the south. Get ready for a few more fireworks and then stop at the gate's threshold, squat down, and thrust your way into a narrow opening where an atomic health unit awaits.

2. **Collect what you can, and reach the central observation chamber.** Stepping into the long and wide runway, you will notice gigantic metal curtains recede to give way to a bold, translucent sky. But your sense of awe will be drawn short by the party assembled on the skyway. Be sure to grab the ammo for the ripper chaingun and the RPG launcher as you move westward along the skyway. When you come upon a narrow wall cutting the skyway in half, climb the north slope and kick in the duct grill. Step inside and traverse the length of the narrow duct to claim an armor and an RPG launcher. Armed with your new weapon, continue forging westward.

> **TIP**
>
> As you reach the entrance to the main chamber's foyer, a sensor triggers a door open back toward the start of the skyway. The small storage area is a veritable sentry drone hive, buzzing with frenzy. Use the long space between you and the sentry drones and put the RPG launcher to work overtime for you.

### In the Central Chamber

1. **Seek out the red keycard.** Upon entering the central observation chamber, head immediately southward, toward the organic growth along the south wall. Crawl inside the squishy interior, fend off creeping protozoid slimers, and grab two very indispensable shrinker crystals before moving forward. Ride the conveyor to the top of the narrow tunnel.

2. **Take the red keycard.** Push open the next door and step in to wrestle the red keycard from a less-than-compliant assault commander. Limit your exposure, and don't give the assault commander time to react as you clear the small wall partition. Be ready to aim and fire at the C-9

canisters next to the assault commander. If he survives the explosion, finish him with one or two shotgun blasts.

3. **Return to the central chamber.** Ride the conveyor escalator back to the central chamber, and then make your way over to its western wall.

4. **Greet a couple of old pals, and yank the blue keycard.** Use the red keycard on the switch along the western wall. Stand back as a slanted platform pushes its way from out of the wall. Climb up the steep platform, and be sure to pick up the devastator ammunition en route to the top. Open the rusty metallic door emblazoned with the Battlelord's contemptuous countenance and step in a ways. It's best to draw the Battlelords out and clobber each with a shower of devastator charges or an all-out RPG shower. When they succumb, go inside the chamber to take the blue keycard. Check the secret compartment behind the broken terminal to claim an atomic health unit and a couple of laser trip bombs.

5. **Penetrate the central cage's lock.** Rush back toward the east side of the central cage. You have earned the right to enter.

## In the Central Cage

1. **Activate the switch to the side door.** As you enter the central cage, look for a switch next to a small computer bank. Activate the switch. It causes a door on the south side of the central cage to open, thus granting you access to the space between the walls of the central cage.

2. **Enter through the back door.** Get out of the cage only to find the newly opened door on the south wall that you will re-enter. Don't let the enforcers stop you from reaching what appears to be an observation deck that looks into the middle section of the cage.

3. **Take down more Battlelords before making tracks.** Press the switch to the right of the observation window, and watch a heavy shield give way to reveal two Battlelords and a holographic image of a yet-unseen alien host.

4. **Battle the two giants.** Dodging their projectiles and explosive pellets, strafe left and right and take advantage of every opening to administer

unhealthy doses of devastator charges. For variety, pelt the Battlelords with RPG rounds too.

5. **Cross the planks to reach the exit.** Jump through the observation opening, and pass over the row of metal planks to reach the circular stage with the holographic horror. Push the switch to its right side, and punch the exposed exit switch.

> **TIP**
>
> To reach the secret exit and visit the maniacal Spin Cycle, half way down the planks, look slightly behind and to your left. Then look up. Shoot the switch to cause a panel on the right side to open. Inside, behold the secret exit. Hover over to the switch and you're on your way to Spin Cycle.

## ADDED ATTRACTIONS IN OCCUPIED TERRITORY

Almost every step along the way in Occupied Territory is fraught with uncertainty and danger. Here, you get to examine one such moment more closely.

### Battlelord, Will You Please Hand Me the Blue Keycard?

By far the most daring maneuver in this level involves obtaining the blue keycard. There is too much at stake. Without the blue keycard, you won't be able to enter the central cage, where the final exit switch awaits. But perhaps no keycard in this game is under such tight guard as this blue keycard. Not one, but two Battlelords are entrusted with the simple mission of annihilating anyone who even comes near.

Don't let the prospect of being rendered a slice of human Swiss cheese detract you from your quest to save humanity. Once you have obtained the red keycard from the southern chamber at the end of the long corridor with the conveyor ramps, activate the central chamber's switch on the west wall. Hop on top of the massive slanted surface pushing its way out from the wall. Halfway up the ramp, pick up the two cases of devastator ammo. Though this is far from a prize fight, every single round is crucial.

Coming upon the emblazoned mug of the Battlelord on the metallic doorway, ready your devastator. Push the door open, and venture in just enough to douse one of the Battlelords before suddenly retreating toward the entry ramp. Jump off the ramp and think quickly. You know the Battlelords are after you. Ideally, you should have enough health, armor, and ammo to pummel both Battlelords before they can even get off the ramp.

However, should they reach the chamber's main floor, you're in for a terrifying game of cat and mouse. The first thing to do is find a position where you can take shield from the chaingun and explosive pellet onslaught. The best place for that is along the northern or southern wall so you can use the central cage as a shield. You can, in fact, run around the central cage and fire upon the Battlelords when you find the slightest opening. But this is at best a tenuous proposition. Something a bit more conservative is to run into the long, webbed hallway to the south. The Battlelords' massive size will prevent them from following you. You can then unload your weaponry almost at will.

With the Battlelords in the pages of history, climb up the ramp to the west chamber a second time and secure the blue keycard.

## COVERT DETAILS

For its apparent simplicity, the Occupied Territory level houses an unusual and assorted collection of secrets. See Table 6.10 for a full list.

### TABLE 6.10: THE SECRETS IN OCCUPIED TERRITORY

| AREA IN LEVEL | SECRET ITEM | HOW TO GET IT |
|---|---|---|
| The entry way | atomic health unit | This item is in the small recess by the threshold of the first door. |
| The skyway | RPG ammo<br>armor | These are inside a narrow duct. The duct is accessible through a grill on the west side of the wall dividing the skyway down the middle. Climb up the ramp to reach the duct grill. |
| | shotgun chaingun ammo | These are in the rocky tunnel that looks like an appendage near the eastern end. The tunnel is accessible only through an exploding wall on its north side, across from an alien hand print. |
| The Battlelords' quarters | laser trip bombs (2)<br>atomic health unit | These can be found behind the computer panel. The secret compartment is accessible through the broken computer monitor to the right of the original place where the blue keycard sits. |
| Central cage | Secret exit | Halfway down the narrow bridge near the exit, look behind you to your left. Shoot the switch high on the wall and hover to the opening on the right side. |

# TIBERIUS STATION

You may not be the first person to walk on the moon. But at least in this adventure, this is the first time you reach the desolate planes and craters of our companion satellite. Like the orbital stations, Tiberius, too, is under heavy alien occupation. Laid out in a vertical north-south floor plan, Tiberius Station also has an extensive duct network. Starting at the southernmost point, your mission is straightforward. Get to the northernmost chamber, where an eager Battlelord Sentry will do his best to render his usual hospitality and keep you from activating the exit switch.

Unless you know about certain shortcuts, your seemingly simple task can become suddenly very complicated. It is possible, in fact, to get through Tiberius Station with a single red keycard. However, you risk missing a large part of the installation. Considering you are facing some very unforgiving opponents, you might want to explore the very generous offerings of weapons and power-ups in this level. The general key to succeeding in Tiberius Station is to blow things up, if there is any doubt. You won't need to ask questions later.

## MAPS AND ROUTE

Figures 6.16 and 6.17 show Tiberius Station to consist of a few chambers of varying sizes connected by a network of hallways and air ducts.

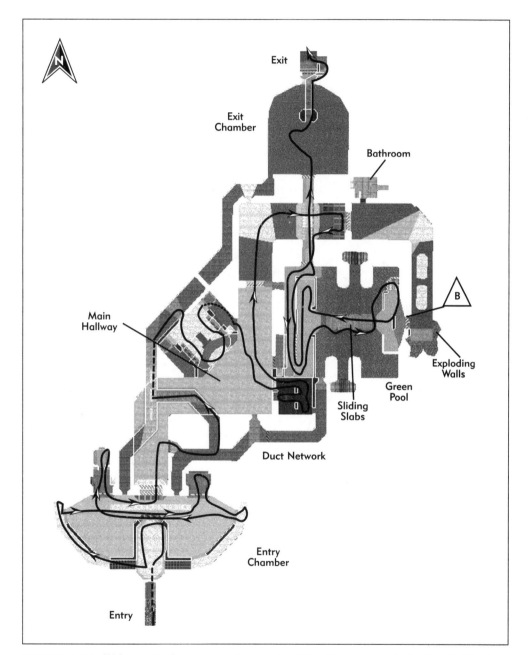

N

Exit

Exit
Chamber

Bathroom

Main
Hallway

B

Exploding
Walls

Green
Pool

Sliding
Slabs

Duct Network

Entry
Chamber

Entry

**FIGURE 6.16:** Welcome to the moon and sorry about the bloody mess, but after all, Tiberius Station is under siege.

**FIGURE 6.17:** The alien infestation has reached our moon bases. Collect your fill as you liberate Tiberius Station.

## THE GOODS

Few other levels in the Lunar Apocalypse episode are as generous in the goods departments, as you can see in Table 6.11.

### TABLE 6.11: THE GOODS IN TIBERIUS STATION

| WEAPONS | AMMO | POWER-UPS |
|---|---|---|
| 1 shotgun | 5 cases | 3 portable medkits |
| 1 ripper chaingun | 4 cases | 3 atomic health units |
| 2 RPG launchers | 2 cases | 2 armors |
| 1 devastator | 1 case | 1 steroid flask |
| 1 shrinker | 3 crystals | 1 holoduke |
| 1 freezethrower | 2 charges | 1 scuba gear |
| 2 laser trip bombs | | 1 pair of boots |
| 2 pipe bomb cases | | 1 jetpack |

## BLAZING THROUGH TIBERIUS STATION

Do you want to avoid much heartache and sorrow? Reap some choice goods, and get through Tiberius Station in a mercifully short time. This section shows you how.

### In the Entry Chamber

1. **Climb out of the goo.** Hop over the door and punch a hole through the grill to get out of the narrow and gooey entryway. Landing on an elevated control platform, find your way down through either long, narrow east or west walkway.

2. **Collect the goods in the east and west side storage rooms.** At the end of the walkway you will run into a monitor and a switch. The switch causes a small storage room at the opposite side of the chamber to open. The storage chamber on the

**TIP**
Look for the cracked lines on the right wall's surface as a telling sign of the correct location for placing the pipe bombs.

east side has two cases of shotgun ammo and a shrinker crystal. The other storage room boasts two armors, a large medkit inside a refrigerator, and a secret panel between the two armors. The panel leads to a small back room with a portable medkit.

3. **Open the gate to the main hallway.** Get back on top of the control platform, and activate the switch overlooking the chamber's exit gate. Get down and enter the main hallway.

## In the Main Hallway

1. **Blow up a hole in the wall.** Drop a pipe bomb near the wall on the right side. Stand back and detonate the pipe bomb. Hop inside the gaping hole in the wall, and take the two cases of shotgun shells.

2. **Take the goods in the computer control room.** Continue along the duct directly due north. Follow it as it makes a couple of sharp right turns and slopes upward. You will come upon two shrinker crystals right in from of a duct grill. Take the crystals and bust through the grill. The compartment in the computer panel on the left side houses a holoduke.

3. **Go after the devastator.** Punch the switch overlooking the main hallway, and race down one of the side platforms to catch the gate across the hallway before it closes. Grab the devastator on the table, and annihilate the enforcers.

4. **Pound your way to the north hallway.** Armed with your new weapon, clean yourself a path to reach the north hallway, past the gate at its north end. As you turn the corner, face off the rushing enforcers. Then run to the east end of the hallway to stand behind the handrail.

5. **Access the overhead bridge.** Hop onto the handrail, aim upward toward the overhead bridge, and then jump. Walk up to the door on the south side; it opens into the central ooze pit.

### In the Central Ooze Pit

1. **Work your way down to the ooze.** Two elevated areas flank the ooze pit on the east and west sides. Your entry point is at the top of the western side. While you are at the top, take advantage of the heavy walls shielding you and pepper the octabrain parade floating above the pit. Walk south along the narrow passage to reach the next lower floor.

2. **Don the scuba gear and dive for the red card.** You will find the scuba gear sitting next to a panel of computers. Slip it on and plunge into the murky toxic waters. Reach the very bottom and collect the red keycard. The keycard is directly below the middle of the flanking area you jumped from.

3. **Reach the eastern flanking area.** Once you have the keycard in your possession, swim across to the eastern area and hop onto the platform on its north side. Activate the platform and get on it to reach the elevated area.

4. **Build a bridge and get out.** Look for the switch in the middle of the elevated area and punch it at once. Four heavy metallic platforms will emerge from the north and side walls to line up in the middle of the pit and form a bridge. Cross the bridge to the west side again.

5. **Get back to the top floor.** Trace your steps back to the top side and get back out of the pit chamber and onto the bridge where you entered. Walk straight north on the bridge to reach the final chamber.

### In the Exit Chamber

1. **Greet the Battlelord with a bang.** The instant the door opens, aim for the C-9 canisters on the left side of the chamber and back away quickly. It matters not if you fall off the bridge. Keep banging at the Battlelord until you watch him crumble. (See Figure 6.18.) Occasionally the Battlelord Sentry will stay back behind the pillar in the middle of the room. If he does, you will have to go hunt him down in the reduced space of the final chamber.

2. **Find the underground passage.** Enter the chamber and look for a duct entrance on the south side of the chamber's only pillar.

**FIGURE 6.18:** Bang this dude hard. He won't go down any other way.

3. **See you next time.** Crawl through the tunnel and then walk out onto the small enclosure with the glowing red light and the exit switch. You know what to do next.

## ADDED ATTRACTIONS IN TIBERIUS STATION

For the amount of pain, suffering, and untold psychological damage you can undergo in this level, it is only fair that you get at least a little something in return. Isn't it? The pool area, east of the main hallway, is a place where you can be almost suitably compensated.

### This is No Pool Party

There are at least two ways to reach the green slimy pool. One involves using the blue keycard, which is found in the elevated computer room west of the hallway. With this keycard you can access the pool through a security latch at the far east side. The second way does not require you to use the blue keycard. Instead, you have to jump from the railing at the end of the north hallway onto the overhead bridge. Then you can simply go through the entrance at the northwest corner of the pool.

If you went in through the east side door, grab the protective boots along the wall overlooking the pool. Then activate the switch in the center of the platform to cause four heavy metallic slabs to line up in the middle of the pool, creating a bridge in effect. Then run over the newly formed bridge across to the east side of the pool.

If you entered through the bridge at the north end, you will find yourself on the top floor of a balcony overlooking the pool. Drop a pipe bomb a short ways into the narrow hallway. When you detonate it, it will open up a crevice in the wall large enough for you to walk into and claim a jetpack. Continue southward to reach the middle level platform. Collect the scuba gear and the shrinker near the north end of the platform. Then activate the switch to cause the heavy metallic slabs to line up in the middle of the pool. Dive into the pool on the north side of the slabs, and swim to reach the wall indenture where the second slab is normally found.

Resurface and push against the wall to uncover a small enclosure holding two atomic health units. Take the atomic health units and go back underwater. Swim to the south side of the slabs, and look for a similar enclosure along the south wall, in the place where the third slab (from the left) is normally found. In this second enclosure you will be able to grab two cases of RPG ammo.

## COVERT DETAILS

Table 6.12 shows the truly staggering number of secrets in Tiberius Station.

| TABLE 6.12: THE SECRETS IN TIBERIUS STATION | | |
|---|---|---|
| **AREA IN LEVEL** | **SECRET ITEM** | **HOW TO GET IT** |
| The entry chamber | portable medkit | This is in a secret compartment behind a panel in the west side storage room. The panel leading to the secret room is between the two armors in the storage room. |
| | shotgun shells access to west side duct network | These are found through the exploding wall, right outside the main gate to the entry chamber. |
| The main hallway | pipe bomb cases (2) | These are in a secret area below the elevated computer room on the west side of the hallway. To get the bomb cases, you must walk through a fake wall right across from a small water fountain under the computer room. |

*(Continued on next page)*

*(Continued from previous page)*

| AREA IN LEVEL | SECRET ITEM | HOW TO GET IT |
|---|---|---|
| The main hallway | steroids<br>chaingun ammo | These are in a secret panel to the left of the door labeled "Radioactive." |
| | RPG launcher | This is in an elevated secret panel at the northwest corner, to the right of the vertical light panel. This panel opens only for a few seconds after a sensor is tripped inside the duct across the way. That duct is only accessible through the exit chamber to the north. |
| The pool area | atomic health units (2) | These are in a secret chamber near the northwest side. To access this area, you must first cause the large metallic slabs to line up in the middle of the pool. Then you can jump in to reach the area, which is at surface level, push against the wall, and then enter the enclosure. |
| | RPG ammo (2) | You'll find these in a similar enclosure along the southeast side. |

# LUNAR REACTOR

Almost twice as large as Tiberius Station, and posing an even greater threat, the Lunar Reactor level sprawls its long hallways, assorted chambers, and multiple secrets over a vast expanse of lunar surface. Complete with crew quarters, working bathrooms, underground toxic disposal canals, a sealed-in courtyard, and crushing tunnels, Lunar Reactor places you in an environment where only your skill, keen reflexes, and intelligence can see you through. There are various places where you must perform difficult maneuvers under extreme pressure. Of course, the piece de résistance in this level is the core reactor chamber and the cinematic escape sequence.

Your objective is to seek out and destroy the core reactor. But without the yellow keycard, the reactor will remain forever sealed and out of reach. Getting the yellow keycard will test the limits of your tenacity. It lies in a tunnel in the north side of the lunar courtyard. Get there, and you will have won only half the battle. The other half requires getting back to the main installation and facing off with the Battlelord, before you blow the reactor to bits.

## MAPS AND ROUTE

It's too bad there aren't guided tours of Lunar Reactor. As you can see in Figures 6.19 and 6.20, finding your way around this level can seem overwhelming.

## THE GOODS

This is a big level. It is only fair that the goods be just as substantial. See for yourself in Table 6.13.

### TABLE 6.13: THE GOODS IN LUNAR REACTOR

| WEAPONS | AMMO | POWER-UPS |
| --- | --- | --- |
| 2 shotguns | 5 cases | 1 portable medkit |
| 1 ripper chaingun | 4 cases | 6 atomic health units |
| 2 RPG launchers | 4 cases | 2 armors |
| 1 devastator | 8 cases | 1 jetpack |
| 1 shrinker | 2 crystals | 1 pair of boots |
| 1 freezethrower | 4 charges | 1 holoduke |
| 6 laser trip bombs | | |
| 2 pipe bomb cases | | |

## BLAZING THROUGH LUNAR REACTOR

Even if you want to blaze through this level, you're still in for a long and perilous haul. Don't worry too much, though, just stick with the plan and you might yet make it.

### In the Entry and the Restricted Area

1. **Explore the ducts.** If you were to venture out immediately, you would find your access blocked by keycard gates in every direction except to the restricted area (to the east). Therefore, it behooves you to see how

**FIGURE 6.19:** If you like fighting fiercely and intelligently and solving interesting puzzles, then you are in your element making your way through Lunar Reactor.

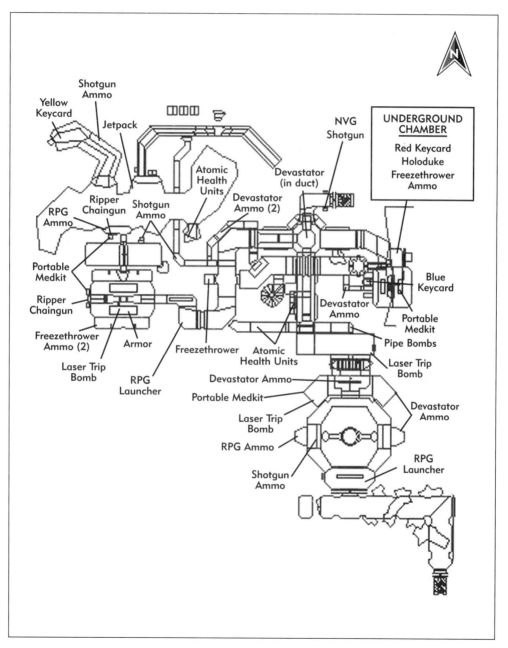

**FIGURE 6.20:** Lunar Reactor boasts a bevy of booty.

far you can go in the ducts. But even before that, take the shotgun and the NVG in the small compartment just outside the entry chamber. Then jump into either one of the ducts to the left or right as you come out to the spot where the corridors converge. You will have to clear the area of protozoid slimers, as they thrive in dark, moist places. Grab the shells and pipe bombs.

2. **Continue moving through the ducts.** Now stand in the middle of the ducts, face south, and jump forward to reach a higher space in the duct network. Reward your efforts with the devastator you just found. Continue north along the corridor and drop into a small space that branches off to the right. You will come upon an atomic health unit. Take the unit and kick the duct grill to emerge just outside the core reactor door.

3. **Fell an assault commander.** With your health properly boosted and you now holding a devastator, head toward the crew quarters. Open the door and be ready to take down the assault commander behind the door.

4. **Grab the blue keycard in the bathroom.** Storm the bathroom at the end of the restricted area. Clear the path of enforcers and their trooper underlings. Then explore the two stalls near to the entrance to collect a laser trip bomb, and most importantly, the blue keycard that grants you access to the crew quarters.

## In the Crew Quarters

1. **Penetrate deep.** Use the blue keycard in the crew quarters latch to the west. Follow the wide hallway and come upon a grilled section of the floor. If you have any, drop a pipe bomb or three down the grill to fry a few protozoid slimers in their juice before they come bouncing after you. Also, fend off any sentry drones patrolling this area.

2. **Ransack the crew's sleeping and slumming quarters.** Open yet another gate labeled "Crew Quarters" and run for the RPG launcher in front of you. Enter the commons area, and battle your way to the north end where you can grab a ripper chaingun and other goodies from the adjacent

cabinets. After grabbing the ripper chaingun, you will almost have to empty its contents on the encroaching aliens. Also, check out the closets for additional items.

3. **Reach the underground sandwich chamber.** Direct your attention to the sleeping chambers on the north side of the crew's quarters. Find the open chute between the cots, and drop into a small restricted space in a flooded and large underground chamber. Seemingly trapped, you must cross the chamber toward the duct directly north of your position.

> **TIP**
>
> When confronting the assault commander by the crew quarters entrance, start running backwards as soon as you open the door. You want to keep your sights on him while giving yourself some room to react and dodge his incoming projectiles. Start firing immediately.

4. **Reach the north courtyard.** Activate the switch in the small space, and run straight across as fast as possible while the giant metal slabs come apart temporarily. You have a matter of mere seconds to make it across. Avoid a wily coyote scene by stopping in your tracks as soon as you reach the grill. Otherwise, you could be plummeting to a precipitous fall and get to see the bottom of the north courtyard face first.

## In the North Courtyard

1. **Make it to the north side.** As soon as possible, take out the turret across the chasm. Then take the RPG ammo nearby and the

> **TIP**
>
> Another way to reach the north side of the courtyard without the help of a jetpack is to take a running start and attempt to land on the glowing blue platform that is visible from your position. Then you can simply teleport to the tunnel to the west, where the yellow keycard is found. The teleporter is hidden behind the computer consoles.

portable medkit in the compartment by the console. If you have a jet-pack, you're in good shape. If not, you will have to get the one at the bottom of the courtyard. This means taking a fall. Luckily, you have a portable medkit with you. So be brave and plunge into the open space below. Then collect the jetpack and elevate yourself to find a wide opening along the mountainside. Land in there and take the yellow keycard near the entrance.

2. **Teleport to the tunnel on the east side.** Now you are ready to get back to the main installation area and go in search of the reactor. However, there is the small matter of reaching the south side of the courtyard. Penetrate all the way to the end of the marble-like tunnel, and pick up the shrinker crystals along the way. Don't be too discouraged by the sight of a mangled human body hanging upside down. At the very end of the tunnel, you will see a teleporter. Get on it and emerge on the eastern platform.

3. **Collapse the tunnel.** Start into the tunnel, but be very cautious. Dispose of the small armada of troopers who will come barreling down the tunnel. When you feel the first set of tremors, you should stop on your feet. As you reach the middle section of the tunnel, entire sections will begin to crumble in succession. Get out of the way of crushing rocks by standing near the edges of the tunnel or, better yet, by running back near the entrance. The rock shifting will cause the south wall of the tunnel to blow open a hole where a duct is conveniently accessible.

4. **Get back via the duct network.** Enter through the duct and cross right over the courtyard back into the main installation. The duct will lead you directly to the area below the grill floor in the hallway outside the crew quarters.

5. **Get the red keycard.** Jump into the disposal canal and follow its downward slope. You will go past an opening on the right side leading to a spiral staircase and toward a giant turning cog. It will do you no good to run up the staircase without the red keycard. So keep going toward the cog. Stop when you are close to the turning cog. Synchronize your movement with the cog, and place yourself in one of its recesses. Then just let it turn you like a revolving door into the eastern end. You will

happen upon an underground computer chamber containing the red keycard as well as a holoduke and freezethrower ammo.

6. **Ascend the spiral staircase.** Go back through the cog in the same way you came in. Trudge up the canal to find the opening along the left wall leading to the staircase. Enter and climb. Use the red keycard when you reach the top to emerge right outside the core reactor quarters. Use the yellow keycard to enter the core reactor chamber.

7. **Cream the Battlelord.** The entrance to the reactor chamber is guarded by a Battlelord. Leave yourself plenty of room to retreat. Because the area is dark, you might also want to break out your NVG. Jump over the dead heap, and enter the core reactor chamber.

## In the Core Reactor Chamber

1. **Reach the floor level and blow up the core reactor.** Go down the flight of stairs in the chamber's entry. Clear the floor area of as many enemies as possible. Then press the switch on the right side to expose the reactor core. A single rocket at the power source should cause it to blow up and take the southern door with it.

2. **Get out quickly.** Go through the hole in the door into a steel gray corridor. Without a moment's hesitation, hoist the RPG, and run eastward to catch a couple of hovering assault commanders in midair as the entire hallway begins to explode behind you.

If you move fast enough, you will see the hallway exploding behind you in the mirror at the far end of the hallway. If you have survived all of this, all that remains to do is to punch the exit switch.

## ADDED ATTRACTIONS IN LUNAR REACTOR

There are plenty of moments during your mission in Lunar Reactor that bear a closer look. One such scenario unfolds when you reach the north courtyard.

### Strolling in the Lunar Courtyard

Besides the compelling reasons to visit the courtyard (fun, challenge, and adventure), you really have no choice. The yellow keycard, which unlocks the core reactor chamber, is found in a remote cave along the courtyard's north mountainside. You need this keycard so you can destroy the reactor and find the exit.

There is only one way to reach the north courtyard. That involves reaching the underground chamber just north of the crew's sleeping quarters. The chute between the cots lets you drop inside the chamber. Once there, timing and execution are essential. You must cross the chamber to reach a narrow platform overlooking the courtyard from its south side. If you don't feel particularly perky, ingest some steroids before punching the switch in front of you. As the metal slabs part momentarily, you have seconds to cross the chamber and reach the grill at the north end.

Apply the breaks as soon as you reach the grill. By now, the metal slabs will have joined again in the middle of the chamber. Kick the grill and come out into the narrow platform. Take out the few troopers gathered there, and destroy the turret mounted on the mountainside across the courtyard. Collect the RPG ammo and the ripper chaingun inside the compartment. Now it's time to make some tough decisions. Your decisions will be narrowed down by one factor: Do you have a jetpack? If not, you should try to jump the chasm to land on the blue platform visible below and to the right from your position. If you have a jetpack, you can hover directly across to the cavernous opening due northwest to reach the western tunnel where the yellow keycard can be found. Going directly is no problem. Start the jetpack and hover up a few dozen feet and head northwest.

To get the keycard the hard way, give yourself every inch to take a running jump onto the platform. Should you miss the platform entirely, be ready to activate your portable medkit as you start to plummet. With any luck, you will survive the fall and be able to collect a jetpack at the bottom of the canyon. Assuming you make it to the platform, resist entering the tunnel. Instead, access the hidden teleporter behind the computer console, and emerge inside the other tunnel on the west side. You will come out facing the gruesome sight of a slightly dismembered human hanging upside down from a rope. Go toward the entrance of the tunnel and take the keycard. Then return to the teleporter.

Back on the east side platform, proceed inside the tunnel, but move with utmost care. First, resist any temptation to run. You will only cause the tunnel to collapse and crush you like a bug. Instead, as you reach the mid point along the tunnel's length, stop to riddle with bullets the thick crowds of troopers rushing you from the tunnel's far side. As you reach an area where a rock juts out from the tunnel's top side, and as you begin to hear deep rumblings, start running back.

Entire sections of the tunnel will collapse in a matter of seconds. If you cannot get back fast enough, try standing near the wall to avoid the falling slabs. When the rumblings and aftershocks subside, find the new opening along the south wall of the tunnel. It is an access point to a duct that crosses over to the south side of the canyon. Hop in and pray for a better tomorrow.

## COVERT DETAILS

Table 6.14 bares every secret in Lunar Reactor.

### TABLE 6.14: THE SECRETS IN THE LUNAR REACTOR

| AREA IN LEVEL | SECRET ITEM | HOW TO GET IT |
|---|---|---|
| Underground chamber at the end of the disposal canal | freezer charges (2) holoduke | These are behind the secret partition in the east wall of the chamber. The only way to reach the disposal canal is via a long duct, starting at the eastern tunnel in the canyon. |
| West side and around the canyon | teleporter | It's behind the rock enclosure at the very end of the canyon's western tunnel. The teleporter places you east at the platform entrance to the collapsing tunnel. |
| | armor RPG ammo atomic health unit | These are in a high location, which you can only hover to, if you posses the jetpack. |
| | ripper chaingun portable medkit | These are behind the computer panel on the elevated platform, just north of the sunken chamber. |
| Sunken chamber | atomic health units | These are behind the secret compartment in the southeast pillar in the corner. |
| | RPG ammo | You can find this on a similar platform on the west side of the chamber. |

# THE DARK SIDE

The Alpha, Beta, and Gamma transports—subway-like boxcars—converge in a central hub. But The Dark Side is a crossroads in more ways than a literal one. It is also your link to Lunatic Fringe, the second secret level in the Lunar Apocalypse episode—if you're clever enough to find the secret exit. The Dark Side is also a place where you might become closer to your own soul as you ponder some very deep questions. For instance, where did the buried monolith come from? What sort of intelligence created it and planted it? For what purpose was it planted, and how long ago? And why are so many women hanging upside down or found in otherwise compromising positions? Oh, the horror and the wonder of it all, baby.

Besides exploring a morgue, blowing up a reactor chamber, visiting a collapsing cave, and taking many free subway rides, you also get to go for a moon walk in The Dark Side. An immense lunar crater is the backdrop for a battle scene involving flocks of darting drones.

You can approach The Dark Side from two angles. You can either set out to find the secret exit and make the rounds in Spin Cycle, or you can go on a longer ride, filled with more danger and possibilities, to reach the regular exit and move on to the next level. To reach the secret exit, you have to gain access to the Gamma transport. That requires you to reach the top level of the central hub. But without the blue keycard, you won't be able to reach the second floor (unless you have a jetpack).

For most people, getting to the top involves visiting the morgue at the end of the Alpha route to get the blue keycard. The story to reach the normal exit follows the same script. However, you must also obtain the yellow keycard from the reactor chamber. This entails a subway ride in the Gamma transport. After that, you're free to board the Beta station and meet your fate in the lunar crater to the north.

## MAPS AND ROUTE

If you enjoy traveling, come along for a trip on The Dark Side. Figures 6.21 and 6.22 show you the routes and connections. But *you* are responsible for your own itinerary.

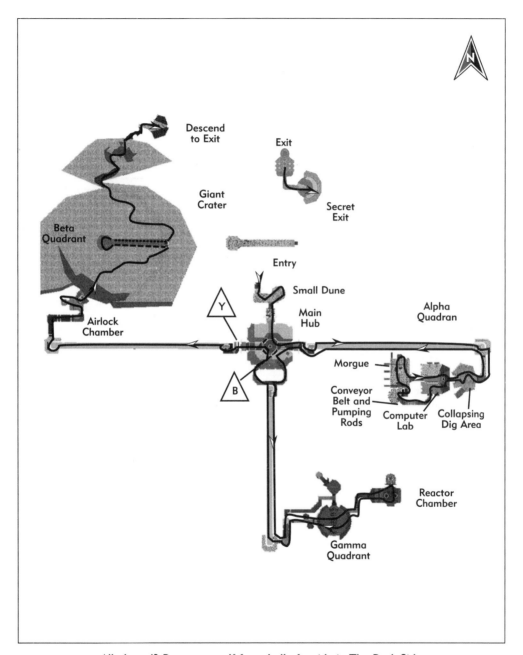

FIGURE 6.21: All aboard? Brace yourself for a hell of a ride in The Dark Side.

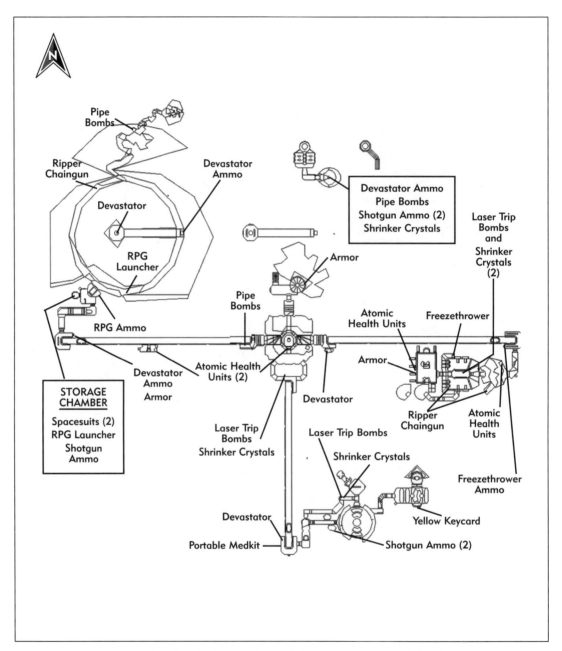

**FIGURE 6.22**: After experiencing the lure of The Dark Side, you might find it hard to tear away and go back to normal life.

## THE GOODS

You will find, as you might have already suspected, that The Dark Side has its goods too. There are plenty to tempt the most righteous among us. Check out Table 6.15.

### TABLE 6.15: THE GOODS IN THE DARK SIDE

| WEAPONS | AMMO | POWER-UPS |
|---|---|---|
| 2 shotguns | 9 cases | 2 portable medkits |
| 2 ripper chainguns | 2 cases | 8 atomic health units |
| 2 RPG launchers | 5 cases | 6 armors |
| 3 devastators | 6 cases | 1 steroid flask |
| 3 shrinkers | 4 crystals | 2 NVGs |
| 1 freezethrower | 6 charges | 1 holoduke |
| 3 laser trip bombs | | 1 pair of boots |
| 10 pipe bomb cases | | |

## BLAZING THROUGH THE DARK SIDE

Whether you want to get to the secret level or complete the Lunar Reactor in its entirety, you must still complete the first leg of the trip. And speaking of extremities, you are about to cover what will seem like miles of territory. See you on the other side, wherever that turns out to be.

### In the Small Dome

1. **Get armored.** Losing no time as you come out the entry door, take out the eggs in the domed room before their slimy hatchling crawl out. Dispense with the enforcer too. Then take the armor, and ride the small platform up to the hub level.

2. **Shoot it out at the hub.** Emerging from the platform, grab the nearby shotgun, and tear through a duo of troopers. Then head for the door to the south and open it. Accommodate the sentry drones and enforcers as best you can. Notice there is also the freezethrower directly ahead. Run straight for it and then use it to freeze the enforcers in their tracks. Check the secret compartment behind the panel to get an atomic health unit.

### In the Alpha Quadrant

1. **Take the Alpha route.** You really have no choice but to take this route, as it is the only way you can possibly go without any of the keycards. Before boarding, pick up the case of pipe bombs. Then push the large switch by the dock to beckon the transporter. At the end of the route, collect two shrinker crystals before proceeding into the collapsible dig at the end of the hallway.

2. **Deal with the pressure.** As you come upon the seemingly tranquil dig, notice the lasers crisscrossing the room. You don't have to violate the lasers to cause a shake-up. Step in a few feet and back out immediately as the dig in front of you collapses and shifts shape. Drop a few pipe bombs to dispose of the enforcers hiding in the crevices. Then explore the dig to collect all manner of goods, including devastator ammo, atomic health, and even a ripper chaingun. Then go into the computer lab behind the blue door.

3. **Take over the lab, and ride the waste conveyor belt.** Sorry. There's just no other way to get to the morgue. (How's that for an ultimate destination?) Storm in pouring lead on all present at the lab, which is divided into left and right chambers with a central corridor. In the left chamber, jump and then squat to get inside the conveyor belt. You will come upon a series of heavy pistons whose function seems all too clear. Clear the pillars by stopping in your tracks and dashing forward just as the piston begins to ascend. You'll wind up plunging into a disgusting tank of assorted refuse.

4. **Get to the morgue on time.** Don't hang down there for too long. Besides a few ferocious octabrains, there really isn't much else to see. Jump out as soon as you can, and take the small platform up to the morgue.

5. **Bounce some bodies and score the blue keycard.** As you reach for the blue keycard, a sensor triggers open the body chambers lining the walls of the room. Within seconds, the morgue will be crawling with protozoid slimers. Hose the place down with your ripper chaingun. Then collect the goods inside the body chambers. (See Figure 6.23.)

**FIGURE 6.23:** Squish, squeal, and squirm. Clear the morgue of protozoid slimers, once you grab the blue keycard.

6. **Head back to the hub.** Pound your way through the crowd of enforcers. The devastator is your best bet.

## In the Gamma Quadrant

1. **Get upstairs.** Use your newly acquired blue keycard in the wall switch, and ride the elevator to the second floor. Collect the NVG and armor, and proceed to the door on the west side.

2. **Get loaded.** Enter the Gamma transport station and look behind the route map on the wall to collect a shrinker and some laser trip bombs. Summon the transport, and, at the end of the route, be sure to claim the devastator ammo and the portable medkit.

3. **Venture in the tunnel.** But only go in a few feet to avoid the ensuing explosion. The place is rigged. Back up and pummel the enforcers. Then proceed into the large pit chamber.

4. **Build a bridge and cross the pit.** Take out as many octabrains before hitting the switch that moves the metal blocks in the pit to align down its center. Cross over to the other side, and head toward the reactor chamber.

5. **Destroy the reactor to claim the yellow keycard.** Upon entering the chamber, take out the snipers across the room on the elevated computer panel that also holds the yellow keycard. Don't go in too far, for you might run into not one but two assault commanders. Should they come after you, don't be too concerned about saving devastator ammo. Standing at a safe distance from the reactor room, aim the RPG at its crown. Pull the trigger, jump out of the way of the crashing ceiling, and then climb over the rubble to get the yellow keycard.

**WARNING**

The radiation levels in the reactor room are very harmful, and you will feel instantly debilitated if you stand too close. After you destroy the reactor, the ceiling of the control chamber comes crushing down. This means that after making impact with the reactor, you should do your best to get out of the way of the crashing ceiling by running toward the entrance.

6. **Trace your steps back.** Collect yourself and find your way back to the transport, and ride it back to the main hub. You are ready to enter the Beta quadrant.

## In the Beta Quadrant

1. **Enter the Beta transport.** Slap the keycard on the entrance, and cash your ticket to enter the Beta quadrant. At the end of the ride, pick up the devastator ammo and watch out for the sentry drone.

2. **Bust into the airlock chambers.** Rip through the aliens standing guard, and look behind the desk for freezethrower ammo. Look in the storage chamber on the east side, and take a space suit, the freezer ammo, and the RPG launcher. Then take your stuff with you to the airlock cage, and step out into an impressive vista of a huge lunar crater with a man-made,

crane-like structure rising high above the crater's center, which is very much like a parabolic antenna.

3. **Pick off sentry drones like clay discs.** The dots growing suddenly larger across the lunar sky are sentry drones homing in on you. Douse them with an assortment of devastator charges, rockets and even shotgun blasts. When the coast is clear, cut a path straight for the bottom of the giant crane.

4. **Deactivate the force field.** Ride the lift to the top of the crane structure. Inside the circular chamber at the very top, you will find a devastator and the switch that turns off the field barring access to the level's exit.

5. **Go through the crack and dig up your own tunnel.** Get back to the crater's ground level, and dash toward the crack directly due north. Proceed cautiously and don't let the assault commander at the end keep you from your goal. Drop a pipe bomb inside the small cave-like aperture, and detonate a hole through the rock.

6. **Confront the object of someone's desire.** Follow the newly dug tunnel into a dark chamber holding a half-buried rectangular structure. Don't succumb to the eerie, alien atmosphere and fight the real alien presence all around you. Postpone your awe for a second, and jump right into the monolith. Doesn't it seem like the only sane thing to do?

## On the Other Side

1. **Just be glad you're alive.** But you're still not out of The Dark Side. Take the shrinker and any other useful stuff around the strangely organic emerald chamber. Obviously, the upside down human females suspended by the

 **NOTE**

To experience the maddening Lunatic Fringe, take a detour for the secret exit, which is found near the end of the level. After jumping through the monolith, turn 180 degrees and look above and to the right. You will see a crack in the green luminous wall. Drop a pipe bomb or hit the crack with your RPG. Then jump through the gaping hole and bingo, there it is.

walls aren't simply decoration. Follow the short hallway into a circular chamber with a water tank at its center.

2. **Freeze-dry your way out.** As you cross the path of the small chamber, a swarm of octabrains descends from the chamber's top. Back off and freeze the house down. Then break everyone's heart, and jump in the pool. Look for the exit switch, and don't look back.

## ADDED ATTRACTIONS IN THE DARK SIDE

It's hard to pick a single feature of The Dark Side to elaborate upon further or examine closer. But there is a technique that you can master now, and who knows, maybe you will put it to use later in similarly tight situations.

### Getting Off of a Moving Train

Why would anyone in their right mind ever want to jump off a fast moving train? Stupidity? Thrill-seeking? Suicidal tendencies? Overdue car payments? Receding hairline? Go figure. One good reason to do it in the Beta quadrant is if you're in desperate need of a health boost. Another might be that the enemies waiting for you at the end of the route are overwhelming and you want to postpone the meeting a little longer. For whatever reason you might want to jump off, if you can jump directly into a small wall recess, you will have two atomic heath units for your troubles and near-death experience.

If you see yourself in the dire need to jump off the train, there is something you can do to cushion the fall. It involves using your cushion. That is to say, your butt. As the train picks up speed, position yourself so that your back is towards the door and you are facing the transporter's switch. Maintain a firm pressure against your back. The ride may be bumpy, especially on your back side. But if you keep trying to push off and back out, as it were, when the crevice on the south wall and the transporter intersect, bingo. You will more than likely pop out of the train like a cork off a bottle of foaming champagne. Okay, maybe more like the bottle cap off a cheap beer. But you get the picture. You will be inside a dark little cove with two glowing atomic heath units and a teleporter booth.

## COVERT DETAILS

For its impressive dimensions, there's only a handful of secrets in the Dark Side, but they are juicy ones at that, as Table 6.16 indicates.

### TABLE 6.16: THE SECRETS IN THE DARK SIDE

| AREA IN LEVEL | SECRET ITEM | HOW TO GET IT |
|---|---|---|
| The Gamma quadrant | secret exit to the Spin Cycle (one of two secret levels in this episode) | You literally have to blow a hole in the northwest wall of the crimson pit that contains the females impaled on giant stakes. |
| The Alpha quadrant | devastator | Blow a hole in the wall by the boarding area to reach it. |
| | ripper chaingun and freezethrower | You will find these inside water holders in the computer lab. The steel panel right by the table near the canisters is a secret door that takes you inside the wall so you can claim the goods. |
| The main hub | atomic health unit | You will find this behind the map, inside the covered area in the main hub. You must push it open and then crouch below to gain access. |
| The Beta quadrant | teleporter cubbyhole | This teleporter is halfway down the path from the main hub to the end of the Beta station. You must jump off the transport to get there. |

# OVERLORD

There had to be moments when you doubted if you would make it this far. Overlord closes down the Lunar Apocalypse episode with a giant exclamation mark. Of course, there are two secret levels that you can venture into if you haven't already.

What manner of beast is this Overlord? If its shape and organic quality seem somewhat familiar, you might recall the gem you found encrusted in the rocks of The Abyss, at the memorable conclusion of the L.A. Meltdown episode. It seems as though you're aboard one such alien ship. Your fears will be confirmed when you reach the egg-laden, octagonal chamber and witness a massive cannon aiming a concentrated energy beam at California's San Andreas Fault. The eggs and their slimy hosts will seem like a minor distraction, when you consider you're actually sharing the floor with the boss for this episode, the sanguine and completely charmless Moon Assault Leader. Also, early in this level, the Battlelord makes a cameo appearance.

## MAPS AND ROUTE

Hop aboard the decisively alien construction of spaceship Overlord. Figures 6.24 and 6.25 help you make sense of the structure's layout.

## THE GOODS

There is much to see and much to lay your hands on in this level, and you will need every bit of it. Table 6.17 lays out the goods in Overlord.

### TABLE 6.17 THE GOODS IN OVERLORD

| WEAPONS | AMMO | POWER-UPS |
|---|---|---|
| 1 shotgun | 5 cases | 3 portable medkits |
| 1 ripper chaingun | 2 cases | 6 atomic health units |
| 2 RPG launchers | 7 cases | 3 armors |
| 1 devastator | 4 cases | 2 scuba gear sets |
| 1 shrinker | 2 crystals | 1 jetpack |
| 1 freezethrower | 4 charges | 2 NVGs |
| 3 laser trip bombs | | 1 holoduke |
| 1 pipe bomb case | | |

## BLAZING THROUGH OVERLORD

There are both lightening fast and more involved ways of reaching your final destination in Overlord. But either way, you must eventually arrive at the same place, inside the large octagonal saucer section. After that you and the histrionic Moon Assault Leader get to exchange bows in a dance of life and death.

**FIGURE 6.24:** You're a virtual stowaway in Overlord. Try not to get discovered too quickly.

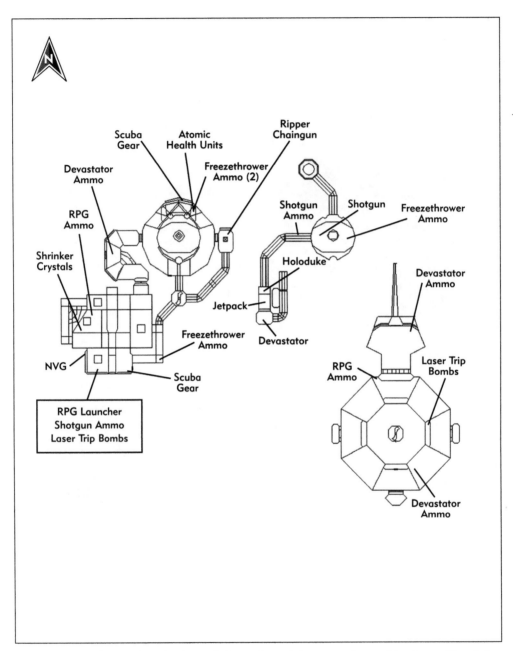

**FIGURE 6.25:** Overlord marks the end of a cycle and the start of something huge. Hopefully, your own cycle will continue to make the rounds.

## On the Bridge and in the Pool Area

1. **Build your arsenal.** Before emerging onto the bridge, look for two cylindrical pillars at the north end of the pool. Stick your upper body out of the water so you can breath normally, and run straight for the secret horseshoe-shaped crawl space. You can enter through what looks like solid wall right next to each pillar. (The wall between the pillars is solid.) Take the healing atom and the two freezethrower charges.

2. **Take the goods from the bridge.** Storm the bridge and collect all manner of goods, including the scuba gear by the control panels. Activate the combination switches to lower the generator rod. From left to right, the four switches should be set as follows: on, off, on, and on. When the rod lowers to the right height, jump on top of its small surface and capture the freezethrower.

3. **Head for the multilevel pipe chamber.** Upon entering through the door on the west side and turning the

> **NOTE**
>
> If you have a jetpack and want to make short work of this level, find the circular duct at the south end of the bridge, blow a hole in it, and enter it with the aid of a jetpack. You'll come upon a rotating helix in the middle of large silo-like space. If this is indeed the case for you, skip the remaining steps and refer to the section headed *In the Major Chamber*.

> **TIP**
>
> Although your first impulse might be to face off against the Battlelord, it might be more prudent to save your strength for the real boss in this level. One useful technique involves drawing the Battlelord out onto the bridge and then simply locking him there. Blow up the C-9 canister next to him and run back to the bridge. (The explosion also blows a tunnel right through the wall.) Encourage the Battlelord to give chase. The lack of room to move will force him to go into the pool. This is what you want. Run into the eastern chamber, and close the door behind you.

second corner, you will have to contend with the Battlelord. If you are not well armed for the occasion, you can try to get past him.

### In the Multilevel Pipe Chamber

1. **Hose the place down.** Before you can venture too far into the multilevel pipe chamber, you will come under fire from troopers, assault captains, and enforcers in every direction. Rely heavily on the ripper chaingun for long-distance engagements. Then whip out the shotgun in closer struggles.

2. **Get on top.** Cross the narrow water canal, and work your way toward the stairs on the west side. Climb to a floor area where you can get a shrinker. Turn eastward and drop onto a lower floor area to reach the eastern stairs. Take these stairs to reach the highest floor level in the chamber. Collect the RPG launcher, and most importantly, throw the switch at the very southwest corner, behind the unfortunate young maiden.

3. **Find the helix silo.** Get back down the first flight of stairs, and bash the duct grill to access it. You will come upon the breathtaking view of an imposing cylindrical opening with a floating helix spinning below you.

4. **Take a plunge for humanity.** This is the only way into the major chamber. Dive below and do your best to avoid the massive turning blades of the helix.

### In the Major Chamber

1. **Blow up the eggs.** Without moving from your landing position, aim at one of the explosive canisters by the large circle of alien eggs around you. The ensuing chain reaction will scramble the eggs beyond recognition. Avoid stepping over gooey egg remains as you collect every possible weapon, before facing the dreaded Moon Assault Leader.

2.  **Unleash the Moon Assault Leader, and put an end to Lunar
    Apocalypse.** Flip the hand print switch to the turret chamber, and pum-
    mel the Moon Assault Leader with every rocket you can release before
    he has a chance to react.

After that, it's open warfare. Your wit and speed can see you through.

## ADDED ATTRACTIONS IN OVERLORD

By far the most shocking, dangerous, and inevitable encounter in Overlord is the tête-
à-tête with the notoriously vicious Moon Assault Leader, the big, bad boss of Overlord.

### Downing the Overlord Boss

The gargantuan rocket-launching Moon Assault Leader is not your average adversary.
You have to hit him with everything but the flower pot to bring him down. Therefore,
it makes sense to avail yourself of every chance to inflict pain upon him. As for your
saving your own skin, you really haven't got many defenses in the way of hardware.
However, your mind can churn out enough cycles per second to outdo the reptilian
brain in the hulking body of the Moon Assault Leader.

If up to this point you haven't used up all your laser trip bombs, deploy them all
where they can harm the Moon Assault Leader but not you. This means you should place
them high along the threshold of the chamber where the untamed alien beast is kept. You
want to be able to run or crouch under the laser projections and give the Moon Assault
Leader a massive headache. This sounds great, you say, but without a jetpack you're as
good as minced meat. Don't fret too much. Luckily, a jetpack and a devastator are
within reach.

To get the jetpack and the devastator, find the crack along the west side of the
major chamber and jump into the water enclosure. Emerge into a J-shaped tunnel that
turns into a very large tank, at the bottom of which is the sought-after jetpack. Venture
further north into an even larger water tank, and claim the devastator from the clutches
of the octabrains. Then head back to the major chamber.

Use your jetpack to deploy vertical rows of tightly packed laser trip bombs. This
maneuver is delicate and requires precision moves. Put off the double lattes for awhile.
Once you've deployed your laser trip bombs along both sides of the threshold in the major
chamber, deploy the holoduke at the south end, if you have it. Then carpet the area just
outside the door with as many pipe bombs as you have. Now comes the moment of

truth: Open the turret door at the north end, and run backwards immediately. As the Moon Assault Leader comes into view, wait a second for him to set off the laser trip bombs, and, at the same time, detonate the pipe bombs with one big bang.

Pull out the RPG launcher and feed a steady pounding to the Moon Assault Leader before he has a chance to fire off a rocket or stomp you like a bug. If you have any steroids left, swallow them. Play a lethal game of keep-away and take every opportunity to unload your weaponry. There is no sense in holding back; you won't have another chance. With any luck, the Moon Assault Leader will be confused by the holo-duke at the south end. You can take this opportunity to get inside the turret chamber, where you can continue pounding the Moon Assault Leader from the rear. If it becomes necessary, you can close the heavy gate to take refuge from the oncoming rain of rockets. Hopefully, by this point, you will have inflicted enough damage on the heinous beast to be able to knock him completely with a few more RPGs. The freezethrower can also be instrumental in delivering the final blow.

No one can blame or judge you too harshly for what you will do to the Moon Assault Leader after his limp, but still warm body bounces to the floor. After all, what the aliens are doing to human females does not exactly speak of gentility. Meanwhile, back on Earth . . .

## COVERT DETAILS

Not exactly overflowing in the secrets department, the Overlord level still offers some nifty finds, as shown in Table 6.18.

### TABLE 6.18: THE SECRETS IN OVERLORD

| AREA IN LEVEL | SECRET ITEMS | HOW TO GET IT |
|---|---|---|
| Bridge and pool | atomic health unit<br>freezethrower ammo | Go through the secret wall openings beside the pillars at the north end of the red pool. |
| | atomic health unit | Inside the pool, find the hand print switch along the south pillar. Activate it to cause the entire pillar to lift and reveal an opening that you can actually swim through as you collect the atomic health unit. |
| Major chamber | RPG ammo<br>atomic health unit | Activate the hand print switch on the map panel in the turret chamber. Then rush back to the south end to climb into a secret chamber in the wall. |

# SPIN CYCLE

If you found the secret exit in the Occupied Territory, all of a sudden you are thrust into the centrifugal world of Spin Cycle. A strong stomach and a robust constitution are vital

if you want to complete Spin Cycle. This, the first secret level in Lunar Apocalypse, could be fanciful and reminiscent of cotton-candy and childhood days riding the merry-go-round at the carnival. Spin Cycle, however, is far from such innocence; it is more of a romp for spirited multiplayer battles than the type of level you would normally encounter in solo matches.

Spin Cycle's design is simplicity itself—it offers a central, circular dome surrounded by a wide, rotating band that spins incessantly counterclockwise. That is it! Around the periphery, there are four narrow walkways that follow the great circle's contour. These walkways appear incidental, as though they were put there as an afterthought. But in reality, you can cling to life and find refuge in these areas from the onslaught you will most definitely experience near the center of the structure.

The centrifugal force of the spinning band in Spin Cycle is real enough. Any time you set foot on it, you will feel its effects. Simple movement will seem hard, almost as though you were twice as heavy. This same undeniable physical force also affects your weapons and their projectiles. This means that you will have to compensate for your acceleration as you aim and fire at your opponents, whose weapons are also affected in the same way. But hovering opponents like the assault commander, assault troopers and captains, and sentry drones are all capable of canceling the centrifugal force by their ability to hover and fly.

## MAPS AND ROUTE

If you were to slice Spin Cycle into four equal pieces, you would see that each one is identical to all the others. But in spite of its very basic architecture, as you can see in Figures 6.26 and 6.27, and its void of secret passageways or hidden chambers, Spin Cycle, by virtue of its cruel inhabitants, can make a person look for a new circle of friends.

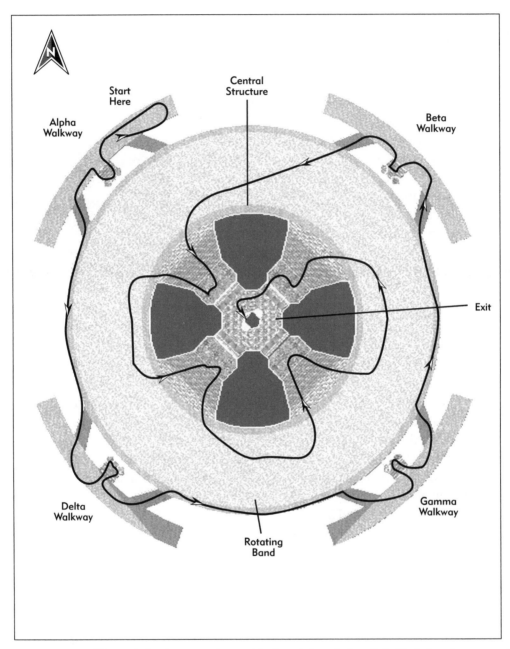

**FIGURE 6.26:** Throw deductive reasoning and logic out the window. Spin Cycle is prime ground for unabashed skull bashing.

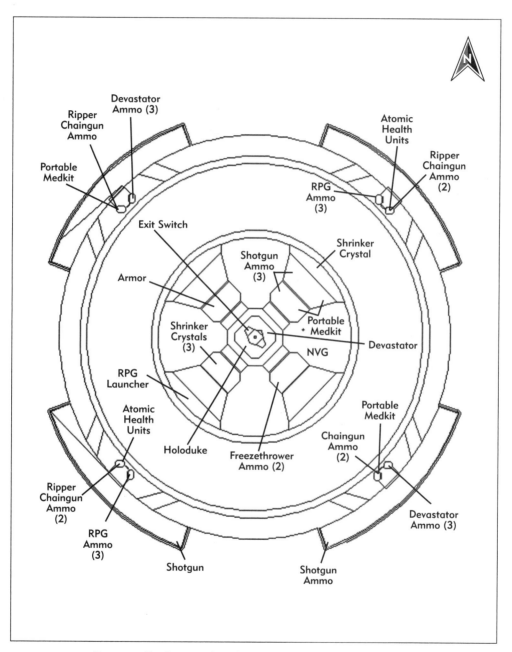

**FIGURE 6.27:** Do yourself a favor and explore the peripheral walkways for their weapons and power-ups before you step on the spinning band.

## THE GOODS

Spin Cycle brims over with weapons and more than a stockpile of ammo. The amount of power-ups in this level is also respectable. Table 6.19 catalogs the goods you can get in this level.

### TABLE 6.19: THE GOODS IN SPIN CYCLE

| WEAPONS | AMMO | POWER-UPS |
| --- | --- | --- |
| 2 shotguns | 5 cases | 3 portable medkits |
| 1 ripper chaingun | 8 cases | 2 atomic health units |
| 1 RPG launcher | 6 cases | 1 armor |
| 1 devastator | 6 cases | 1 NVG |
| 2 shrinkers | 3 crystals | 1 holoduke |
| 1 freezethrower | 3 charges | |

## BLAZING THROUGH SPIN CYCLE

There really is not one particular way of solving Spin Cycle. In fact, there really aren't any puzzles to solve. The exit is in the central structure. All you have to do is unlock all of the gates. Then waltz inside and push the exit switch. "Waltz," however is only a figure of speech. Actually, most of the dancing in this level occurs around the ever-spinning band. There are four external gates, which are plainly visible from the periphery. There are also four internal gates. The spaces between the gates serve to contain pockets of your loathsome alien foes.

Switches in the peripheral chambers open the external gates. The internal gates, however, work in tandem and open only when you activate each of the four switches, one outside each gate. By the same token, the same four inside gates can be closed together by pushing any of their switches. Use this level to sharpen your fighting, shooting, and defensive techniques. But if you want a semblance of a plan, consider the steps that follow.

### In the Perimeter and on the Spinning Band

1.  **Score everything you can.** Starting with the Alpha walkway, near where you first materialize, explore the curving corridor to get everything from shotguns and shrinkers to shotgun shells, RPG ammo, and atomic health

units. Each of the four walkways (labeled Alpha, Beta, Gamma, and Delta) has a small chamber near its center. Enter each chamber, press the central switch, and take the goods from the cylindrical containers.

2. **Ride the spinning band.** Armed to the teeth, get on top of the band and fight off the sentry drones before they get too close. If you are being pummeled too hard, jump off the band and find shelter in any of the four perimeter walkways.

3. **Face the central structure.** Once you have decreased the drone, trooper, and captain population to a more manageable level, focus your attention on the assault commanders who like to hang out near the central structure's entrances. Get off as many RPGs as possible as you circle past the assault commanders.

## Around the Central Structure's Entrances

1. **Grab more weapons near the entrances and throw every switch.** Every one of the four entrances in the central structure has something useful to offer. However, your foray to the center may be stopped short by droves of floating troopers and other hovering enemies. Once you take possession of the shrinker, you will have a better time

**TIP**
Although one of the entrances appears to be blocked by a metal door, the door will open the moment you push it.

of cutting the opposition down to size. Also, take a second to push each of the four buttons in the entrances.

2. **Make a dash for the final exit.** Once you push the last of the switches, all four doors will open simultaneously. You can then step in and rush toward the exit switch in the central pole in the middle of the chamber. Or, you could be rendered into a lifeless mass of tissue and bone by, not one, but two Battlelords who will materialize the second you set foot inside the chamber.

## ADDED ATTRACTIONS IN SPIN CYCLE

If you aren't able to reach the exit switch before the Battlelords converge on you, you will definitely have a fine mess in your hands. However, your cunning and resourcefulness can help you through this dire situation. The first thing to do is to get out of the line of fire. It's useless to confront one Battlelord, let alone two, if your health is lower than one hundred percent and you don't have a powerful weapon like the devastator or the RPG launcher. But even if your health isn't what it once was and your weaponry is starting to dwindle, you can still triumph over the Battlelords.

As the Battlelords give chase, one is bound to get in front of the other and be

> **TIP**
>
> An effective technique for dispensing with assault commanders when they are near the central structure, is to aim your weapon to the left of your intended victim, and shoot after the spinning band has carried you past the target. Let the laws of physics work for you and drive the projectile home. Similarly, when you are aiming at targets moving ahead of you over the band, aim to the left of the target. You want to time your projectile for the moment when the target intersects it curving path. (See Figure 6.28 for an illustration of the technique.)

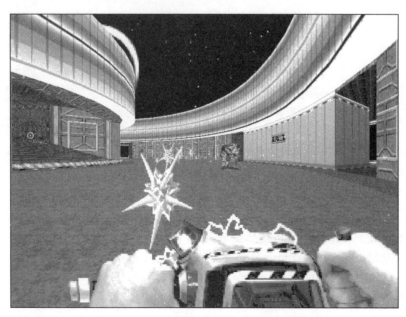

FIGURE 6.28: Shoot to the left of your intended target to connect just at the right time.

subject to friendly fire from behind. If this happens, avail yourself of the chance to pound the Battlelord from the front and double the damage he sustains. You can also always buy breathing room by confining the Battlelords in the central chamber. Pushing any of the switches in the chamber's entrances causes all of the doors to close at once. Knowing this, you can also draw one of the Battlelords outside of the chamber and keep his compadre captive inside. With only one Battlelord to worry about, you should be able to outmaneuver him and hit him with your best shots, as you are both spun in the incessant cycle of life and death.

Having taken care of the first Battlelord, employ a similar technique to deal with the second menace. When the Battlelord's heavy armor hits the deck, run past his smoldering remains and punch the exit switch inside the central chamber.

# LUNATIC FRINGE

Are you here by design or because you stumbled upon the secret exit in The Dark Side? No matter. Lunatic Fringe is a wild romp over the edge that will have you questioning just how reliable your senses are. But take heart—you are not seeing things. The reality of this level, as in real life, is that reality is fundamentally relative. If this sounds like circumlocution, you better get used to going around in circles, quite literally. Solving the puzzle of Lunatic Fringe will have you doing what amounts to chasing your own tail. The careful observer, however, will begin to see a pattern and act accordingly.

If you are not entirely sure of where you are, how are you ever going to find the exit? And it's not just that. You'll never get to wander about your whereabouts if you don't survive the first few instants in Lunatic Fringe. You have to be ready to fight from the word go. The central chamber, where the exit switch is heavily guarded by two Battlelord Juniors, will remain a question mark until you throw the proper switches, all four of them.

## MAPS AND ROUTE

"Simple enough," you might think after giving Figures 6.29 and 6.30 the once over. However, wait until you make the rounds in Lunatic Fringe before you render a more qualified opinion.

## THE GOODS

You don't get just one, but two chances to score goods in Lunatic Fringe. The two realities of this level let you double-dip into the bag of goodies as Table 6.20 shows.

| TABLE 6.20 THE GOODS IN LUNATIC FRINGE | | |
| --- | --- | --- |
| **WEAPONS** | **AMMO** | **POWER-UPS** |
| 2 shotguns | 2 cases | 1 portable medkit |
| 1 ripper chaingun | 2 cases | 3 atomic health units |
| 1 RPG launcher | 4 cases | 1 armor |
| 1 devastator | 2 cases | 1 steroid flask |
| 1 laser trip bomb | | 1 holoduke |
| 1 shrinker | 2 shrinker crystals | |
| 1 freezethrower | 2 charges | |
| 2 pipe bomb cases | | |

## BLAZING THROUGH LUNATIC FRINGE

Stick to the path outlined below, and find out why sometimes the closest distance between two points isn't always a straight line. (Keep in mind, you might be oscillating between two visions of reality with different physical laws.)

### In the Entry Spot

1.  **Emerge into the daylight.** Push the small switch behind you to open a screen panel and come out into a small platform overlooking the large central chamber and a narrow walkway extending to both sides around the chamber.

FIGURE 6.29: Once inside, sane or not, there is no easy escape from Lunatic Fringe.

**FIGURE 6.30:** No, you're not quite ready for a straitjacket and a padded cell. Lunatic Fringe just makes you think you might be missing a screw.

2. **Activate the switches.** Notice the switch on either side of the screen with the map of the United States. Use your handgun to activate each of these switches.

3. **Cash in while you can.** Walk along the ledge to the right and collect every weapon and power-up along the way. Protect yourself as you go, and be ready to fend off hovering assault captains and their insubordinate troopers.

## In the Same Entry Spot

1. **Contain your astonishment.** When you complete the round and come upon the same entry spot, you will see what appears to be a different panel. In fact, even the central structure will seem to have changed. It is and it has. The panel now shows what appears to be a picture of a distant alien planet.

2. **Activate the last two switches.** After you activate the last two switches, listen for the hissing sounds of several openings forming at various heights along the central structure.

3. **Get inside.** The current view in the large screen determines the route you should follow to get in. If it's North America, you can enter either through the small opening right across from the actual screen or by jumping from the ledge along the east side into an elevated opening in the structure. But if the view is of the alien planet, then you can enter either by jumping from the south tip on the ledge or by walking down the stairs through a side door on the west side.

## Inside the Central Structure

1. **Hop around a bit, if you feel lucky.** Collect any useful stuff you can grab. It is possible to jump into the small apertures housing atomic health units. You take a chance in falling down and sharing the floor with the Battlelords, but any reward usually involves an element of risk.

2. **Get to the central platform.** Get a good angle from one of the many elevated openings, and jump into the green glowing enclosure in the center. Pay no mind to the incessant growls of the Battlelord s below, and take the atomic health units and the freezethrower ammo.

### Back to the Front

1. **Throw the hand print switch.** Get back on the platform on the south side, inside the chamber. Look for the hand print switch along the left side of the opening into the outside. Throw it and jump out of the window through the side window on the left side, where you can see a panel lowering in the middle of the screen with the alien world. If you try to get out of the front opening after throwing the hand print switch, you will see only the North American continent on the panel, and the opening you saw earlier will seem like it was only a hallucination. But it wasn't.

> **TIP**
>
> Unless you are eager for a show-down with the two Battlelords patrolling the area, you should enter through either the back door at the south end or through the front. Both of those locations are on higher ground from the Battlelords, where it is very difficult for them to spot you in their lethal sights.

2. **Get small and get out.** As you come upon the opening in the panel, you will notice that it's way too small to crawl in. But almost at the same time, you will be hit by a shrinker emanation that will allow you to filter through the small opening and reach a larger area as you start to regain your normal size. Then just hit the exit switch.

## ADDED ATTRACTIONS IN LUNATIC FRINGE

If you're not entirely happy unless you have a major confrontation at least once a day, then proceed to the account of how you might work out some natural aggression with the Battlelords in Lunatic Fringe.

## A Memorable Encounter

After you have determined that you are not crazy and have activated all four switches around the screen with the alternating views, try a little deception to confound the Battlelords in the central chamber. Enter the central chamber through either of the elevated areas, and drop a good dosage of pipe bombs into the space below. Detonate them in bunches to cause major damage.

Run out to the periphery and deploy the holoduke in front of one of the side entrances. Back off and quickly plant some laser trip bombs like spokes of a wheel with the main structure at the hub. As either or both of the Battlelords give pursuit, entice them to cross over the laser trip bombs. Switch to the RPG launcher, and proceed to dish out as many projectiles as you possibly can.

If, by good fortune, both Battlelord Juniors are after you, usually the one in front will receive friendly fire from his pal behind him. By backing off continually, and releasing projectiles as the surviving Battlelord Junior gives chase, you should be able to finish him in less than one full circle around Lunatic Fringe.

# 7

# Shrapnel City

Alas, welcome home at last, Duke Nukem. But once again, so sorry the reception is not exactly befitting of one whose legendary deeds could fill volumes. You fought bravely and sometimes savagely in Lunar Apocalypse. You saw action in what now seems like countless orbiting stations and surface installations. And never once did you question your role as humanity's savior. It's just something you seem to do so well.

In Overlord, the last mission of Lunar Apocalypse, you penetrated an alien ship to discover a massive turret pointed at California's San Andreas Fault. With providence on your side, you also battled the boss of the episode, the Moon Assault Leader, and put him out of commission permanently. To say it wasn't easy would be a major understatement; but you were never big on words, Duke, and complaining just isn't your nature. That's all history now, anyway. Now you're back on Earth. Unfortunately, things haven't really changed for the better since you left. In fact, they are positively out of hand. Thank God you're back.

## RAW MEAT

It's hard to think of a better place to cut your teeth in Shrapnel City than Raw Meat's sushi bar. Culinary delicacies aside, Raw Meat serves up an intricate complex of chambers, tunnels, and interconnected underwater passages. Speaking of liquids, wait until you check out the wet bar. The dance floor also offers a relief for sore eyes; and speaking of eyes, no matter how you slice it, the main dish in Raw Meat is the food. There are obviously two types of clientele who frequent Raw Meat. The dining areas on the first floor will seem ordinary enough, but wait until you find the underground eatery. By the looks of the table scraps, you might guess the diners down there like their meat, well, very rare.

Making the cut in Raw Meat is much like a three-course meal. First, tease your taste buds for the ensuing action while you are still in the outside area. Next, partake of the main dish as you devour your opponents in the dining chambers, where you must also score the blue keycard. Finally, top off the evening's meal with a few libations at the bar and some live entertainment. Of course, your culinary experience won't be complete until you visit the kitchen, where you can score additional power-ups and weaponry. And, finally, find the passage to the main pool, where you can nab the red keycard. This keycard opens the door that grants you access to the back door—perhaps the best way to leave Raw Meat after your violent binge.

## MAPS AND ROUTE

Raw Meat features a totally different sushi bar. If the food doesn't kill you, the diners will. Check out Figures 7.1 and 7.2 to whet your appetite.

## THE GOODS

Raw Meat gives you plenty of reasons why you might want to stop in, even if you are not particularly hungry or don't care for Japanese food. Table 7.1 shows you everything you can collect in this level.

### TABLE 7.1: THE GOODS IN RAW MEAT

| WEAPONS | AMMO | POWER-UPS |
| --- | --- | --- |
| 1 shotgun | 7 cases | 1 portable medkit |
| 1 ripper chaingun | 7 cases | 4 atomic health units |
| 1 RPG launcher | 2 cases | 2 armors |
| 1 devastator | 2 cases | 2 steroid flasks |
| 1 shrinker | 2 shrinker crystals | 2 jetpacks |
| 1 freezethrower | 1 charge | 2 NVGs |
| 1 laser trip bomb | | 1 holoduke |
| 3 pipe bomb cases | | 1 scuba gear |

**FIGURE 7.1:** However experimental your culinary leanings, abstain from ordering the sliced eyeball in Raw Meat.

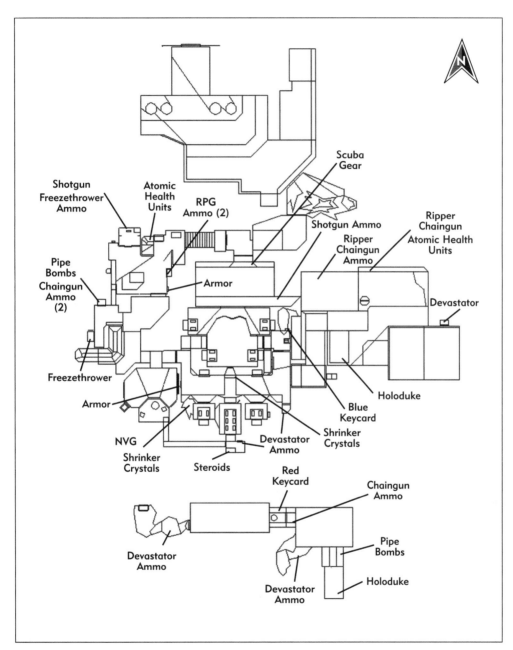

**FIGURE 7.2:** Even if you decide to stay away from the culinary delights, don't neglect to collect all you can in Raw Meat.

## BLAZING THROUGH RAW MEAT

Despite its voracious appetite for human flesh and suffering, you can really make a short meal of Raw Meat, if you follow the main course outlined below.

### In the Cul-de-Sac

1. **Load up on weaponry.** Dash to the wall compartment north of your location on the rooftop and grab the devastator. Get near the rooftop's ledge to entice a sentry drone and an enforcer or two to come after you.

2. **Take a plunge.** Get a running start and jump along the side of the building, from where you got the devastator. You want to land on the ledge that skirts the building on the north side of the cul-de-sac. At the end of the ledge, you can claim an atomic health unit and a ripper chaingun.

3. **Eat sushi and don't pay.** Work your way toward the ramp entrance to the sushi bar and proceed cautiously.

### In the Sushi Bar's Entrance

1. **Forget the reservations.** Stepping onto the restaurant's ramp, you will become fodder for a group of enforcers. You are also in the sights of a turret mounted high up on the wall. If necessary, back out into the cul-de-sac to avoid being mobbed and so you can work your devastator with some elbow room. When the moment is opportune, rush back onto the ramp, aim your weapon upward, and destroy the turret as you make it to the door.

> **TIP**
> You want to thin out the alien marauders, even by one or two, before you take a plunge to face additional enemies in the cul-de-sac below.

2. **Dine and dash.** Walking into the restaurant's foyer, take out the turret in the small space due directly south. Then rush to that same spot to collect some crucial devastator ammo. Proceed into each of the dining rooms

along the left wall, and collect all the goods you can. The large dining room in the center hides a secret area behind the table. When the table sinks under your weight, crouch to enter the small chamber. Then collect more ammo for your devastator and the steroids on top of the metal box with the fans.

3. **Take a major shortcut and cash in your chips.** With a three- or four-step running start, jump right into what might

> **NOTE**
>
> If you want to visit the alien dining quarters, be sure to flip the switch on the east wall on your way out. It opens a door into the more exclusive dining areas of the sushi bar.

seem like a solid wall to the left of the greeting geisha near the restaurant's main entrance. You will reach a dark rectangular area that leads directly to the cash register. Open the small compartment behind the register to get the blue keycard. It grants you entry to the bar. Then get out into the restaurant's main hallway, using the same way you got in.

## In the Bar

1. **Mingle with some reserve.** The bar crawls with pig cops and other unsavory characters, and assault commanders play the role of bouncers. So keep a low profile by ducking, creeping around corners, and otherwise disposing of your opponents by picking your shots carefully.

2. **Enjoy a few libations and a floor show.** At your earliest convenience, get to the wet bar at the south end, make the rounds to consume every power-up and ammo. You also might want to grab the RPG launcher behind the speaker on the right side of the stage. Just beware of the rushing waves of pig cops. When you have had enough of the bar scene, move to the kitchen, on the north end of the bar, and don't be too alarmed at the food-preparation techniques you will see displayed. They're not exactly in accord with the fundamentals of hygiene and sanitation.

## In the Kitchen

1.  **Face the heat.** Take the chefs by surprise, and douse the place with lead. A couple of pipe bombs will also help clear the air before you raid the kitchen. Take all the weapons, ammo, and power-ups you can find. Look in the cold room for a freezethrower and shotgun ammo. The wine rack also hides two cases of RPG ammo.

2.  **Do the dishes.** Find a water tank next to the oven grill (to the right of the walk-in cold room) and, taking a deep breath, jump in. Follow the tunnel leading south and then east. You will come into the main pool area where an octabrain or two might live.

## In the Main Pool Area

1.  **Get the scuba gear.** Emerge from the pool to take the scuba gear along the north side. Then dive right back in.

2.  **Get the red keycard.** Head east toward the end of the pool, where you will find the red keycard. This key will let you get out of the sushi restaurant through the back door.

3.  **Get back to the kitchen.** Now that you have the red keycard, retrace your route back to the kitchen sink. Jump out dripping wet and head for the back door.

## Into the Back Alley

1.  **Endure another battle.** Use the red keycard on the latch and venture out, but expect another enforcer ambush. Your devastator weapon will help you cut a path through the wall of alien flesh.

2.  **Avoid a serious concussion.** The instant you reach the top of the ramp out of the back alley, you will sense a deep rumbling. This is a sign to run back inside as fast as possible. In a matter of instants, a huge explosion causes an entire wall to crumble in the adjacent building. The explosion also unearths the tunnel to the exit.

3. **Reach the tunnel and find the exit.** When the aftershocks subside, get back outside, and crawl through the demolished side of the building. Make your way among the rubble to the glowing red exit switch at the very end of the tunnel.

## ADDED ATTRACTIONS IN RAW MEAT

This level is really large, and there are plenty of things to discover on your own. Regardless of where your meandering takes you, the alien dining hall is a must-see for anyone with even a mild interest in intergalactic culinary experiences.

### Power Lunch with the Big Boys

There are obviously two types of clientele who frequent Raw Meat's sushi establishment. Those who like to eat the standard sushi fare, and those who like their meat, well, even more raw. The dining areas along the restaurant's main hallway seem ordinary enough. However, there is a large dining hall reserved for the alien elite. And judging by the look of the remains on the tables, it is obvious the aliens' appetite is quite insatiable.

You might want to visit the alien dining hall for a couple of reasons. Maybe you are just interested in alien nutritional habits. Or perhaps morbid curiosity drives you to see the spoils. But maybe a more sensible reason would be that you missed the shortcut to the cash register area and wish to collect the blue keycard the hard way.

If the alien dining room is open, step right on in. However, if the entry way is blocked, you have to throw a key switch in the large dining room along the hallway. (The switch is inside the small chamber behind the table.) Stepping inside the alien dining hall, you will run into what appears to be the aliens' dessert, a group of surrounded, bound human females. There are also a good number of explosive tanks lying about the place and especially around the bound women. Bite your lip and press the trigger to blow up a tank. Run out of the hall to avoid suffering any damage from the big explosion.

When things cool down a bit, step inside and proceed to sweep up the remains. Collect all the weaponry and armor you can carry. Then move eastward to find the cash register area. Don't expect to find a helpful cashier. Instead, get behind the counter, and take the blue keycard from the compartment. Now that you have the blue keycard, you can proceed to the bar where you are sure to pick up a good fight.

## COVERT DETAILS

You would expect there to be scores of secrets in Raw Meat, but there are only two, as you can see in Table 7.2.

| TABLE 7.2: THE SECRETS IN RAW MEAT | | |
| --- | --- | --- |
| **AREA IN LEVEL** | **SECRET ITEMS** | **HOW TO GET IT** |
| Sushi bar entrance | blue keycard | Jump into what looks like a solid wall to the left side of the geisha near the entrance. The secret passage leads you to the cash register room, where you will ultimately score the blue keycard. |
| Wall behind the wet bar | freezethrower | Find the hand print switch on the menu to the left of the wet bar and activate it. Then rush into the secret enclosure behind the wet bar. |

# BANK ROLL

Legal tender, it's what it's all about. Isn't it? By day, you sell your soul to the man for the privilege of keeping up with others who are also sweating to keep up with others. Occasionally, you enjoy the fruits of your labor, but more often than not, you're being squeezed into pulp by the cogs of our run-away economic machinery, which seems more intent on feeding itself than clothing the masses.

Bank Roll, like the institution it represents, seems unfeeling, uncaring, and ultimately self-serving. In spite of its smug exterior, Bank Roll is really a fun level to play. Perhaps it's the emphasis on action and clever puzzles. Or maybe it's the very convincing bank, complete with its foyer, main office, and giant safe box. You are sure to discover other reasons on your own.

Although it might be tough to get into the bank, let alone speak to a loan officer, your ambitions run much higher. You want nothing less than to get to the bank's safe box and crack it wide open. The bank's entry requires

**FIGURE 7.3:** One thing you can bank on after visiting Bank Roll is that you will probably want to do your own banking.

**FIGURE 7.4:** Don't let Bank Roll take you to the cleaners; grab what you can from the comprehensive cache available.

you to have the blue keycard. Once inside the bank, you will need to obtain the red keycard for clearance into the safe box.

## MAPS AND ROUTE

You can almost see the cogs of the business machinery at work in the design of Bank Roll, as portrayed in Figures 7.3 and 7.4.

## THE GOODS

However stingy and tight lending institutions tend to be, Bank Roll is exceptionally generous when it comes to the goods at your disposal. Table 7.3 shows you the bottom line.

### TABLE 7.3: THE GOODS IN BANK ROLL

| WEAPONS | AMMO | POWER-UPS |
| --- | --- | --- |
| 1 shotgun | 4 cases | 1 portable medkit |
| 1 ripper chaingun | 1 case | 4 atomic health units |
| 1 RPG launcher | 1 case | 1 armor |
| 1 devastator | 1 case | 2 steroid flasks |
| 1 shrinker | 1 shrinker crystal | 2 jetpacks |
| 1 freezethrower | 2 charges | 1 NVG |
| 2 laser trip bombs | | 1 holoduke |
| 3 pipe bomb cases | | |

## BLAZING THROUGH BANK ROLL

Why wait in line for your turn when you can blaze through and make out like a bandit? Stick to your guns and the plan below, and you just might make it out alive on the edge of town.

### En Route to Main Street

1. **Take down some pig cops.** Coming out from the crack on the wall, grab the pipe bomb case, dash for the shotgun on the ledge, and jump down onto the street level—all the while dodging blasts from a couple of pig

cops perched on a ledge across the alley. Get the portable medkit inside the trash Dumpster.

2. **Claw your way to Main Street.** Advance toward Main Street, but be careful of pig cops and enforcers jumping out of nowhere. The place where the alley narrows is particularly perilous because you can be easily ambushed by no less than a pig cop, an enforcer, and another RPV-mounted pig cop. (Deft footwork and a devastator would be most appropriate in this situation.)

## On Main Street

1. **Visit the offices across the street from the bank.** The blue keycard is in an upstairs office, and without it, you are forever locked out of the bank. Look for the first entrance along the north side of the street. As you walk up to it, a sensor opens it and a window to your right.

2. **Get some goods before you go up to the office.** Grab the atomic health unit atop the soda machine and the ripper chaingun from on top of the other vending machines; then it's impossible to overlook the freezethrower. Now head for the elevator.

3. **Storm the office and take the blue keycard.** As you step inside, be ready to deal with a couple of bel-

> **TIP**
> Get ready to back out as soon as the door and window open. Waiting to run you down behind the door is an RPV. The window on the right also makes you an easy target for the pig cops inside. If you can release a shot from your RPG launcher and do away with the RPV, then you only have to worry about the pig cops. And once you know they're there, the pig cops are sitting ducks. Dump a bomb or two in their enclosure, and detonate it from a safe distance.

ligerent enforcers who materialize out of thin air. Behind the partition, take care of the pig cop, and push the button on the desk as you reach for the steroids. Then take the blue keycard from the lowering bookshelves. As you exit, grab the devastator that was hidden behind a wall picture.

### In the Bank

1. **Hold up the place.** Take out the turret mounted high outside the bank's entrance, and then use the blue keycard to get in. Deal with the first of several pig cops, and step just outside the foyer, hiding partially behind the plant. From this position, fire upon the pig cops congregated in the main office. Also, hit the turret by the right side of the foyer so you can move more freely.

2. **Get to the main office.** Be sure to jump in through the small side window because the regular entry is lined with laser trip bombs. Press the desk button to unlock the door to the safe and to reveal a hiding place above the desk (behind the painting, naturally), which stores a jetpack. Proceed to the area in the back that houses the safe box.

### In the Safe Box Zone

1. **Throw three switches in a row.** The safe box will remain bolted shut until you find the red keycard. For that reason, dispose of the few enforcers and troopers standing guard in the steel chamber of the safe. Walk behind the desk and throw all three switches. This opens up the three-stage door on the south wall.

2. **Get through the cogs.** Hop onto the circular platform to get the protective boots. Notice how the giant cogs turn, sensing your move on the platform. Get off and walk toward the Beta platform. (Each platform is conveniently labeled.) Again, hop on and then walk into the space leading to the Delta platform. Get on the last platform and face west directly. As

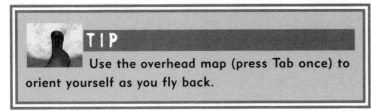

TIP
Use the overhead map (press Tab once) to orient yourself as you fly back.

the cog turns, its opening reveals a small recess on the wall behind it. Using this small window of opportunity, jump off the platform and rush toward the wall recess. Ride the platform up into a dark corridor.

3. **Score the red keycard.** If you have your devastator handy, destroy the pig cops in the corridor as you reach for the plainly visible keycard. Also take the jetpack and the other goods behind the wall compartment. Fly back to safety and the safe box. Use your newly acquired jetpack to get back to the safe box area.

4. **Crack the safe.** Use the red keycard and then walk up to the safe and push it open. The door swings outward to reveal a very nasty scene indeed. Throw a pipe bomb inside and immediately close the safe box door. Detonate the pipe bomb and grab a hold of something, for the place is about to shake.

5. **Reopen the safe and fight to the end.** Although mostly everyone and everything inside the safe is either dead or dying, don't count on it completely. In fact, the explosion blew up a large tunnel and a Battlelord has crept up from underground. You can choose to confront the Battlelord, or simply dash for the exit at the north end of the tunnel. The choice, as always, is yours.

## ADDED ATTRACTIONS IN BANK ROLL

Although the pace in Bank Roll moves quite steadily, it really crescendos when you are finally ready to deal with the safe box. For this reason, this particular scenario is worth examining more closely.

### Cracking the Safe and its Contents

Stand outside the safe box with the red keycard in hand, check yourself to be sure you have a good dose of health. If it is anywhere below 90 percent, give yourself a boost with the portable medkit. Then, reach for a pipe bomb. Stick the red keycard in the slot, and walk up to the heavy safe box door. Press on it and the massive door will swing open toward you. Don't gawk at the horror in there longer than you need to. (Although the place is buzzing with octabrains and there are dozens of alien eggs everywhere you look, perhaps what is most disturbing is the image of human females hanging upside down from the ceiling.) Throw the pipe bomb near the eggs and the ever-present explosive tanks. Then rush back out and close the safe box door behind you.

The entire building will rumble as the explosive charges go off inside the safe box. You will hear a mixture of explosions and alien flesh splashing the walls red. It is pos-

**NOTE**

Before you move on to the next level, you can also choose to explore the ledges around the buildings on Main Street. You can either use the jet-pack or climb along a portion of the tunnel along the southeast side. It leads to the ledge of the building overlooking the alley on the south side.

sible and likely that an octabrain or two might make it out of the safe box. If this is the case, use the ripper chaingun to put any survivor down. You want to save your devastator and RPG ammo for one last opponent, should he get in your way. The last hurdle to overcome is none other than the Battlelord. Formidable though he is, he can fall under the force of your devastator, especially if you manage to catch him while he is facing the other way.

Open the safe a second time. Step in looking left and right for any signs of alien life. You might have to quell another octabrain, but you are really mostly concerned now with the Battlelord. He likes to hang near the right corner. So waste not a moment in pouring whatever you have left in him. If he reacts quickly and gives chase, you can either run back out to the steel chamber or find refuge along the cracks in the newly dug tunnel on the northeast side of the safe box. From either of these places, you can manage to keep the Battlelord in your sights. However, it is easier to avoid his ripper chaingun and explosive pellets if you are not confined to the small spaces, as you are in the tunnel. When the Battlelord crumbles under the weight of your attack, just head for the exit switch.

## COVERT DETAILS

There are only a handful of secrets in Bank Roll, and Table 7.4 summarizes them for you.

| TABLE 7.4: THE SECRETS IN BANK ROLL | | |
| --- | --- | --- |
| AREA IN LEVEL | SECRET ITEMS | HOW TO GET IT |
| ATMs across from the bank building | ripper chaingun | Push either of the ATMs and jump through the small opening. |

| AREA IN LEVEL | SECRET ITEMS | HOW TO GET IT |
|---|---|---|
| In the bank's lobby | holoduke | Use the handgun to hit the switch high on the angular wall on the north side of the narrow lobby. The phone booths at the opposite end will lower to reveal the holoduke. |
| Main office in the bank building | jetpack | Expose the jetpack behind the painting on the south wall. |
| Third floor office across from bank | devastator | Enter the building through the garage door. Ride the elevator to the top. Push the switch on the desk behind the wall divider. Grab the blue keycard and on your way out, look at the place where a painting once hung. A devastator is hidden behind it. |
| Chamber with giant cogs | atomic health unit | Once you reach the Gamma platform, spin the walls to reveal a crack in the west wall. Blow a hole in the wall and run in to claim the atomic health unit. The hole connects you back to the outside of the giant safe. |

# FLOOD ZONE

If you like it wet and wild, you will love it in Flood Zone. Get ready to spend half the time underwater and the other half climbing along precipitous paths on rocky mountainsides. Flood Zone is basically a piece of downtown Los Angeles that went under during the last big earthquake. Of course, the alien's power beam targeting the San Andreas Fault from space didn't help matters.

To find the elusive exit in Flood Zone, you must travel high and low in search of all three keycards. Start out with the blue keycard. It sits atop a set of rock stairs at the west end. With the blue keycard you can get inside the underwater alien egg nest, which is also at the west end. Not only do you need to go in there for the yellow keycard, but you must also destroy every egg. With the yellow keycard you can finally gain access to the square, half-sunk building. Inside this building you must access the bottom floor to activate the switch that reveals the hiding place for the last and final red keycard.

This level is highly populated with octabrains, assault commanders, sharks, and even a Battlelord. To make a tense situation even more so, you have a limited oxygen supply so your underwater excursions must be rather methodical.

## MAPS AND ROUTE

Figures 7.5 and 7.6 let you see surface and submerged views for Flood Zone.

## THE GOODS

You will not be diving for pearls in Flood Zone, but pearls are the last thing you could wish for when your life could be snuffed out at any moment. The top side also holds many weapons and other useful finds, which will seem more precious than any treasure anyone could hope for. Table 7.5 tallies the goods in the Flood Zone.

### TABLE 7.5: THE GOODS IN FLOOD ZONE

| WEAPONS | AMMO | POWER-UPS |
|---|---|---|
| 1 shotgun | 5 cases | 2 portable medkits |
| 2 ripper chainguns | 6 cases | 5 atomic health units |
| 1 RPG launcher | 7 cases | 1 armor |
| 1 devastator | 9 cases | 1 steroid flask |
| 1 shrinker | 1 shrinker crystal | 1 jetpack |
| 1 freezethrower | 2 charges | 2 NVGs |
| 2 laser trip bombs |  | 1 holoduke |
| 2 pipe bomb cases |  | 2 scuba gears |

## BLAZING THROUGH FLOOD ZONE

It's easy to feel overwhelmed in this level. The place teems with alien life, which means yours could end anytime. Also, solving the puzzle of Flood Zone could have you guessing indefinitely. That's why this section is here, to keep you from second guessing yourself.

**FIGURE 7.5:** Don't hold your breath for too long. You're about to make a splash in Flood Zone. These maps show the top and the submerged areas.

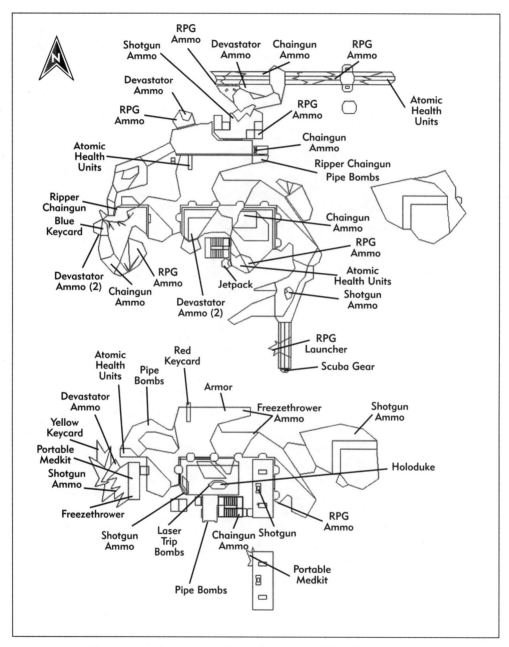

**FIGURE 7.6:** Water, water almost everywhere—welcome to Flood Zone.

## In the Elevated Entry Tunnel and Main Waterway

1. **Get ready for a dive.** Look behind you and take the scuba gear in the compartment. A few steps on the left you will find the RPG launcher. As you come out of the tunnel where a water stream comes out of the rocks, you will be confronted by an octabrain. Use your RPG launcher for the first time. Then plunge into the depths.

2. **Travel westward.** Move either over or under the water's surface; but either way, open yourself a path through the herds of octabrains and rogue sharks, and continue moving east. As you get near the end of the water way, look for an underwater tunnel that leads to a small concrete platform.

3. **Climb after the blue keycard.** Find the rock path along the curving south wall, and climb a few large rocks to reach the blue keycard. Then, get back into the water. It's time to visit the west side egg nursery.

## In the West Side Egg Nursery

1. **Blow up the nursery and take the yellow keycard.** Use the blue keycard on the latch for the alien egg nursery. Drop a pipe bomb or use your favorite method for hitting one of the incubator accelerator tanks. Close the door and bide your time for a few seconds. Then go back inside and collect the yellow keycard. Get to the east side of the waterway.

## Inside the Submerged Square Office

1. **Get to the bottom of things.** Enter the submerged office in the east side of the building. Use the keycard on the latch, and go all the way down to the bottom floor, using the sunken stairway.

2. **Push the right switch.** Go inside the large reception area, and push the switch along the

**SEE ALSO**
See the section *Added Attractions in Flood Zone* for a full account of what to expect and how to survive on top of the square building.

front wall. It raises the metal window covers, and it also causes the neon Alley Cat Lounge sign to lift a few meters. Swim out toward the Alley Cat Lounge, and open the door behind the sign to uncover the red keycard.

3. **Hover over to the other side.** Get back into the submerged office, and take the flight of stairs all the way to the top of the building, which is well above the water level. After surviving one of the most intense battles you are likely to face anywhere, anytime, climb along the rocks on the south side to pick up an atomic health unit. Also, push the solid rock wall at the end to pick up a jetpack. Activate it and hover to the Alley Cat Lounge's rooftop.

## On the Alley Cat Lounge's Rooftop

1. **Wear a hard hat.** Use the red keycard to enter the hard-hat area. Fight off the leaping enforcers, and move north toward a water brook. Continue ascending into a straight long tunnel that might have been a subway route or a tunnel for a train.

2. **Dive into the hole.** Move east along the tunnel, watching your back for octabrains creeping up behind you. When you come upon a small opening in the tunnel, just let yourself go and drop all the way to the bottom, where water will soften your fall.

3. **Face the switch and take your leave.** Jump out of the water facing north to reach a small platform right in front of the exit switch.

## ADDED ATTRACTIONS IN FLOOD ZONE

One of the many tenuous moments in Flood Zone occurs when you reach the rooftop of the square building. If you can survive the onslaught in this heavily contested area, the human race might still have reason for optimism.

**WARNING**

You don't want to stick your head out of the water and sit there for very long. A strategically placed turret is perched at eye level and can fry your head in no time at all.

### Showdown on the Square Building's Rooftop

When you finally reach the rooftop of the half-submerged building, don't expect any fanfare. First of all, you should know that there are several hidden areas nestled in the rock tops, and all of them overlook the very exposed rooftop where you stand. As soon as you open the door leading to the rooftop, get ready to pummel several assault commanders making their way over the waterway from an area above and to the right of the Alley Cat Lounge. Don't make the fatal mistake of rushing to the west side of the rooftop. You would only increase the number of enemies that are free to roam. Instead, retreat to the stairs if you are overwhelmed by the commanders. The weapon of choice to deal with matters on the rooftop is the devastator. You need the most effective means of tearing down opponents with the least effort. See Figure 7.7 for a snapshot of the action you can expect on the rooftop.

When the action on the east side of the rooftop subsides somewhat, climb over the small rock outcropping to get an atomic health unit. Then, press against the smooth, flat rock to uncover a jetpack. Strap it on and get ready for your next daredevil, yet coldly calculated, maneuver.

Move over to the west side of the rooftop, and anticipate another commander onslaught. This time, however, the commanders will come rushing at you from an

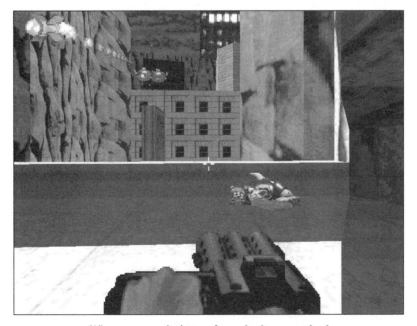

**FIGURE 7.7**: When you reach the rooftop, don't expect fanfare.

opening in the rocks above and to the left of the once legendary Alley Cat Lounge. If you keep your back pressed against the wall as the commanders slice their way through the air, you will keep a nearby Battlelord from joining the party. "How nearby is the Battlelord?" you ask. So nearby he could almost jump right on top of you. In fact he is perched in a large recess on the rocks above your head.

When you have taken out most or all of the commanders, fire up your jetpack and fly as fast as you can across the waterway. When you have gone far enough, turn 180 degrees to face the Battlelord from your elevated position in mid air. Then use your complete freedom of movement to avoid the Battlelord's projectiles, while you shower him with a few rockets of your own. When he succumbs under the pounding of your RPGs and devastator combination, continue toward the exit.

## COVERT DETAILS

The secrets abound in Flood Zone, as Table 7.6 makes plainly obvious.

### TABLE 7.6: THE SECRETS IN FLOOD ZONE

| AREA IN LEVEL | SECRET ITEMS | HOW TO GET IT |
| --- | --- | --- |
| Large cave serving as an egg nursery on the northeast side of the main waterway | devastator and shrinker crystals | Drop a pipe bomb or use the RPG launcher on the bottom section of the wall. Penetrate the tunnel, and battle a good number of octabrains. Rise to the air bubble in the nursery, and collect the goods. |
| On the rooftop of the square building | jetpack | Climb over the rock boulder on the south side of the rooftop. Grab the atomic health unit, and then push the flat rock at the end. Watch it lift, and grab the jetpack before the rock comes down. |
| Rock stairs at the west end | blue keycard | Climb over the large rock stairs starting at the south side of the short building at the far west. |
| Small chamber at the east end of the Alley Cat Lounge | ripper chaingun ammo | Use either the jetpack to rise to the small rock platform halfway up from the water level to the top of the Alley Cat Lounge, or simply jump there if you are at the top of the lounge. Push against the second window from the end, and enter into the small chamber with the ammo. |

# L.A. RUMBLE

Far away from the countryside or anything remotely close to nature, L.A. Rumble is a big pile of concrete, steel, glass, and other materials forged by the hands of humans. But for all the trappings of culture and sophistication, the action about to unfold will be anything but civilized. Hollywood Boulevard and the East Town Towers provide a suitably cosmopolitan backdrop. To make sense of L.A. Rumble, you will have to take care of business inside both towers. But getting from one tower to the other without a jetpack might present a bit of problem. Don't forget you are in Los Angeles, and the landscape could change quite unexpectedly, for this is tremor country.

## MAPS AND ROUTE

Figures 7.8 and 7.9 show you the layout of L.A. Rumble, once a place of fame and glamour.

## THE GOODS

Known for its lavish ways, L.A. Rumble includes a plethora of weapons, ammo, and power-ups. Check out the pickings in Table 7.7.

### TABLE 7.7:  THE GOODS IN L.A. RUMBLE

| WEAPONS | AMMO | POWER-UPS |
|---|---|---|
| 1 shotgun | 5 cases | 3 portable medkits |
| 1 ripper chaingun | 3 cases | 3 atomic health units |
| 1 RPG launcher | 5 cases | 1 armor |
| 1 devastator | 5 cases | 1 steroid flask |
| 1 shrinker | 1 shrinker crystal | 1 jetpack |
| 2 freezethrowers | 2 charges | 1 NVG |
| 2 laser trip bombs | | 1 holoduke |
| 2 pipe bomb cases | | |

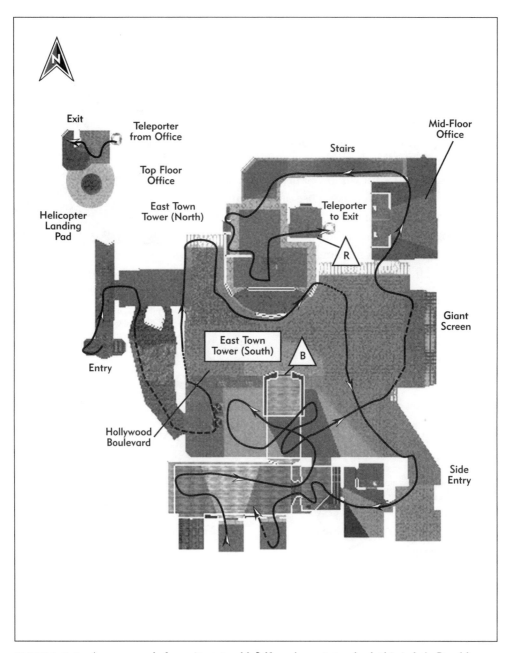

**FIGURE 7.8:** Are you ready for quite a tumble? If you're not, too bad, this is L.A. Rumble.

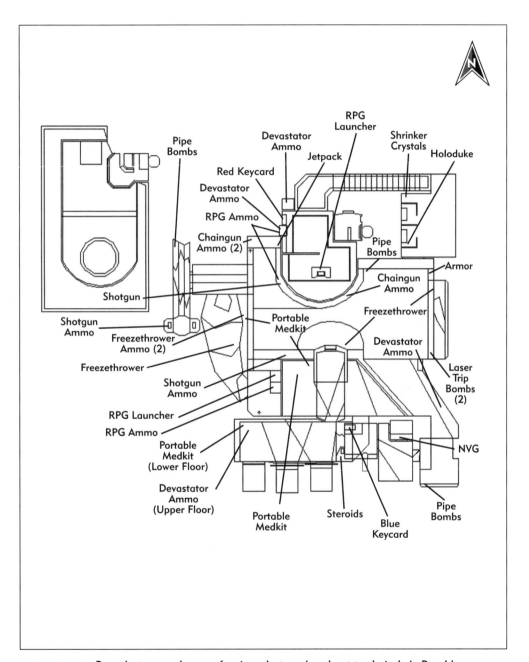

**FIGURE 7.9:** Pray that some day you forgive what you're about to do in L.A. Rumble.

## BLAZING THROUGH L.A. RUMBLE

Get ready for urban assault tactics and guerrilla-type warfare in the streets and buildings of L.A. Rumble. Although blue and red keycards are available in this level, you only really need to score the red one. It opens a teleporter that beams you directly to a landing pad on top of the north of the East Town Towers. Waiting nearby is your getaway helicopter. But first, you must make it inside the north tower. Without a jetpack, it takes a few neurons to figure out how.

### On the East Side

1. **Dig a tunnel.** Crawl out of the manhole, grab the shotgun shells nearby, and walk down the tunnel. Step through a cross-shaped hole along the tunnel's wall, and emerge into a dark passage leading out to Hollywood Boulevard. Halfway up the dark passage, drop a pipe bomb or use your RPG launcher on the south side wall to open up a big, gaping tunnel.

2. **Take a walk around the perimeter.** Climb along the rubble and cross the length of the tunnel to reach the lower side of the south tower. Hop on the air ventilators to collect an RPG launcher and some ammo. Look towards your left, and hop onto a lower ledge that lines the building front on the east side. Follow the narrow ledge north first, then east, and then around the half-circle of the north tower. Among the items you can collect in this short jaunt are ripper chaingun ammo and more RPG ammo. Drop off the ledge when you've collected everything you possibly can. Start heading down the hill toward the side entry to the south tower.

### In the South Tower

1. **Take over the first floor.** Step in cautiously and deal with the obstinate pig cops in the only language they understand, the language of hot lead. Access a laboratory-like chamber with embryo flasks, dispense with a few more pig cops, and then blow a big hole in the lab's west side wall.

2. **Going up?** Proceed into the next large rectangular chamber, and drop into the empty shaft of the elevator on the far end to pick up a devastator. Then hop aboard the functioning elevator. It takes you to a similar

rectangular chamber filled with undesirables. Count on a few more encounters with alien enforcers in this part of the building. Eventually, work your way to the front side of the building, where you will find yourself overlooking Hollywood Boulevard from the building's roof.

3. **Cause a major stir.** Stepping out onto the building's rooftop, walk up to the earthquake warning sign. A bone-jarring rumble will shake the place up. Notice how part of the concrete structure below the giant screen is rearranged in the short, but strong, quake.

4. **Jump toward freedom.** Surely by now, you have noticed the two floor levels in the north tower that are plainly open and inhabited by aliens. If you had a jetpack you could simply fly over. However, if you like to use your jetpack as much as most people do, chances are that your fuel may not carry you across. The next best alternative is to jump, but clearly the gap seems to be way too wide. Here's a way you can do it: Align yourself with the right column below the giant screen. (See Figure 7.10.) Use the crosshair to help you. Back up as much as you can, and take a running

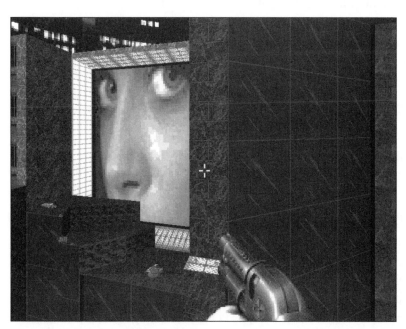

**FIGURE 7.10:** Line your crosshair with the column, and throw caution to the wind as you launch yourself to reach the awning.

jump toward the column. You will land on the awning below the giant screen. The idea is to reach the point furthest to the north along the broken awning, so you can hop right into the mid-floor office of the south tower.

### Inside the North Tower

1. **Dislodge the office workers.** Storm the office, and cut a path to the wide stairway along the north side.

2. **Get the red keycard and flee.** When you come upon the top-level office, hope that you can catch everyone on their break and rain your wrath upon them. Grab the red keycard and all the other visible power-ups and weapons on the shelves.

3. **Take the RPG launcher, and hit the desk switch.** A panel will open momentarily in the square office. Rush over to get inside. Riddle the troopers and captains assembled there, and grab anything that you can, and of course, we're not talking office supplies.

4. **Teleport to the landing pad and take off.** Use the red keycard on the latch behind the desk, and step inside the teleporter. Emerge in a small control area overlooking the helicopter you hope to ride out of L.A. Rumble. Walk right over to the exit switch, and pound it one last time.

## ADDED ATTRACTIONS IN L.A. RUMBLE

Expect to fight for every yard in L.A. Rumble, especially in the early going, when you attempt to skirt the boulevard's perimeter and when you finally manage to penetrate the south tower in the East Town Towers complex.

### Skirting the Boulevard

There is a ledge that starts on the west wall and goes around the north tower, ending up against the eastern wall. There are also key sniper spots all along the boulevard because the surrounding buildings are very tall. It's a scary thought, but at any moment, you could be under someone's sights. It makes sense, then, to take out at least some snipers, lest you become too exposed for your own good.

Stepping out of the tunnel you dug in the dark passage, notice the first set of sniper pig cops at the north end, standing on the ledge where you want to reach yourself. Take cover behind the metal air units, hop from the small one to the bigger one, and grab the RPG launcher and its ammo. Set your sights and send one or two rounds in their direction. Drop from the air unit to a small space near the very front of the building, but still on a ledge, and look to the right for the next group of snipers. Again, make handy use of the RPG launcher and your God-given talents. Figure 7.11 shows a detail of this action.

Now you can jump onto the ledge on the south wall and begin your perimeter run. When you reach the place where the ledge stops along the east wall, you will be in plain view of another group of snipers mounted high upon the awning below the giant screen, all the way across the boulevard. This too is a prime opportunity to launch long range shots at the sitting enforcers. Rely heavily on your crosshair, but watch out for the hair trigger. Remember you're carrying the RPG launcher.

After taking out a few more snipers, jump over the small gap and continue along the ledge. Pick up everything you can along the way. Begin circling the front side of the north tower.

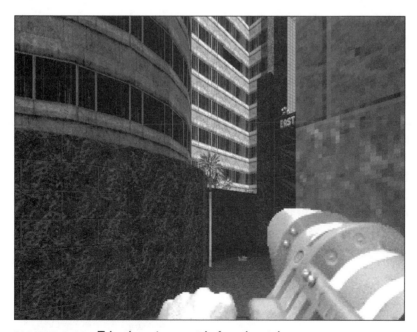

**FIGURE 7.11:** Take the snipers out before they take you.

## Penetrating the South Tower of East Town Towers

If you don't have a jetpack, the only way to reach the north tower is by jumping across, in hop-scotch fashion, from the south tower to the giant screen's awning and then to the middle floor of the north tower. But getting to the top of the southern tower isn't exactly a matter of hopping on an elevator and enduring a bit of muzak. In fact, if you're not on your toes every second, you probably will never get off of the bottom floor.

As you descend down the sloping side street leading to the tower's entrance, make wise use of the RPG launcher and pelt the congregated pig cops from a good distance away. Enter through the open door, and dispose of the single trooper. Before entering the second lab-like chamber, walk up to the panel on the right and push it open to claim more ammo for your devastator. If you need them, also pick up the NVGs on the counter top.

**WARNING**

Stop immediately after collecting the pipe bomb case. You don't want to step any farther east along the ledge. A few instants after you do, you would hear the assault commander's rocket piercing through the air. If you survived the initial hit, then you would see a small dot growing large very quickly as the commander descends upon you from high above. Avoid loss of limb and life by getting off the ledge at this point.

Before stepping into the lab, drop a few bombs behind you. As soon as you cross the threshold into the lab, wait an instant to hear the growl of the enforcers and then hit the detonator.

Pick up the survivors with impunity. While in the lab, grab the blue keycard if you want to open the front door to this building; otherwise, ignore it. But one thing you don't want to pass up is the hidden atomic health unit. Crouch and push the cabinet at the very left; the adjacent cabinet will open. Crawl in quickly and take the glowing blue atomic health unit. Back off a ways and blow a hole in the lab's north wall.

Run right through the hole, and drop into the empty elevator shaft at the far end of the dark rectangular room to pick up a devastator, should you need one. And who doesn't? Then get on the functioning elevator, and ride it to a very similar chamber a few floors up. Come out firing your devastator. If you are forced to get near the back of the room, an enforcer will sense your presence and come spinning out of the empty elevator shaft. Don't be afraid to overheat the devastator. It's a rugged weapon, after all. Once things have simmered in the chamber, go around the wall on the east side to come out overlooking the boulevard, and get ready to cross over to the north tower.

## COVERT DETAILS

There are three secrets you should know about in L.A. Rumble, and Table 7.8 points them out.

**TABLE 7.8: THE SECRETS IN L.A. RUMBLE**

| AREA IN LEVEL | SECRET ITEMS | HOW TO GET IT |
|---|---|---|
| Secret tunnel at the east end | freezethrower | Blow up the side wall of the dark passage as you emerge from the entry tunnel. Crawl through the rubble inside the tunnel, and collect the freezethrower. |
| Top of the stairs in the north Tower | devastator ammo | Push the landscape painting as you reach the top level office. |
| The southern tower's bottom-floor lab | atomic health unit | Push the cabinet at the far left, then crawl in the middle cabinet to collect the item. |

# MOVIE SET

Give the aliens a few weeks in Los Angeles, and the next thing you know, they think they can take over tinsel town too. Movie Set is a nice little diversion into a not-so-reputable Hollywood studio. And once again, the aliens seem to relish playing roles normally destined for humans and a few talking pigs and dogs. But for all the enthusiasm normally shown by newcomers to the industry, don't expect high production values or moving artistic statements from the alien directors and their second rate thespians. Their sensibilities really seem more in tune with the B-movie, drive-in splatter genre. And there is probably nothing the aliens would like more than to have you star in their first feature snuff flick.

The Movie Set consists of two stages where low-budget, sci-fi send-ups are currently under production. About half of the entire space in this level is taken up by an open lot for outdoor shootings, literally. Although the exit switch is only a short distance from your entry point, you will have to collect all three keycards before you take your final bow and leave Movie Set behind. You can also choose to branch off into Tier Drop, the first secret level in Shrapnel City.

## MAPS AND ROUTE

In lieu of a script for the Movie Set, check out Figures 7.12 and 7.13 for a preview of coming attractions.

## THE GOODS

Besides the usual studio equipment, props, and cameras, Movie Set has a few items useful to your cause, as shown in Table 7.9.

### TABLE 7.9: THE GOODS IN MOVIE SET

| WEAPONS | AMMO | POWER-UPS |
|---|---|---|
| 1 shotgun | 2 cases | 3 portable medkits |
| 2 ripper chainguns | 2 cases | 8 atomic health units |
| 1 RPG launcher | 3 cases | 1 armor |
| 1 devastator | 5 cases | 1 steroid flask |
| 1 shrinker | 1 shrinker crystal | 2 jetpacks |
| 1 freezethrower | 2 charges | 3 NVGs |
| 2 laser trip bombs | | 1 holoduke |
| 2 pipe bomb cases | | |

## BLAZING THROUGH MOVIE SET

There is no point in hanging out at a soda fountain waiting to be discovered. Take your destiny in your own hands. Blaze through Movie Set, and rise to major stardom in no time flat.

### At the Start

1. **Get the blue keycard.** Without the blue keycard, you can wander all you want in the open lot, but you will never get inside the filming stages. Naturally, your first move is to find the keycard in question. Look behind you at the entry point—near the south end of the open lot—and pick up

**FIGURE 7.12:** Are you prepared for the role of your life on the big screen?

**FIGURE 7.13:** Don't look for a casting couch; just collect as many of these props as you can in Movie Set.

the shotgun shells sitting on top of the lane divider. Grab a shotgun and duck from the sights of two pig cops inside a small chamber. Dispose of the pig cops quickly, perhaps with a pipe bomb. Climb over the cash registers, and grab the portable medkit that you pray you don't have to use up too quickly. Climb back out from the small room, and head east toward a dingy vending machine area, where you can snatch the blue keycard by the public phone.

> **WARNING**
> The dark, dingy tiled room is a prime spot to be ambushed by pig cops. It also isn't unusual for an assault commander to show up unexpectedly.

### Inside the Stages

1.  **Make the devastator yours.** Use the blue keycard to enter stage 17A. The first chamber is a warehouse of sorts with various wooden crates. You will have to battle a few enforcers before you can attempt to claim the devastator, which is a somewhat tricky proposition. Walk up to the crates lined up along the south wall. Push the middle panel of the crate in the center. Quickly, as soon as you hear the top crate slide open, jump onto the stage light and from there into the open crate.

2.  **Score the yellow keycard.** Go north and enter stage 17B. The production under way on this stage has to do with some gratuitous desecration on the moon, which is sure to bring a flashback or two of your days in Lunar Apocalypse. Take the studio crew by surprise, and storm out

> **WARNING**
> The crate containing the devastator also packs a couple of unpleasant surprises in the form of two sentry drones. It would be suicidal to jump into the crate with such carriers of death. Play it safe by drawing the drones out of the crate and destroying them before taking the devastator.

holding the yellow keycard. Now it's time to enter the actual film scene back on stage 17A.

3. **One more card to go.** Open the door to stage 17A, and step inside the back side of the set. Drop a few pipe bombs onto the lower stage before delivering your lines, which are basically, "I'm here to kill you and take the red keycard." Access the capsule prop, and reach inside the pilot's chair to take the red keycard. Your next destination is the small chamber at the extreme north end of Movie Set.

4. **Push a crucial switch.** Clear out of stage 17A, and cut through the warehouse area toward the small door at the north end of stage 17B. Use the red keycard and step inside the small chamber. Do you hear some hair-raising growls in the distance? Stepping into this chamber conjures the dreaded Battlelord. Pound the switch on the right side. Look at the monitor to see the garage-style door lift at the very south end of Movie Set.

> **TIP**
> While you're visiting stage 17B, consider locating and securing one of this level's two jet-packs, if you don't already have one. This power-up could come in quite handy in the next level.

5. **Dash to freedom.** With all physical barriers removed, make your way back south. If you go out in the open lot, you will have to face a newly materialized Battlelord and his sidekick, the assault commander. However, if you stay inside the stages, you might avoid a painful confrontation. The choice, as always, is yours.

## ADDED ATTRACTIONS IN MOVIE SET

If you ever wanted to shoot a scene at an open lot location, step out to the open lot. But beware of the wrath of two formidable enemies, the dreadful Battlelord and his bloated cohort, none other than the fatuous assault commander.

### Shooting onto the Open Lot

After stepping into the north chamber to push the switch that lifts the exit door (way back at the south end), you are basically clear to leave the set. However, the call of the wild and the growling of the Battlelord in the open lot might be too much to resist. And, of course, there is another potent reason to prolong your stay: You can uncover the secret of the billboard and reap handsome rewards.

Moving very quickly, and staying indoors, outrun the Battlelord to reach the southernmost door on stage 17A. Hoisting a high impact weapon like the RPG launcher or the devastator, step out facing north, and open fire at the encroaching Battlelord. He will soon be joined by the assault commander. Deliver an unhealthy dose of punishment. (See Figure 7.14.) Then sidestep back inside the stage, and close the door behind you. Leave the confused aliens cooling their heels and other extremities outside, and dash back to the north side, inside stage 17B. Open the door and, facing south this time, repeat the same procedure as before. One or two solid RPGs will do the assault commander in. The Battlelord may outlast him, but not for very long.

**FIGURE 7.14:** You will soon find out why an open lot "shoot" isn't as glamorous as it is portrayed in the movies.

### The Secret of the Billboard

By now, you might have suspected the billboard hides something. For one thing you may have been hit enough times to know the shots come from somewhere on the east side of the open lot. Before you go investigating what lies behind the billboard, clear the way by firing randomly, but aiming mostly in its center section.

Now there's the matter of getting up there. If you have a jetpack, then you've got no problem; and if you don't, that's no problem either. Just go around the helicopter crash site, and jump along the rubble until you reach a large piece of asphalt you can climb on. From there, it's just another short jump to a narrow walkway below the giant billboard. Walk along to the 3D Realms logo, and step right in. Collect the atomic health unit, climb the ramp, and take two cases of devastator ammo and the freezethrower. Then be immediately on guard for another assault commander.

There is not much time to plan your moves. Before you know it, the assault commander will be furiously pounding the billboard with his devastating, albeit unusually propelled rockets. Your best option is to drop off the platform to reach cover. Then, reach for your newest acquisition, the freezethrower, and, still inside the billboard, step into his line of sight and bombard the assault commander until he freezes solid in mid air. With a flash of flair, flick out the lowly handgun and break the crystallized commander.

## COVERT DETAILS

Do you want to hear about the dirty little secrets of Movie Set? Table 7.10 gives you the inside scoop.

| TABLE 7.10: THE SECRETS IN MOVIE SET | | |
|---|---|---|
| **AREA IN LEVEL** | **SECRET ITEMS** | **HOW TO GET IT** |
| Stage 17A | jetpack | Jump right through the projection screen showing the blue planet. |
| Warehouse for Stage 17A | devastator | Push the middle panel of the central crate along the south wall. Then jump onto nearby stage lights, and from there jump into the open crate, where the devastator is kept along with a couple of sentry drones. |

| AREA IN LEVEL | SECRET ITEMS | HOW TO GET IT |
|---|---|---|
| Stage 17B | secret exit | Press the letter on the fin of the rocket to uncover the secret exit right on the side of the rocket. If you step through the door and press the exit switch, you will come out in Tier Drop. |
| Vending machine room | atomic health units (3) | Get inside the small chamber at the south end of the open lot. Push the cash register machine on the right side (there are two machines). Run quickly to reach the secret area behind the vending machine before it raises from the ground to block the space again. |
| Movie billboard on the open lot | atomic health unit devastator ammo (2 cases) freezethrower | Fly into the bottom right or top center portion of the billboard. Without a jetpack, access the billboard from the north side, in the area where the helicopter crashed. Hop along the debris and onto a large piece of cement. From there jump to the narrow walkway below the billboard. Step in through the 3D Realms logo. |

# RABID TRANSIT

This level takes place entirely in the dingy underground. The backdrop is a subway system with two trains and only one route in the shape of a large O. The trains run counterclockwise on a fixed schedule, arriving closely together at the east boarding deck and separated by a few seconds at the west deck. This bit of information is not trivial, when you consider you might have to jump off a moving train or run along the tracks.

Your initial entry point is near the center point of the oval route, in a tunnel close to the east boarding deck. Your ultimate destination is the U-shaped chamber to the south, inside the system's route. The only area outside the periphery of the route is the west boarding deck. This is also the place where the red keycard can be found. The red keycard, as you have correctly guessed,

**WARNING**

Step in front of a moving train, and you become instant road-kill.

opens the south latch into the U-shaped chamber. However, access to the west boarding deck is only possible with the aid of the blue keycard. Rabid Transit punishes carelessness and rewards fighting skills, dexterity, and sheer guts—all qualities synonymous with the Duke Nukem name.

## MAPS AND ROUTE

What better way to get a handle on Rabid Transit than to view the actual route map, as shown in Figure 7.15. Figure 7.16 will help get you oriented to collect everything you'll need.

## THE GOODS

It's dark, dingy, and savage, but Rabid Transit does offer a few good reasons to take a couple of rides on the trains. Table 7.11 shows you the goods.

**TABLE 7.11: THE GOODS IN RABID TRANSIT**

| WEAPONS | AMMO | POWER-UPS |
| --- | --- | --- |
| 1 shotgun | 3 cases | 2 portable medkits |
| 2 ripper chainguns | 1 case | 5 atomic health units |
| 1 RPG launcher | 3 cases | 1 armor |
| 2 devastators | 5 cases | 1 steroid flask |
| 1 shrinker | 1 crystal | 1 NVG |
| 1 freezethrower | 2 charges | 1 holoduke |
| 5 laser trip bombs | | |
| 2 pipe bomb cases | | |
| 2 pipe bombs | | |

**FIGURE 7.15:** How do I get there from here? Getting around in Rabid Transit is never easy.

**FIGURE 7.16:** You will discover that going around in circles sometimes gets you things.

## BLAZING THROUGH RABID TRANSIT

You can't get around the fact that you must go around to get anywhere in Rabid Transit. Here is a simple but effective itinerary so you can make all your connections.

### Around the East Boarding Deck

1. **Get some goods right away.** Emerge from the rubble of the tunnel through the revolving doors and into a bookstore. Watch out for the turret at the south end and the encroaching troopers and captains. If you grab the chaingun ammo from on top of the shelf, several pig cops will materialize on the scene.

2. **Take it to the boarding deck.** Mow down a few pig cops as you move into the vending machine area to collect a shotgun. Then look behind the Lunar Apocalypse movie poster, and jump into a small enclosure to grab a ripper chaingun.

> **WARNING**
>
> As far as anyone knows, without a jetpack, it is impossible to get the blue keycard, which rests on an elevated platform at the south end. For that reason, if a jetpack doesn't figure in your arsenal, you should go back to the last level and collect one. If not, your stay in Rabid Transit may well be eternal and not just transitory.

3. **Take out the laser trip bombs.** Stand at a good distance and attempt to detonate the laser trip bombs barring access to the trains. A square shotgun blast usually does the trick, but it's hard to fail with a pipe bomb as well.

4. **Wait for your train to come in.** Notice how the

> **TIP**
>
> Expect to hear a few sentry drones' engines whip up to a frenzy as soon as you reach for the ripper chaingun. Save yourself from serious damage by shutting the compartment as quickly as you can. If you move fast enough, you can expect to hear the drones crash on the wall outside.

second train arrives almost right behind the first one. Get on the last car of the second train. Scoot next to the opposite door. The train makes only one stop. And it is on the west boarding deck.

## At the First Stop

1. **Don't get off yet!** The first time you come around the west boarding deck, you will notice the entire area is behind metal curtains. It does no good to get off because you still have not scored the blue keycard. Stay in the car and spray bullets at the pig cops patrolling the sealed deck.

## Your First Jump

1. **Get off at the right time.** As the train approaches the south end of its route, get ready to jump off. The right moment is when you see a red-lit platform where a few pig cops guard the blue keycard. Jump off confidently. A small recess below the platform gives you just enough space to avoid being squished by the next passing train.

2. **Get the blue keycard.** Activate your jetpack to reach the platform and wrestle the blue keycard from the pig cops. Look across the way and notice a small yellow latch that leads to the U-shaped chamber, where freedom awaits at the bottom of the wet area. However, don't go for it prematurely; your next move is to penetrate the west side.

3. **Run on the tracks.** It sounds dangerous and it is, but the alternative is to try boarding a moving train, having only a small window of opportunity and no room for a second try. The best time to run is right after a train passes. Run directly back to the west side to put the blue keycard to use.

## On the West Boarding Deck

1. **Bust the pig cops.** As soon as the metal curtains lift, you are at the end of a large rectangular area covered with aliens in blue uniforms. The RPG launcher or devastator is hard to beat in this situation.

2. **Clear the stairway.** Step just inside the stairway, and fire an RPG toward the dark north end, where a bunch of alien eggs are almost ready to hatch. A major explosion will rattle the entire area, causing a tunnel to form, which connects the stairway and the deck at the north end. Also, suddenly the entire boarding deck will become crowded with octabrains.

3. **Get the red keycard at the top of the stairs.** As you begin your ascent, you will hear the hair-raising growl of the Battlelord, who materializes at the bottom of the stairway.

4. **Get back on the tracks.** As soon as you notice a train go by, jump back on the tracks and then use the red keycard on the latch at the south end.

## In the U-Shaped Chamber

1. **Trash two assault commanders.** Move along the perimeter steps, and try to make each one of your RPG shots count. Avoid hitting the bound female at the bottom of the U-shaped chamber to prevent additional octabrains from materializing.

2. **Dive for pearls.** Although not exactly pearls, there is a shrinker at the bottom of the pool—and a couple of octabrains.

3. **Slide through the final tunnel.** Head directly into the inviting opening at the south end of the pool. Swim upwards into a cavity, where the glowing red switch beckons you to come home in no uncertain terms.

# ADDED ATTRACTIONS IN RABID TRANSIT

By far the most intense moment in Rabid Transit occurs on the west boarding deck. Getting the red keycard at the top of the dark stairway involves engaging some of your toughest enemies. You can't avoid the confrontation, but you can try to control it and pace it in such a way that is advantageous to your cause.

## The Bloody Battle for the Red Keycard

Once you have cleared the dock from the initial wave of pig cops, things will appear to be calm. But don't let your guard down for a second. In this section of Rabid Transit, your enemies materialize only after you take certain actions. Knowing what these actions are allows you to be ready for the ensuing alien attack.

Stepping into the threshold of the stairway, aim north and fire an RPG at the egg hatchery at the north end of the tunnel. A violent explosion rattles the place and causes a multitude of octabrains to materialize in the deck area. Holding your position just inside the stairway, you have an ideal angle to release RPGs at the octabrains outside, as shown in Figure 7.17. Additionally, you can use the dividing wall as a shield from the octabrains' mental energy blasts.

> **TIP**
>
> You can also reach the red keycard by crawling through the hole you created when you fired the RPG launcher. This way you can avoid the stairs altogether, and prevent the Battlelord from materializing.

When the octabrains' remains are spread over the deck, get out and approach the north end very cautiously. You want to avoid crossing the stairs because that would only mean that you would be triggering a Battlelord to crash the party. As you get near the

**FIGURE 7.17:** Use your protected position inside the stairway, and do away with the octabrains before making your next move.

north side where the explosion dug a tunnel, be ready to unload a few more RPGs or devastator rounds on the assault commander lurking in the dark. The best time to catch him is when you first hear his sadistic laugh echoing from the tunnel. Fire directly into the gaping dark hole, and prevent the commander from joining you on the boarding deck.

## COVERT DETAILS

Rabid Transit houses a good number of secrets, and Table 7.12 lists them all for you.

**TABLE 7.12: THE SECRETS IN RABID TRANSIT**

| AREA IN LEVEL | SECRET ITEMS | HOW TO GET IT |
|---|---|---|
| West boarding deck | RPG ammo | Jump on top of the mail drop box, and push against the wall to open a secret compartment. |
| Dark stairway | freezethrower ammo (2) devastator RPG ammo | Push the left side of the wall at the south end. Enter the alien chamber, and collect the freezethrower ammo in plain view. Then activate a control panel at the bottom right corner of the large screen to uncover an adjoining chamber along the east side. This chamber houses the devastator and RPG ammo. |
| U-shaped chamber | devastator ammo (2 cases) RPG ammo (1 case) | Use your jetpack to lift yourself on top of the bookshelf on the left side. Then hop onto the next bookshelf. This causes the first bookshelf to lower and reveal a small chamber with the goods. |
| Vending machine area | holoduke | Jump on top of the magazine dispenser at the southwest corner. It will lower to show a small chamber where you can crouch and grab the holoduke. |
| Hole at the north end of the tracks | atomic health unit devastator ammo (1 case) steroids | Blow a hole in the north wall, step in, and claim the loot. Of course, you have to negotiate the timing of the trains to avoid being run over when you are in this area. |
| East boarding deck | ripper chaingun | Push the Lunar Apocalypse poster, and jump into the enclosure to grab the weapon. |

# FAHRENHEIT

Who turned up the temperature? This level puts you back above ground, in a part of the city where a TV studio and a fire station dominate the landscape. There is also a small and cozy apartment nearby, a courtyard, and an open warehouse. Like in most major cities, the environment might seem crowded and encroaching. But unlike in most cities, Fahrenheit's environment is run by the aliens you seem to know all too well by now. Sentry drones and assault commanders have a strong presence in this level. But even if you get past them and make it all the way to the exit, you must still face the Battlelord and two of his enforcer minions.

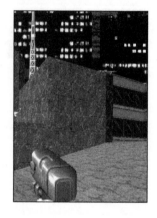

Fahrenheit strikes a pleasing balance of inside action and frisky outdoor encounters. In Fahrenheit, you might start to realize just how effective weapons like the freeze-thrower and the shrinker are in crowded situations. You only need to score the blue and then the red keycards. After that, you are practically home free—except for the small matter of an encounter with the Battlelord. Although the blue keycard is plainly visible at the north end of the waterway, the red keycard is a bit tougher to locate. It is hidden in the fire station's pole, which is inaccessible until you reach and push the appropriate switch. The assault commanders around the fire station complicate matters to a much higher degree. You might not come out smelling like roses, but if you use your weapons judiciously and maintain your health level, you will prevail over Fahrenheit.

## MAPS AND ROUTE

Although you could use the maps to fan yourself, Figures 7.18 and 7.19 can help you cope with the heat you will experience in Fahrenheit.

## THE GOODS

Fahrenheit offers almost everything you need to make it through, even if you start the level nearly empty-handed. Table 7.13 shows you the goods.

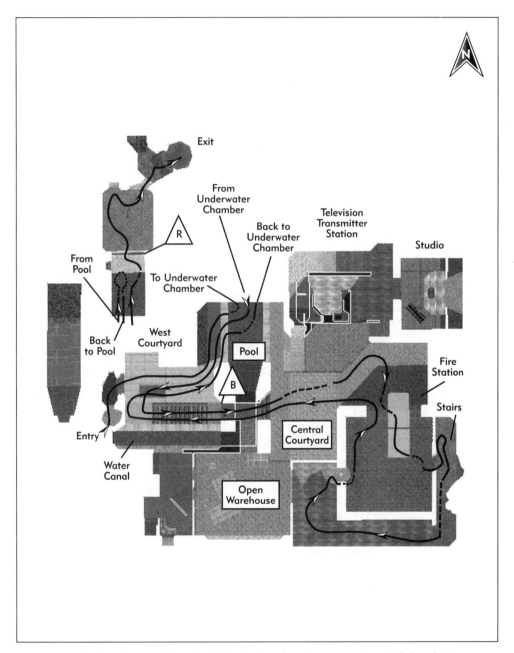

**FIGURE 7.18:** You will see hot action in both closed and open quarters in Fahrenheit.

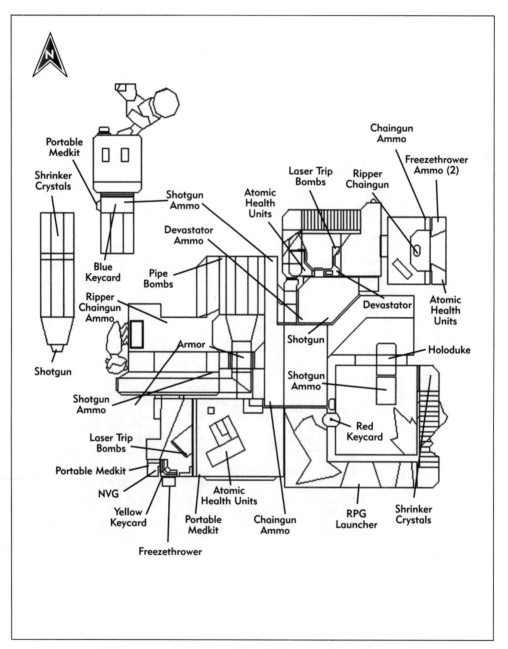

**FIGURE 7.19:** All three keycards are available in Fahrenheit, should you decide to uncover every secret and reap every useful item.

## TABLE 7.13: THE GOODS IN FAHRENHEIT

| WEAPONS | AMMO | POWER-UPS |
|---|---|---|
| 2 shotguns | 4 cases | 4 portable medkits |
| 1 ripper chaingun | 4 cases | 3 atomic health units |
| 2 RPG launchers | 2 cases | 3 armors |
| 1 devastator | 3 cases | 1 steroid flask |
| 1 shrinker | 3 shrinker crystals | 1 NVG |
| 1 freezethrower | 2 charges | 1 holoduke |
| 2 laser trip bombs | | |
| 1 pipe bomb case | | |

## BLAZING THROUGH FAHRENHEIT

If you want to explore this level in depth, consider visiting the nearby apartment and the television transmitter station. But to make tracks as quickly as possible, stick to the plan below.

### In the West Courtyard

1. **Kill the pig cops, and loot the area.** Push the metal surface to slide a big Dumpster out of the way and emerge in a small courtyard. Battle a couple of pig cops, and pick up the shotgun shells and chaingun ammo. Head for the north end of the courtyard.

2. **Cook some octabrains in their juices.** Climb on the ledge of the canal, and grab the pipe bomb case. Drop a couple of pipe bombs in succession, and detonate them simultaneously to make short work of the octabrains below. Then dive in and continue north into a larger underwater chamber covered with green growth. Come up for air.

3. **Take the blue keycard, please.** Hop onto a small platform at the north end of the pool, and grab the blue keycard. Notice that the large gate in front of you requires a yellow keycard. Grab the portable medkit as you dive back into the pool, and head for the west courtyard again. Go down the ramp and use the blue keycard on the gate.

### In the Central Courtyard

1.  **Work your way to the fire station.** To better your odds, take out the turret high up in the northwest corner of the courtyard. Then grab the ripper chaingun ammo at the south end. Before rushing toward the fire station, as you ascend the inclined asphalt, look southwest in the direction of a warehouse area. If you haven't already felt its firepower, notice the turret mounted high in the corner. If you have your RPG launcher, take it out and be done with

    > **TIP**
    >
    > Expect to hear the very low and ominous laughter of the assault commanders guarding the pole. You should have your RPG launcher ready to fire straight ahead at the first sign of movement. To avoid being reduced to puree, keep a prudent distance by running back into the lower part of the tunnel, if necessary. Normally, the second assault commander stays behind, so you will have to deal with him separately, which is probably a good thing.

    it. Then get ready for a four-alarm fire in the station.

2.  **Set the fire station on fire.** Would that you could; but first, you must get what you came here for—the red keycard. Several pig cops will die if necessary to keep you out of this area. Pound them hard and when you get a chance, hop on top of the fire truck to claim a holoduke and a case of shotgun shells.

3.  **Blow a hole in the wall.** Either use the RPG launcher or drop a pipe bomb on the east side of the truck to blast an opening into the stairs leading to the top side of the station. Step into the hole and grab the shrinker crystals near the entrance. Then start your ascent into the dark stairway.

4.  **Open the pole and slide down.** Reaching the top area of the fire station, notice a switch on the right side, next to the cylindrical enclosure that hides the pole. Push the switch to uncover the elusive pole. Slide down it and land on top of the red keycard at the bottom. Trace your steps back to the west courtyard. Get back in the water and swim north again.

### In the North End

1. **Open the last gate and meet some old faces.** Be ready to jump back in the water and get out of harm's way, for as soon as you open the door you are faced with a less-than-hospitable Battlelord and two of his pet enforcers.

2. **Battle the Battlelord with courage.** An effective technique in this seemingly hopeless situation is to jump in and out of the water like a pogo stick, unloading your arsenal as you break the surface and then rapidly dropping to avoid retaliation. It also helps if you sidestep left and right to keep them guessing.

3. **Knock out yet another hole.** Enter the medium-sized chamber, previously held by the Battlelord, and grab the RPG launcher behind the compartment. Back off a few steps, and blow another hole into the north wall of the chamber. Climb along the jagged edges of the tunnel. Then descend into the area to the right to find the exit switch.

## ADDED ATTRACTIONS IN FAHRENHEIT

If you haven't had enough fun yet, there are a couple of other places in Fahrenheit that are certainly worth visiting. These places include:

- A nearby cozy apartment
- A television transmitter station with truly questionable programming

### The Cozy Apartment

Tucked away in the southwest corner of Fahrenheit, there is one small but cozy apartment. It overlooks an open warehouse area with a few crates of varying dimensions. The apartment has a TV showroom, complete with multiple screens. In addition, a wet bar and plenty of well drinks make the atmosphere even more alluring. The only way to reach this little oasis in this asphalt desert is to cross the open warehouse area. The sentry drones and enforcers patrolling the area aren't exactly keen on letting just anyone get by, much less you. But you aren't exactly expecting an open invitation either.

So, enter the warehouse carefully, expecting leaping enforcers to pounce on you at any moment. The freezethrower or shrinker will work wonders on the first wave of offenders. But these weapons aren't as effective against sentry drones. Switch to the ripper chaingun or the shotgun to keep the drones from dive bombing into you.

Hop onto the smallest crate and from there into the next larger one. At this point, you should be able to peek inside the windows of a small open space that leads directly into the small apartment. Jump from the middle crate up onto the narrow ledge right by the windows. Use the wall space between the windows for cover as you assassinate the pig cops inside. Then face eastward and jump onto the larger and longer of the crates to claim an atomic health unit. After that, you're clear to enter the apartment. Hop back onto the ledge, and from there go right through the window and get inside the apartment. These series of movements are graphically depicted in Figure 7.20.

> **TIP**
>
> A most effective way for disposing of the Battlelord and his pals in this very confined situation is to rely almost exclusively on your freezethrower. If you have enough charges and can maintain a sustained attack where you can unload the equivalent of one charge (twenty-five blasts), then you can shatter his majesty with a simple bullet.

Once inside the apartment, be sure to pick up the devastator and RPG ammo along the north side. Notice the very dark wall next to the RPG ammo. It hides a message for you, but you will need the NVG to read the message; deciphering it is another matter.

Head toward the south end, where the entertainment center is found along with a cushy sofa and the aforementioned wet bar. Get up on the couch to reach for the yellow keycard. Also, don't pass up the steroids on top of

> **NOTE**
>
> If you intend to visit the TV station, you will first have to get the yellow keycard, which, fortunately for you, is inside the cozy apartment.

one of the bookshelves. The painting behind the couch hides a secret compartment where a freezethrower is kept. Also, if you want to read the secret message on the dark wall, you should grab the NVG on the bookshelf. Having reaped a few goods, you might as well take a load off on the couch, and take in a few moving pictures on the sets.

**FIGURE 7.20:** This is how you get to the cozy apartment.

## The Television Transmitter Station

Don't even think about visiting the transmitter station, unless you have a yellow keycard on you. (If you don't, check out the nearby apartment at the southwest corner of Fahrenheit.) From the central courtyard, head north toward a ramp leading directly to the main door of the station. Use the yellow keycard and smoke the enforcer pages dispatched to guide you on a private tour of the facilities. The ripper chaingun and the shotgun may prove somewhat ineffective in such tight quarters. So without any vacillation, whip out the shrinker and reduce your enemies to the size of bugs. Then step on them.

Proceed up the stairs, resist going into the closed studio doors, and take possession of the security control room. There are only a couple of assault captains in the monitoring room. Be sure not to miss the devastator next to the monitor on the left side.

Take stock of your health. If it needs it, you can give it a boost with the atomic health unit behind a small door near the back of the room. The door actually opens into the back of the monitoring system. Feeling good and mighty powerful, head toward the closed studio doors. Face them squarely and throw them open. Before the doors have finished opening completely, back out to the security control room as you fire a steady stream of devastator charges. If the assault commander hovering near the door manages to expel a rocket, you can sidestep out of the way inside the security room.

Continue sidestepping and unloading charges. The freezethrower is also an excellent weapon from this distance. As soon as the assault commander turns blue, like a grotesque, hovering ice statue, switch to another weapon and break him. Inside the studio you will find a ripper chaingun and some ammo on top of a bookshelf.

## COVERT DETAILS

Fahrenheit is hot for action as well as secrets. Check out Table 7.14 to see for yourself.

### TABLE 7.14: THE SECRETS IN FAHRENHEIT

| AREA IN LEVEL | SECRET ITEMS | HOW TO GET IT |
|---|---|---|
| Security room | atomic health unit | Open the narrow door at the back of the security room inside the television transmitter station. |
| Studio room | freezethrower ammo<br>atomic health unit | Walk right through the curtains behind the stage. |
| Cozy apartment | Portable medkit | Break every bottle and glass on the wet bar shelf, before you can simply walk right through it. |
| | freezethrower | Climb on the couch and look behind the painting. |

# HOTEL HELL

If it weren't for the dubious clientele, Hotel Hell might actually be a nice place for serious power lounging. The decor is somewhat Spartan, to be sure, but the hourly rooms are cozy and, above all, functional. The upstairs pool and bar are also a nice amenity. You almost want to order a martini and take in the sun by the poolside deck. Yet, this is Hotel Hell, and its alien management—headed by the Battlelord Sentry and his squadron of enforcers, troopers, pig cops, and RPVs—don't believe in carrying your baggage or taking tips. Forget the leisurely life. In fact, if you don't watch yourself in this level, forget life period. Hotel Hell is also your connection to Freeway, the second secret level in Shrapnel City.

A hotel of ill repute, otherwise known as the Wham Bam, dominates this level. The flickering neon sign outside foreshadows the seediness inside. The hotel is flanked by a wide alley to the north. A large street meets the hotel's main entrance on the east side. To the south, the hotel's side door opens onto a narrow street. On the way to the secret exit, Hotel Hell pays homage to a legendary adventurer and doctor of anthropology, a man inseparable from his bull whip, brim hat, and leather jacket. Might you have heard of him?

## MAPS AND ROUTE

Don't get lost in a second rate hotel. The maps in Figures 7.22 and 7.23 can keep you from straying into an early and final bed.

## THE GOODS

Before checking out of Hotel Hell permanently, make it a point to grab all the loot you can get. As Table 7.15 shows, there is quite a bit of stuff you can lay your hand on.

| TABLE 7.15: THE GOODS IN HOTEL HELL | | |
|---|---|---|
| **WEAPONS** | **AMMO** | **POWER-UPS** |
| 1 shotgun | 5 cases | 3 portable medkits |
| 1 ripper chaingun | 3 cases | 5 atomic health units |
| 1 RPG launcher | 2 cases | 2 armors |
| 1 devastator | 3 cases | 1 steroid flask |
| 1 shrinker | 1 shrinker crystal | 2 NVGs |
| 2 freezethrowers | 1 charge | 2 holodukes |
| 2 laser trip bombs | | 2 scuba gear |
| 3 pipe bomb cases | | |

## BLAZING THROUGH HOTEL HELL

In this hotel you are charged by the hour, so make every minute count. In fact, if you get done before time expires, consider staying for seconds to reach the secret exit.

**FIGURE 7.21:** Peril awaits at every turn in Hotel Hell, so take stock of your surroundings and avoid serious trouble.

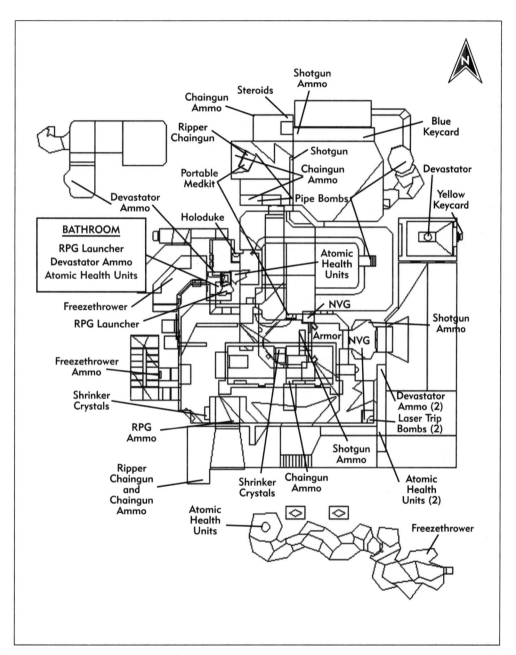

**FIGURE 7.22:** There are two keycards in Hotel Hell, and you will need them both to reach either of the two exits.

## In the North Side Alley

1. **Score a shotgun and down a few bad pig cops.** Hop out of the tunnel you reached at the end of Fahrenheit into a wide alley on the north side of the Wham Bam hotel. Take the shotgun sitting on top of a wooden wall and destroy the pig cops who are sure to sniff you out. Notice there really is no place to go, as the security latch by the door requires you to have a blue keycard.

2. **Grab the blue keycard.** Luckily for you, the blue keycard is in the near vicinity. Hop onto the wooden wall and face north, toward a ventilating unit on top of the short building. Hop again to land near the unit. Finally, a third hop onto the ledge running east and west will place you in plain view of the keycard.

3. **Check into the hotel.** Use caution when you open the door, for there might well be a pig cop on the other side. When you reach the end of the hallway, a blast will open a large hole on the north side of the wall. From this point on, you know you are in for quite a bang inside Wham Bam Hotel.

## Inside the Hotel

1. **Load up on heavy firepower.** Cut a quick right at the end of the hallway, and enter the gaping hole into a dilapidated bathroom. Pick up the RPG launcher from the tiled floor and the devastator ammo on the broken sink.

2. **Skip the soda but take the crystals.** Rush toward the south end of the open foyer, and hop on top of the soda vending machine to take two shrinker crystals.

3. **Face the action outside.** Step out the side door to the south into a narrow side street. You will be instantly met by an assortment of enforcers, pig cops, and an RPV or two. So use every trick in the book, and maybe write a few, to advance into the main street toward the east.

## In Front of the Hotel

1. **Stay clear of the entrance.** As you turn north onto the main street, you will be facing an upward slope and several of your favorite enemies, including pig cops, enforcers, and another RPV. As inside the hotel, avoid stirring the Battlelord Sentry by staying away from the entrance. Stand your ground or retreat back to the side street to make the street safer for yourself.

2. **Fight the enforcers from a distance.** Advance northward toward the east office, but stop short of crossing the front entrance of the hotel. By now you will have noticed the enforcers inside the east side office at the end of the street. Pull out the ripper chaingun, turn on the crosshair, and do what you don't get paid to do, but will do gladly.

> **TIP**
> The reason you step out through the side is simple. You want to avoid a bruising battle with the Battlelord Sentry, who has a permanent shift at the front desk. If you were to engage him now, there would not be much place to run or hide. However, facing the Battlelord Sentry is not nearly as Herculean an effort as overcoming a true Battlelord.

3. **Rush toward the east side office.** Once the enforcer office party is over, rush past the hotel's front entrance, avoiding detection, and jump right through either window into the office.

## In the East Side Office

1. **Beef up your arsenal and uncover the yellow keycard.** Take the devastator on top of the desk immediately. Then walk toward the compartment on the east wall to claim the yellow keycard.

2. **Keep the devastator handy.** Next thing you know, an assault commander shows up to intercept you. Don't be caught off guard. Be ready to point, aim, and fire in the direction of the sinister laughter that cuts the air like a cold, serrated boning knife.

3. **Head back to the hotel.** If you feel brave enough, go ahead and enter through the front door. Engage the Battlelord Sentry and knock him out with three to five solid RPG hits. If you want to play it safe, just dash back the way you got to the east side office.

4. **Get to the top floor.** Inside the hotel's lobby, find the elevator and use the yellow keycard to ride up to the hotel's bar and pool area.

### In the Bar and Pool Area

1. **Step up to the bar.** When you open the elevator door, you can be easily overwhelmed by a mob of enforcers. Avoid this sad fate by dropping a few pipe bombs and then closing the door quickly. From the safety of the elevator, detonate the pipe bombs to stop the enforcer menace before it can mount an offensive.

2. **Check out the wine list, but don't overlook the power-ups.** Look around behind the bar counter for a wooden panel at the north end. It is a secret door into a dark and gray hallway where you can take a portable medkit. The hallway leads to the top of a large water tank holding the freezethrower—and a shark. Grab the scuba gear and the case of pipe bombs from the compartment at the end of the hallway.

3. **Dive for the freezethrower.** If you don't already have it, it is really worthwhile to add this weapon to your cache. But even if you have one already, you can always use the extra charges.

4. **Make it to the poolside.** Get out of the tank and walk around behind the bar into the open area where the L-shaped pool is found. Overcome whatever opposition you find from the roving troopers and captains in this area. Then hop onto the small platform at the north side of the pool, overlooking the initial alleyway where you entered this level. Across the street, you will notice the windows opening on the top floor of the building, revealing a room crowded with aliens of the enforcer ilk.

5. **Fight the enforcers from afar.** The ripper chaingun is a good choice to dispense with the enforcers from where you stand. Turning on the crosshair

and the mouse pointing function, you can zero in on individual enforcers. With the enforcers no longer a threat, jump below into the alleyway.

### Back in the North Alley

1. **Reach the top floor of the building to the north.** As in the beginning, hop your way to the ledge of the top floor. Then jump inside the rectangular room.

2. **Go through the duct and down the chute.** Bash the grill on the east side of the room, and hop into the air duct.

3. **Dive to freedom.** Follow the duct as it turns sharply to the south. Then let yourself fall into a semi-circular pit. At the bottom, you will find the exit switch leading to Freeway.

## ADDED ATTRACTIONS IN HOTEL HELL

Because this level is a junction to the secret level Freeway, finding the secret exit is worth exploring in some detail, naturally.

### Exploring for the Secret Exit

Up to the point where you reach the pool, every step for finding the secret exit is exactly the same as when you are only headed for the normal exit. But when you are finally there, you can go either way. Should you choose to go for an extra romp you wouldn't ordinarily see in the course of your playtime, then by all means embark on a search. Who knows what secrets and surprises might await you there.

In the pool area, walk up to the waterfall that feeds the pool on the west side. Step right into the waterfall. You will come out into a natural, rocky terrain at the foot of another, this time natural, waterfall. Head west and explore the north banks along the small water hole to find a freezethrower. Eventually you will come upon a recess in the rocks where a couple of tall palm trees grow. The secret exit to Freeway is well hidden behind the palm trees. Throw a pipe bomb at the foot of the trees to uproot them completely.

Before marching over to the switch, let your sense of exploration heed the call of its primeval instincts. Push against the bloody hand print switch on the broken wall to your left. As the crack widens, step right through the fire into the tunnel just west of the secret exit switch. Follow the sinewy path all the way to the end, where you will

find a chamber of sorts with a high ceiling and an atomic health unit sitting on top of a heavy cylindrical stone. But that's not all you will see. You seem to have happened upon perhaps a pagan temple of doom. If the unfortunate college-professor-turned-explorer's body impaled on the wall could speak, he would tell you to be careful.

Realizing the seriousness of the situation, grab the atomic health unit and back out as soon as humanly possible. A good dose of steroids will help you reach the exit before the entire tunnel

collapses around and on top of you. Though Duke likes his hair flat on top, this is not the way to achieve it. Having replenished your vitality and health, get back to the secret exit switch and pound it decisively.

## COVERT DETAILS

If truth be told, there are but a few secrets to behold in Hotel Hell, but Table 7.16 comes clean about them.

### TABLE 7.16: THE SECRETS IN HOTEL HELL

| AREA IN LEVEL | SECRET ITEMS | HOW TO GET IT |
| --- | --- | --- |
| Hotel bar (upstairs) | portable medkit<br>scuba gear<br>pipe bomb case | Push the wooden panel on the north wall, behind the bar countertop. It opens into a dark, gray hallway. |
| Hotel bar | holoduke | Push against the wine bottle rack to uncover a small secret area where the holoduke is kept. |
| Remote tunnel, near the secret exit | atomic health unit | Teleport to the area by stepping into the waterfall of the rooftop hotel pool. Follow the tunnel toward the west. The atomic health unit lies on top of a large cylindrical rock. |

# STADIUM

Stadium is the inevitable and much-awaited match of the millennium. A proverbial show-down of colossal proportions, Stadium pits the home-town favorite, Duke Nukem, against the formidable Cycloid Emperor. What's at stake in this final battle is much more than fabulous ratings or the home team's pride. The future of our world rests squarely on your shoulders, Nukem. Please don't let us down. You never have before.

## MAPS AND ROUTE

Considering the straightforward architecture of Stadium and the opposition's caliber, the maps shown in Figures 7.23 and 7.24 might somehow seem superfluous. But think of what's at stake. Every bit of knowledge can become a decisive advantage in Stadium.

## THE GOODS

Power-ups, weapons, and ammo are quite bountiful in Stadium. Of course, judging by the caliber of your opponent, you need everything you can get. Table 7.17 shows you what you can have, should you live long enough to collect. In addition, a *Duff Beer* dirigible floating over Stadium is a veritable weapon and power-up piñata. Fly as high as you can right above the center of Stadium and blow up the blimp to cause a shower of goodies to fall upon the grass of Stadium.

### TABLE 7.17: THE GOODS IN STADIUM

| WEAPONS | AMMO | POWER-UPS |
| --- | --- | --- |
| 1 shotgun | 4 cases | 1 portable medkit |
| 1 ripper chaingun | 3 cases | 4 atomic health units |
| 1 RPG launcher | 3 cases | 2 steroid flasks |
| 1 devastator | 2 cases | 3 NVGs |
| 2 shrinkers | 2 shrinker crystals | 1 holoduke |
| 1 freezethrower | 3 charges | 2 steroid flasks |
| 4 pipe bomb cases | | 1 jetpack |

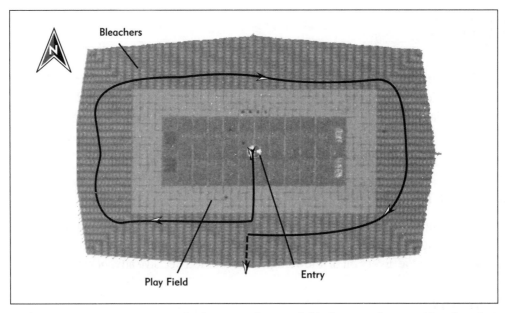

**FIGURE 7.23:** It's game time in Stadium, a wide-open field where anything could and might happen.

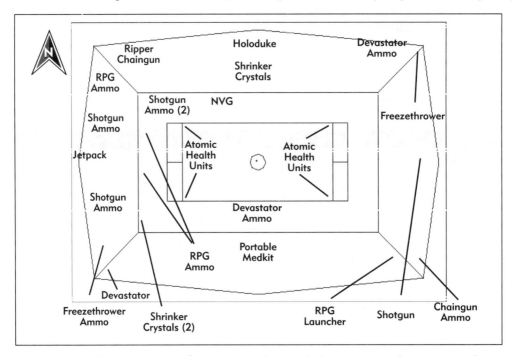

**FIGURE 7.24:** Even if you enter Stadium scarcely armed, there are enough weapons and power-ups to help you overcome the Cycloid Emperor.

## THE MATCH OF THE MILLENNIUM

The kick-off in this level occurs when you emerge from a radioactive manhole cover right at the 50 yard line. The mastodon Cycloid Emperor across the field would like nothing better than to blow you away even before the starting whistle blows. There is absolutely no sense in standing up to the Cycloid Emperor toe-to-toe. It would be a brave but foolish move. Instead, you must use your head, Duke. In a match of fire-power, the Cycloid Emperor has the clear advantage. Your only chance in hell of defeating the Emperor is to remain alive. That means not getting hit. A single hit from the Cycloid Emperor's built-in devastator arms could easily render you into expensive grass fertilizer.

At first glance you might think that there is absolutely no place to hide in Stadium. And you are right. But there are actually a few things you can do to limit the Emperor's target range. For one thing, his

> **TIP**
>
> If a cheerleader gets nailed, you can count on adding a couple of assault cammanders to the alien line-up. This might not be such a bad thing after all. If you can create a cross fire among them, the short tempered aliens will fight among themselves, giving you a chance to pick up heavier artillery and power-ups.

massive stature prevents him from climbing onto the bleachers. Secondly, his single eye compliments his single-minded approach to battle. He lives to force you to retire from the game before your time. You can turn this to your advantage. By now you have probably figured out that you need to climb on the bleachers as soon as possible. And if you take to the air, the better off you will be.

If you hop on the bleachers, you want to draw the Cycloid Emperor as close to the bleachers as you can. When he bumps against them, the Emperor's hell-bent nature will keep him trying, in vain, to climb. This renders him practically immobile. If you manage to climb as high as you can in the bleachers, you will also have succeeded in severely limiting the Emperor's fire range. His projectiles might land close, but without much of an angle, you can breathe somewhat tenuously as you plan your next move.

A minor inconvenience in all of this is that a group of troopers at the east end, or dog pound seats, can fire at you from a distance. You can pick them off even with your pistol. As to which side of the stadium to run to, it is up to debate. You should consider which weapons are available and which you would like to get first. Also, keep in mind that the spirited group of cheerleaders in the north end of the fifty yard line, can, and probably will get nailed by the Cycloid Emperor if you rush to the north.

If you are sitting at the fifty yard line at the top of the bleachers and you don't have about forty to fifty RPG rounds or sixty to seventy charges in the freezethrower, you have no choice but to run around the field collecting what you need. This means getting somewhat exposed. If you are fortunate enough to have a jetpack with you, you can become an elusive target in the air, and drop down in key spots to collect the ammo and firepower necessary. Of course, you should attempt to deflate the hovering blimp at the first opportunity. You will then have just about every weapon and power-up littering the field. Another power-up that can help you even the odds a bit are the steroids. There are two flasks in Stadium—one at the Bad Ass end zone and the other one in your own. Ingest the pills, and you will dash across the terrain like a fearless running back, dodging, cutting, and zigzagging around your opponents. You should try to circle the Cycloid Emperor as you keep him in your sights to pound him with everything you've got (see Figure 7.25).

There won't be another battle in Shrapnel City. But if you overcome him, your children and your children's children's children might live to see a better tomorrow. A tomorrow where people can live together and prosper.

**FIGURE 7.25:** Rain your wrath upon the Cycloid Emperor from high above. It might be your only chance.

# TIER DROP

If you found the secret exit in Movie Set, then you are in for a very special treat in Tier Drop. This secret level is delightful in the four looks and feels it gives you. Four long, wide corridors connected in a simple square design form the perimeter of Tier Drop.

Each side of the square has an opening into a very peculiar central courtyard. Depending on which side of the perimeter you approach it from, the courtyard will seem like an entirely different place each time.

Tier Drop asks you to put aside, if only for a while, your common notions about time and space. At each corner of the courtyard, you will find dimensional wells, which appear like ordinary holes in the ground, that will drop you onto another tier in the Tier Drop level. In fact, you might conceive Tier Drop as being four slices of reality stacked on top of one another. Of course, knowing that your concept of what's real and what isn't has just gone out the window isn't exactly reassuring. But take heart, you can solve this level by visiting only two of the tiers.

## MAPS AND ROUTE

To keep you from straining your eyes, Figure 7.26 shows you the two separate tiers among the level's four tiers that are necessary to blaze through the level. Figure 7.27 and 7.28, on the other hand, shows each of the four individual tiers and the locations of all the goodies on each. A line map for this level looks quite interesting, but it isn't very functional for demonstrating the places where these items can be found.

**FIGURE 7.26:** There is much more to Tier Drop than what you necessarily see.

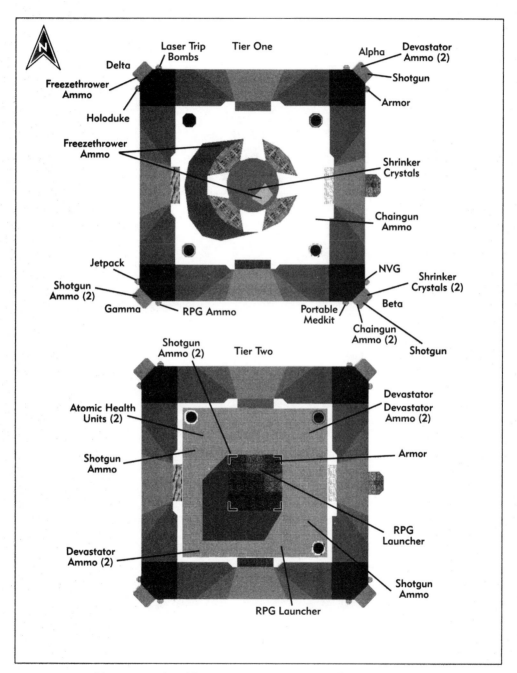

**FIGURE 7.27:** You may not be able to trust your own eyes in Tier Drop . . .

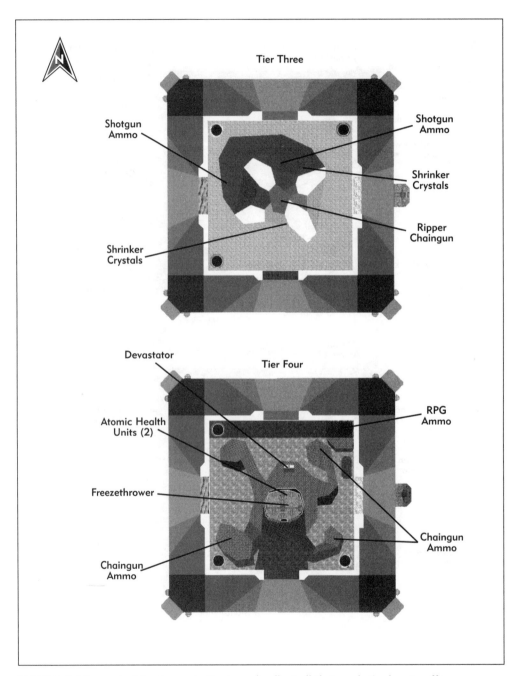

## THE GOODS

There is a considerable cache of power-ups, weapons, and ammo, as Table 7.18 clearly points out.

| TABLE 7.18: THE GOODS IN TIER DROP | | |
|---|---|---|
| **WEAPONS** | **AMMO** | **POWER-UPS** |
| 2 shotguns | 9 cases | 1 portable medkit |
| 1 ripper chaingun | 7 cases | 3 atomic health units |
| 1 RPG launcher | 3 cases | 1 steroid flask |
| 1 shrinker | 4 cases | 1 jetpack |
| 1 devastator | 4 cases | 1 NVG |
| 1 freezethrower | 4 charges | 1 holoduke |
| 3 laser trip bombs | | 1 armor |
| 2 pipe bomb cases | | |

## BLAZING THROUGH TIER DROP

You can spend a good while exploring every facet of Tier Drop and still not get the entire picture. To get through in a timely and efficient manner, stick with the following outline, but don't be afraid to strike out on your own.

### The Initial Round

1. **Come out and make the rounds.** Get out of the small enclosure and dash around the four corners of Tier Drop: Alpha, Beta, Gamma, and Delta. Pick up everything of value along the way. Pay particular attention to the large and small enclosures in each corner. Your survival and success depends on how much firepower and power-ups you can accumulate early on. Also, if you move fast enough, you can avoid attracting the enemies inside the courtyard.

### The Quick Descent to Tier Four

1. **Drop down to tier four.** After making a full tour around the perimeter, get back to your initial point near the east side entrance to the courtyard.

Make a quick right and drop right into the red glowing well. You will emerge in the northeast corner of tier four.

## On Tier Four

1. **Dispose of the assault commanders.** Use the shotgun to pluck the assault commanders, who normally hover around the south end of this tier.

2. **Climb the central structure for the final struggle.** Climb along the slanted metal of the central structure to reach its top. Move toward the north side where you can take a devastator. Then walk around to the front doors bearing the Battlelord's likeness. Open the doors and do your best to overcome the Battlelord. Then run in and punch the exit switch.

## ADDED ATTRACTIONS IN TIER DROP

The blazing section only introduced you to two of the tiers in Tier Drop. The other tiers have their special features, dangers, and rewards, as you will see in the following short descriptions.

### Tier Two

This tier offers the most polished look of all. It has smooth, cement floors and a perfectly square structure in the center. The central structure, however, is practically carpeted with the web-like matter that seems all too prevalent in and around alien egg nests. The RPG launcher and armor are compelling reasons for venturing into the central structure. The peripheral power-ups and weapons, which include a devastator and two atomic health units, are yet another reason why anyone should spend the time visiting this tier. Tier two, however, is a pig cop stronghold. Take the necessary firepower and precautions, should you decide to drop in for a visit.

### Tier Three

Characterized by a rocky, jagged architecture, this tier is perhaps the most vicious of them all. Tier three is a veritable octabrain spawning ground. If you like using the shrinker, consider entering tier three to grab two crystals. Battling the herds of octabrains inside the courtyard isn't always wise. You will be better off drawing the octabrains to chase you into the periphery, where you can more neatly pluck them off in the air, without being overcome on all sides.

## COVERT DETAILS

The secrets in Tier Drop aren't exactly top secrets, and finding them is not exactly rocket science. Table 7.19 catalogs the secrets, such as they are.

| TABLE 7.19: THE SECRETS IN TIER DROP | | |
| --- | --- | --- |
| AREA IN LEVEL | SECRET ITEMS | HOW TO GET IT |
| Alpha corner | shotgun<br>devastator ammo (2 cases) | Push against the steel panel. |
| Beta corner | shrinker crystals (2)<br>shotgun<br>ripper chaingun<br>ammo (2 cases) | Push against the steel panel. |
| Delta corner | freezethrower charge<br>pipe bomb case | Push against the steel panel. |
| Gamma corner | shotgun shells (3 cases)<br>RPG ammo (2 cases) | Push against the steel panel. |

# FREEWAY

Life at the end of Freeway is about to begin for you. You obviously decided to explore the secret exit in Hotel Hell, and you found it near a manhole cover. Now you're about to emerge out of the drain tunnel into Freeway. This former piece of civilization is built around intersecting roadways. A wide underpass runs east and west. The even wider overpass runs north and south. Surrounding buildings, tunnels, and other chambers offer ample opportunity for exploration. Just don't expect any type of courtesy or road-side manners from the aliens along *this* Freeway.

The path to the exit in Freeway is fairly straightforward, but you must pay a heavy toll to get there. Everyone you meet along this "Freeway" wants not just a piece of the action but a piece of you. With scores of sentry drones, pig cops, RPVs, enforcers, and even a few Battlelord Sentries, you are easily stretched to your limits. How well you fare in Freeway depends largely on how well equipped you are when you enter.

Even if your arsenal is measly at the beginning, there are some good spoils along the roads. Your route in Freeway takes you to the overpass. There, you must climb into an apartment on the east side to grab the blue keycard. Then you will be able to penetrate a compression chamber of sorts, where the red keycard is found. It sounds simple and it would be, were it not for the possibility of becoming a road-side casualty at any moment.

## MAPS AND ROUTE

Don't count on the kindness of strangers to give you directions in Freeway. Rely on Figures 7.29 and 7.30 to get your bearings.

## THE GOODS

The spoils in Freeway are catalogued in Table 7.20.

### TABLE 7.20: THE GOODS IN FREEWAY

| WEAPONS | AMMO | POWER-UPS |
| --- | --- | --- |
| 2 shotguns | 7 cases | 2 portable medkits |
| 1 ripper chaingun | 1 case | 3 atomic health units |
| 2 RPG launchers | 4 cases | 2 steroid flasks |
| 1 shrinker | | |
| 1 devastator | 5 cases | 1 jetpack |
| 2 freezethrowers | 1 charge | 2 NVGs |
| 2 laser trip bombs | | 3 armors |
| 3 pipe bomb cases | | |

**FIGURE 7.29:** Plan a route and stick to it, if you want to reach your destination in Freeway.

**FIGURE 7.30:** Perhaps the most difficult items to obtain are the two you need the most in Freeway, the blue and red keycards.

## BLAZING THROUGH FREEWAY

Life on the road has never been easy, and in Freeway it doesn't get much better. The following plan is not exactly a road map to life, but it can help you reach the end of Freeway.

### In the Drain Tunnel

1.  **Collect some weapons and power-ups, and overcome a few octabrains.** Look behind you to grab a shotgun and some shells. If you have a pipe bomb or an RPG launcher, blow a hole at the end of the tunnel to uncover an atomic health unit and RPG ammo. Then start heading eastward.

2.  **Head east and pummel the octabrains.** As you start heading east, three octabrains will try to stop you from reaching the end of the tunnel, where you can collect an RPG launcher. Besides the octabrains, a sentry drone also patrols the east side of the tunnel. If you don't have a heavier weapon, rely on the shotgun and your strafing to open yourself a path past the serrated teeth of the octabrains.

3.  **Blow a hole in the tunnel.** Take your RPG launcher and point it toward the crack along the north side of the tunnel. Punch a hole right through the tunnel where you can crawl out and face the action in the dark underpass.

### In the Dark Underpass

1.  **Get a devastator and an atomic health unit.** With your shotgun leading the way, come out of the tunnel slowly. Look for the glowing red eyes of the pig cops across the underpass, and fire with impunity. If necessary, fall back into the tunnel to avoid diving sentry drones and a couple of roving RPVs. When the moment is opportune, dash across the way to grab a devastator by the trash can. Kick the trash can to uncover an atomic health unit.

2.  **Reach the east side of the underpass.** Use the devastator you just scored to open a path up to the east side of the underpass. Grab the

shells behind the wooden crate, and then hop on top of it to take the RPG ammo.

3. **Cut a path through the narrow alleyway to reach the overpass.** Climb along the narrow walkway at the east end of the overpass, and follow it as it turns north.

### On the Overpass

1. **Hold your position for a while.** If you were to rush out onto the overpass, you would be immediately greeted by a group of enforcers and a Battlelord Sentry. Your odds go dramatically down whenever you face the speedy enforcers and the firepower of the Battlelord Sentry in open spaces. Peek out of the alleyway enough to attract the attention of the enforcers, who will come pouncing after you in seconds. Sidestep behind the wall for protection, and then sidestep and fire your single shell shots at the encroaching enforcers.

2. **Deal with the Battlelord Sentry.** Come out of the alleyway to get a good angle at the slower moving the Battlelord Sentry at the south end of the overpass. If you can get off three to five RPGs and avoid the incoming fire, the Battlelord Sentry will not be a factor any longer.

3. **Climb the downed building and get a jetpack.** Dash across the street to take the devastator ammo. Then hop on top of the downed building at the north end. What will seem like a cloud of drones hovering over the building will suddenly focus on you. If necessary, you can run back into the alleyway for protection. Eventually, drop into the gaping hole in the middle of the leaning building. Fight off the single enforcer below, and then grab the jetpack and shells before hovering out of the downed building.

> **WARNING**
>
> The alleyway is mined. Be ready to back out as soon as you turn north and take a couple of steps. The pig cops patrolling the alleyway will die in all likelihood, but you don't have to suffer the same fate.

4. **Hover over to the apartment on the east side.** Take out the enforcers as you drop in from the skies. Explore the room to take the blue keycard along the east side of the apartment. Also, take a moment to explore all the goods to be had in the apartment. There is a case of pipe bombs on top of the soda machine and two cases of devasta-tor ammo behind the bookshelf under the slanted portion of the ceiling.

**TIP**

Although you can explore another chamber behind the place where you found the blue keycard, you should contemplate whether it's a wise idea. You can blow a hole in the wall behind the blue keycard to reach a chamber that holds one ripper chaingun and a freezethrower charge. However, the second you cross inside the chamber, two Battlelord Sentries will appear out of nowhere on the overpass below.

5. **Hover back to the street level.** Use the blue keycard on the small latch on the west side of the street. Watch out for the pig cop just behind the lifting wall. Then climb aboard the small platform, and ride it to the top.

## On the Top Floor of the West Side

1. **Storm the room with the conveyors.** Stepping off of the platform, do away with the two enforcers, flip the switch that turns off the two con-veyor belts in this room, and reach the chamber at the north end—other-wise known as the compression room.

2. **Get the red keycard in the compression room.** Grab the two cases of RPG ammo, and then go inside the dark room that is dominated by a large compression platform capable of flattening any and everything that gets caught inside. Fight the enforcers and reach the north side. Lay down five or six pipe bombs before you use the blue keycard on the latch to open the steel gate. Then, open the latch, step back, and deto-nate the bombs. If all goes as expected, every enforcer behind the gate is no longer a factor. Take the blue keycard and get back to the main street.

### In the Southern Alleyway

1. **Fight off the pig cops behind car 54.** As you come near the southern alleyway, the police car turned on its side will blow up. Behind it, a squadron of pig cops will come out to shoot and ask questions later. If you have RPG ammo left over, drop a couple of rounds into their tightly packed group.

2. **Open the last door.** Use the red keycard to open the narrow door in the alleyway. Dispose of the pig cop waiting there. Then open a second door, and be ready to confront the last two octabrains standing between you and freedom. If you haven't had a chance to use the shrinker or the freezethrower, this is the perfect opportunity.

3. **Hit the exit switch.** Hop over the dead octabrain bodies, break the glass covering the switch, and then punch it decisively with your clenched fist.

## ADDED ATTRACTIONS IN FREEWAY

The mayhem and destruction in Freeway can escalate even higher if you invite two Battlelord Sentries to the party. And how do you do that? All you have to do is enter the chamber behind the explosive wall in the west side apartment.

### Accommodating Two Battlelord Sentries on the Overpass

If a freezethrower charge and a ripper chaingun are enough reasons to enter the chamber behind the blue keycard, then go ahead and blow a hole in the wall and enter the chamber. Step into the dark chamber, and claim the freezethrower charge and the ripper chaingun. The alien growls you will hear almost immediately will let you know that the guests have arrived. Get out of the dark chamber, and unload a couple of RPGs on the Battlelord Sentries below. It will be hard for them to hit you where you are. However, you can't stay in the apartment forever.

Activate your jetpack and hover toward the south. Come down near the end of the south overpass and jump right through a dark window that leads you into a secret chamber. You can find protection in this chamber and, at the same time, you will also have a clear view of the street outside. However, when you first jump inside, you will have to contend with two enforcers. Take the devastator ammo on the bed, and pummel the Battlelord Sentries outside with a combination of your devastator and RPG launcher. You can then proceed to use the blue keycard en route to the upstairs west side apartment.

# The Birth

Somebody's gonna have to pay for screwing up your vacation. Just when you thought the world was at last free of the alien menace, along comes some bad news. A select task force of alien invaders and their newly arrived allies have a choking stronghold on some of our towns and cities. The sad truth about what's happening to Earth women is at last revealed in shocking graphic detail.

In the scene surreptitiously captured on film by an undercover operative, a woman is seen thrashing helplessly on a surgical table, bare arms and legs flailing in the obvious throes of labor pain. Her bulbous belly looks fully ripe. Bipedal aliens with reptilian features surround her. Known as protector drones, these aliens play the part of murderous midwives with a single mission: to usher in a new, crossbred intergalactic race, half human, half God-knows-what. So . . . what are you going to do about it, Duke? Look away? By now it sounds like a worn cliché, but it still holds true: the future of the world is in your manly hands.

## IT'S IMPOSSIBLE

Your mission, should you decide to accept it, is to penetrate the Impossible Mission Facility and reach the booby-trapped and heavily secured white chamber. Once there, you must activate a set of key-switch combinations. Only then will you be able to unlock the door leading to the exit. But you must get real smart to do it. In fact, just meters from the exit, you can measure your might against a brand new and horribly hostile alien, the dreaded protector drone. On the up side, you can experiment with the new expander weapon and see the uninflated results first-hand.

As with many other Duke Nukem 3D levels, there is a pervasive theme running throughout It's Impossible. If you've seen the TV series—and is there anyone who hasn't?—or the recent hit movie, you're in for some seriously tense action and edge-of-your-seat excitement with minor intermissions to catch your breath or heed nature's untimely calls. If you still can't guess at the series, then utter the immortal staccato beat of "ta-ta, ta ta ta-ta." Anyone can figure it out—it's not a mission *im*possible.

## MAPS AND ROUTE

Despite its being the first level in The Birth episode, It's Impossible is nearly impenetrable. As shown in Figures 8.1 and 8.2, the maps reveal a sprawling installation spreading mostly east-to-west with a variety of chambers, including barracks, a mess hall, and a briefing room.

## THE GOODS

The Impossible Mission Facility will definitely try your mettle, but it also has the potential to stock your arsenal, as Table 8.1 shows:

### TABLE 8.1: THE GOODS IN IT'S IMPOSSIBLE

| WEAPONS | AMMO | POWER-UPS |
|---|---|---|
| 1 shotgun | 4 cases | 1 portable medkit |
| 1 ripper chaingun | 3 cases | 3 atomic health units |
| 1 RPG launcher | 1 case | 2 armors |
| 1 shrinker/expander | 1 crystal/2 expanders | 1 steroid flask |
| 1 devastator | 2 cases | 1 jetpack |
| 1 freezethrower | | 1 NVG |
| 3 laser trip bombs | | 1 holoduke |
| 4 pipe bomb cases | | |

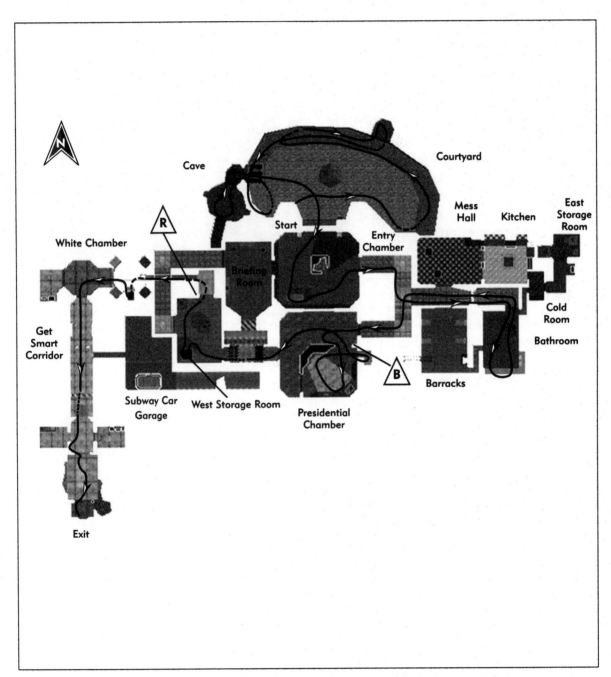

**FIGURE 8.1:** To solve the puzzle of It's Impossible's Impossible Mission Facility, follow this route.

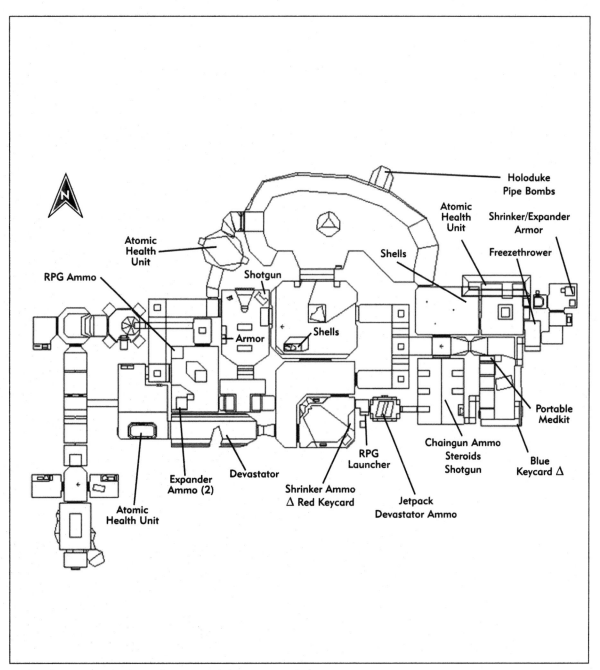

**FIGURE 8.2:** Despite its being heavily booby-trapped, the Impossible Mission Facility is also stacked with all kinds of weaponry and useful items.

## BLAZING THROUGH IT'S IMPOSSIBLE

You're off to a most suitable beginning to The Birth. It's Impossible will test what you're made of and challenge your resolve. Find the small white chamber, drop in from the air duct, and reach the exit switch in heroic fashion—or die trying.

### In the Rainy Courtyard

A dark sky hangs over the courtyard and heavy raindrops fall on your head. A tall rocky wall encloses the kidney-shaped courtyard. Before long, you feel the heat from the turret mounted high up on the wall. It's time for action.

1.  **Get wet and take out the turret.** Run to the southeast end of the courtyard, where you can jump onto the ascending ledge. Get a move on and find a second, very narrow ridge along the northwest side of the wall. This ridge ascends from west to east and leads directly to the turret's enclosure.

2.  **Score big, quickly.** Shoot the turret out and step into the small opening to take a holoduke and a case of pipe bombs.

3.  **Get your first atomic health unit.** Run to the southwest end, along the ledge, and press on the handprint switch. Jump to the courtyard's floor, and run below the makeshift bridge into a dark alcove. Take the atomic health unit, and get set for your next move.

### In the Entry Chamber and into the Eastern Wing

The entry chamber is the midpoint between the eastern and western wings of the Impossible Mission Facility building. You must first focus on the eastern wing, which contains a mess hall, the barracks, and a spacious community bathroom. In this sector, you must obtain the blue and red keycards.

1.  **Get some shells and another gun.** Open the portal to the Facility and deal with the troopers. Then get the shells and the gun that are sitting on the table at the southwest corner of the chamber. Turn on the tape player at your own risk.

2. **Reach the boys' room.** Find your way to the door on the east side, and follow the gray corridor as it bends south and then east again into the bathroom at the end of the hallway. Expect to meet some resistance from a couple of troopers.

3. **Powder the opponents in the can and get the blue keycard.** Proceed cautiously inside the bathroom and shove your weapon at anything that comes near. Two octabrains are known to lurk here, so be careful. Luckily for you, there's also a chaingun near a urinal. Grab the blue keycard on the counter and head to the Presidential Chamber.

## In the Presidential Chamber

Directly south of the entry chamber lies a chamber with pictures of a few illustrious dead presidents lining its walls. The entrances to the Presidential Chamber are protected by an energy shield. This is no big deal, because *you* have the blue keycard.

1. **Storm up the hallway into the chamber.** Dispose of the zealous pig cop and activate the second and fourth switches (from left to right) to gain entry into the chamber.

2. **Deactivate the shields and get the red keycard.** Use the blue keycard to lower the shields to the Presidential Chamber. Ward off the pig cop, some troopers, and a leaping enforcer as you collect not only the red keycard, but a shrinker crystal as well.

3. **Get the RPG and scram.** Walk up to the terminal near Abe's mug and activate it. To your right, a door suddenly opens. A pig cop might come bouncing out; behind him, the small enclosure hides a most precious RPG launcher.

4. **Uncover a secret and score a jetpack.** As you grab the RPG, push against the metal wall to open a secret door into a small, serene courtyard with an open ceiling. Here, you can collect your thoughts for a second and also strap on a jetpack and stock up on Devastator ammo. Get back into the Presidential Chamber. The crate room is your next destination.

### In the Lower Crate Room

The darkened crate room is at a lower floor level than the Presidential Chamber. It houses expander ammo and laser trip bombs. A couple of suicidal drones stand guard. If you have the red keycard, you'll be able to open up a janitorial closet leading to the central white chamber.

1.  **Reach the crate room.** Leaving the Presidential Chamber, turn your sights westward. Press the first and third switches (from left to right) to open the gate into a small passageway where you can ride a platform to the floor below. Continue west into the dark crate room.

2.  **Dispose of the drones and collect the cache.** Draw the drones out and pelt them with your weapon. Enter and feel for the front of a large crate at the southwest side. It will open and reveal the expander ammo. Leap onto the crate in the middle of the room and collect three laser trip bombs.

3.  **Access the janitorial closet.** Use the red keycard to open the closet. Step inside and crawl up through the duct. Near the end of the duct, you'll see the cylindrical, central white chamber below. You're about to drop in for a visit.

### In the Central White Chamber

The smooth, almost antiseptic, central white chamber holds the key to unlocking this level wide open. But getting in and activating the right switches is not altogether uncomplicated. For one thing, laser trip bombs line the only entrance. And then, once you drop in, any step you take sets off sensitive alarms, causing you to contend with a swarm of aliens.

1.  **Set off the laser trip bombs from afar.** Drop a pipe bomb at the top of the duct and back away quickly. For added protection, move all the way back to the dark crate room. And *then* detonate the bomb.

2.  **Drop in and position yourself.** Climb back up into the duct and drop in, but once you hit the ground, don't move an inch! Jump onto the computer

console. Then jump again onto a small pillar, to be able to view the large red switch above the screen (see Figure 8.3).

3. **Push all the right switches.** Trip the switch by shooting it with a bullet. Then turn to face the switches behind the receding panel on the opposite wall. Jump back onto the computer console, taking care not to fall over onto the floor. Aim steady and hit the first, third, and fourth switches. The small confines of the chamber will soon be carpeted with the enemy. But most importantly, the heavy gate opens to the long hallway exit.

**NOTE** As an elegant alternative to dropping unannounced into the white chamber, and with the aid of the jetpack, you can just float down into the chamber and activate the switch above the computer console. Then, simply hover over to the switches behind the panel in the opposing wall and activate the first, third, and fourth switches.

**FIGURE 8.3:** If you move an inch inside the white chamber, you're inviting some very unpleasant company. Instead, jump on the console and activate the first switch.

### Get Smart In the Long Hallway

The final stretch in It's Impossible is a long hallway with doors . . . behind doors . . . behind doors. At its end, an innocuous phone drops you into a sunken portion of the hallway where the exit awaits. Here lurks the greatest challenge of this level, in the shape and form of the dreaded new enemy in this episode: the blood-lusting protector drone.

1. **Drop in again.** Walk up to the phone and push. You'll drop into what seems like an empty hall flanked by doors on each side.

2. **Blow up the doors and get out.** Grab the pipe bomb you find in the middle of the floor. Then drop it near the far door. Drop a few more pipe bombs in front of the flanking doors. Get back to the point where you dropped in, and then detonate the pipe bombs.

3. **Fight the last battle.** This is a good time to pull out the RPG launcher and get off a couple of shots, before the protector drones blocking the exit can get to you and mess you up badly. The ripper chaingun is a good weapon for this situation also, so long as you have enough ammo and time to use it. With the lizards out of the contest, lunge for the exit switch and emerge victorious.

> **TIP**
>
> For extra protection, and considering that you're about to face some serious opposition in very tight quarters, leave the area altogether before detonating the pipe bombs. You can be completely out of harm's way if you get back upstairs (where the phone is). Just press the spacebar to reach the higher floor level. Then detonate your bombs before you drop in again.

## COVERT DETAILS

The Impossible Mission Facility is the stuff of espionage, covert operations, and almost ridiculous secrecy. Table 8.2 gives you an account of every secret.

## TABLE 8.2: THE SECRETS IN IT'S IMPOSSIBLE

| AREA IN LEVEL | SECRET ITEM | HOW TO GET IT |
| --- | --- | --- |
| Community bathroom | portable medkit | Activate the device on the wall next to the sink. Race to the first stall and jump above it into the area where a portion of the wall has receded. Step inside and grab the portable medkit. |
| Barracks | jetpack devastator ammo | Get on top of the bed at the southwest corner of the barracks and push. The entire bed lifts to connect you with a serene, skylit room where the jetpack and the Devastator ammo are up for grabs. |
| Courtyard | holoduke case of pipe bombs | Climb the ledge on the north wall. Step into the wall crevice where the turret is also found. |
| Presidential chamber | RPG launcher | Activate the computer station near honest Abe's mug, and race toward the narrow secret door on the east wall. Once inside the small secret closet, push a second secret door to access the small, serene courtyard that also connects you to the barracks. The courtyard has a jetpack and ammo for the Devastator. |
| Subway car garage | devastator atomic health unit | Crawl through the duct past the first door in the corridor exit. The Devastator is behind the metal door west of the subway car. The atomic health unit is inside the car. To open its door, you must activate the wall switch to the right of the air duct. |

# DUKE-BURGER

All preparations are under way as the new Duke-Burger franchise hosts its grand opening in a week. But certainly not if you can help it. If the public only knew the heinous truth, the not-so-subtle connection between Duke-Burger and the Society for Preparation of Canine Hamburgers (S.P.C.H.), just across the street, there would definitely be many upset stomachs.

Indeed, this is one fast-food joint that should never be allowed to serve anybody anything. If the colossal amounts of cholesterol, fat, and other chemical byproducts won't do you in, certainly, the shoot-first-and-ask-for-your-order-later service philosophy will leave you hungry. In fact, you might have to get your own fries.

To solve this level, you must gain entry into Duke-Burger, reach the kitchen area, and then make your way to the conveniently located underground conveyor belt, which connects (not coincidentally) to a meat preparation room inside the S.P.C.H. building. To get inside the Duke-Burger, you must first find the blue keycard. After that, secure the red keycard and with it gain access to the tunnel and the conveyor belt.

## MAPS AND ROUTE

As shown in Figures 8.4 and 8.5, Duke-Burger reigns over an entire street block, with the S.P.C.H. at its north end. By the time you finish your tour of Duke-Burger, you might feel somewhat like a disgruntled health inspector.

## THE GOODS

Duke-Burger offers something for everyone . . . as long as you like dog. But, if you can remain open-minded to the questionable cuisine, you might get a chance to stockpile your arsenal. Table 8.3 gives you the details.

### TABLE 8.3: THE GOODS IN DUKE-BURGER

| WEAPONS | AMMO | POWER-UPS |
|---|---|---|
| 1 shotgun | 4 cases | 2 portable medkits |
| 1 ripper chaingun | 1 case | 1 atomic health unit |
| 1 RPG launcher | 1 case | 2 armors |
| 1 shrinker/expander | 1 crystal | 2 steroid flasks |
| 1 devastator | 2 cases | 1 scuba gear |
| 2 freezethrowers | 3 charges | 1 NVG |
| 3 laser trip bombs | | |
| 3 pipe bomb cases | | |

**FIGURE 8.4:** Inspect Duke-Burger and declare it unfit for human consumption.

**FIGURE 8.5:** Meat lovers, beware. Duke-Burger serves dog food.

## BLAZING THROUGH DUKE-BURGER

You may never think of a hamburger in the same way after you've paid a visit to Duke-Burger. You might even consider becoming a vegetarian and championing the cause of animal rights. But even if your intestinal fortitude can stand it, you must still break into Duke-Burger and find the connecting tunnel to the S.P.C.H., where a key switch grants access to the exit.

### In the Periphery

The gigantic Duke-Burger, complete with its drive-thru window, dominates the whole of this level. Until you get the blue keycard, you'll have to hang out in the periphery and slug it out with RPVs and the newly built pig cop tank. Slim odds at best. Your first concern then, is to get the blue keycard and slip inside the Duke-Burger (see Figure 8.6).

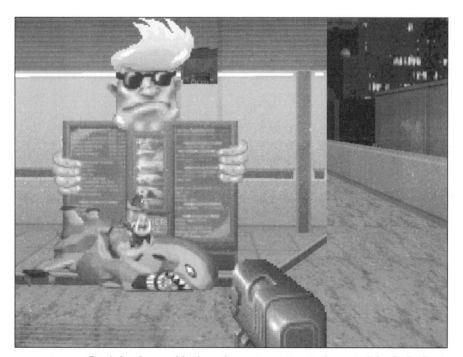

**FIGURE 8.6:** Don't be deterred by less-than-courteous employees of the Duke-Burger chain. Just take the blue keycard and continue your exploration.

1. **Place your order for the blue keycard.** Run around the right side of Duke-Burger to reach its north end. Walk up to the menu board and push the button.

2. **Reach the elevated compartment.** Jump onto the board, and then jump a second time into the small wall recess to grab the blue keycard and the shrinker/expander.

3. **Go inside Duke-Burger.** Use the blue keycard on the security gate at the south end, and step into the still-unfinished dining area.

## Inside Duke-Burger

Once in the belly of the beast, Duke-Burger, you need to find the red keycard. Without it, you can't reach the underground conveyor belt that leads to the S.P.C.H. building and eventually to the exit. The pace inside is quick and you must move fast to reach the serving area, the girls' bathroom, and the kitchen area. Ultimately, you'll want to wrestle the red keycard from the manager's office. This keycard connects you to the tunnel connecting to the building on the north.

1. **Demand service.** Blast your way right up to the serving counter. Jump over the counter and take the atomic health unit by the drive-up window.

2. **Slip a few pipe bombs.** Throw a few pipe bombs into the food prep area through the narrow crack over the rows of hamburgers and fries.

3. **Get to the girls' bathroom.** Run into the bathroom at the end of the hallway, and get ready to battle the protector drones hiding in the stalls.

4. **Get small.** Because a force shield blocks the door to the food prep area, you must get there through the small vent at foot level in the girls' bathroom. Stand in front of the mirror and pull out your shrinker/expander. Aim at your reflection to get small.

5. **Demand to see the manager.** In the food prep area, defeat the enforcer and continue northward toward the manager's office, which is at the end of the hallway and to the left. Take both the red keycard and the shotgun on top of the manager's desk. Then punch the switch on the side of the desk and

climb over the tallest crate to collect the freezethrower from the secret compartment. Don't forget to collect the expander ammo atop the crates, too.

6. **Heat things up in the cold room.** Use the red keycard on the security gate and step inside the cold room. Make mincemeat of the pig cops gathered there, and if it doesn't scare you to do so, reach for the Devastator weapon inside the meat-pounding machine. Then find the sloping conveyor belt and walk down into the tunnel. You have to walk in the opposite direction of the motion of the belt. Turn northward, fight off the enforcers, and emerge into the meat-prep area of the S.P.C.H. building.

## In the S.P.C.H. Building

The seemingly respectable Society's offices at the north end of Duke-Burger hide a sad reality behind the fresh paint job and the shine of the real-wood veneer: nothing less than the systematic wholesale slaughter of dogs to satisfy the demanding palates of Duke-Burger aficionados. From the meat-prep area, through the canine chambers, and into the front desk, you must visit each room inside this building. The key switch will uncover a passage to the final exit.

1. **Reach the meat-prep room.** Run down along the conveyor belt until you reach the end. Then jump into the slaughter room where many a Rover won't recover.

2. **Get an RPG.** Press the switch on the northeast side of the room. Press it a second time and step into the revolving door to come out inside a small chamber housing an RPG. Get the heavy gun, and press the same switch a third time to get out.

3. **Move into the canine chambers.** Find the narrow passageway in the north wall, and follow

> **TIP**
>
> If you press the *wrong* switch to get out of the secret area, you might get squished to death by the rotating wall. Be sure that you press the switch on the left side to guarantee that you leave the secret area semi-intact.

the corridor into the grim canine chambers. Battle the troopers and a ferocious protector drone in this area. Blow up the cell on the northwest end, and climb onto its second floor to find a secret area with a case of pipe bombs.

4. **Check out the front desk.** Take the small opening at the northwest corner of the canine chambers to access the front desk. Battle the enemies in this area, and be careful to avoid the exploding walls. The place could be crawling outside with pig cop tanks. Find the switch behind the front desk counter and activate it. Then run out to the new opening that leads into the rectangular chamber exit. Deal as gracefully as you can with the protector drones, and then get a move on.

## COVERT DETAILS

Duke-Burger has a few specials on the menu. Table 8.4 lists every secret found in Duke-Burger.

### TABLE 8.4: THE SECRETS IN DUKE-BURGER

| AREA IN LEVEL | SECRET ITEM | HOW TO GET IT |
|---|---|---|
| Northeast end of the S.P.C.H. building | RPG launcher | On emerging in the meat-prep room, press the light switch on the northwest corner. The entire corner of the room rotates to form a revolving door. Step inside and claim the RPG launcher. To get out, press the switch on the same location and push out through the revolving door as it turns in the opposite direction. |
| Doggie chambers | pipe bomb case | Blow up the bottom cell in the northwest corner. Then jump onto the top-level cell and push against the secret door to gain entry into a small corridor where the pipe bombs are. |

*(Continued on next page)*

*(Continued from previous page)*

| AREA IN LEVEL | SECRET ITEM | HOW TO GET IT |
|---|---|---|
| Area above drive-thru | pipe bomb case<br>expander charges (2)<br>portable medkit | Stand on top of the narrow food table on the west wall. Then jump forward and side step to the right at the height of your jump to reach the hollow area above the drive-thru. (If this technique seems too difficult, and provided you have a jetpack, step outside and elevate yourself on the outside of the drive-thru wall. Fly into an invisible door right inside the ceiling. To find the correct spot to move into, fire a few rounds with your ripper chaingun and take note of the area where the bullets fail to make an impact. That's where you want to go in. (See Figure 8.7.) |
| Storage room with crates and desk (at the northwest corner, inside Duke-Burger) | freezethrower | Blow up the chair behind the desk, and then squat down and push the switch. Climb over the crates in the corner, and grab the freezethrower inside the secret compartment. |

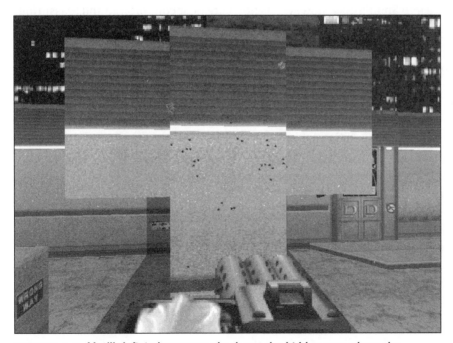

FIGURE 8.7: You'll definitely want to check out the hidden area above the drive-thru window. It offers some loot that's too good to pass up.

# SHOP-N-BAG

There's always something calming and reassuring about a well-lit grocery store with its neatly stacked rows of cans and colorful products wrapped in plastic skins gleaming proudly under buzzing fluorescent tubes. It's more than the combined sense of order and predictability and the strangely soothing effect of piped-in Muzak. It's as though, so long as the shelves are full, you can rest assured that the economy and society's infrastructure work as well-lubed capitalist machines, and the goods are delivered in timely fashion . . . provided the price is right. Supply and demand, you think dreamily, makes sense.

Stepping into Shop-n-Bag, however, is nowhere near comfortable and reassuring. You've probably heard a thousand shopping horror stories, but when it comes to merely dropping in for a gallon of milk and a bag of junk food at the Shop-n-Bag, you're about to write your own horror story.

## MAPS AND ROUTE

As shown in Figures 8.8 and 8.9, Shop-n-Bag is more than a mere shopping experience. It's a downright life-and-death struggle.

## THE GOODS

Table 8.5 inventories the type of goods you can expect to find fresh at Shop-n-Bag, a store that strives to help patrons "check out" promptly.

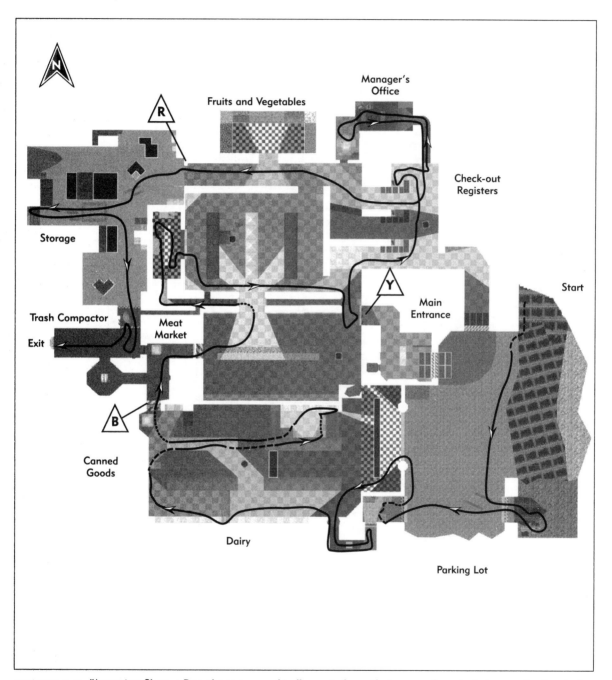

**FIGURE 8.8:** "Attention Shop-n-Bag shoppers, we kindly remind you that we are here to help you check out at any moment."

**FIGURE 8.9:** Shop-n-Bag covers your basic food groups, and then some.

## TABLE 8.5: THE GOODS IN SHOP-N-BAG

| WEAPONS | AMMO | POWER-UPS |
| --- | --- | --- |
| 1 shotgun | 6 cases | 2 portable medkits |
| 1 ripper chaingun | 2 cases | 3 atomic health units |
| 1 RPG launcher | 4 cases | 1 holoduke |
| 2 shrinker/expanders | 2 crystals | 2 armors |
| 2 devastators | 2 cases | 2 steroid flasks |
| 1 freezethrower | 1 charge | 1 scuba gear |
| 3 laser trip bombs | | 2 NVGs |
| | | 1 pair of boots |

## BLAZING THROUGH SHOP-N-BAG

Your shopping list includes all keycards in this order: blue, yellow, and red. Ultimately, you want to reach the warehouse at the northwest corner. There, you must open an industrial-sized trash compactor and figure out a way to sneak past it to the exit switch.

### In the Parking Lot

The southeast quadrant of Shop-n-Bag is a large parking lot flanked by a demolished building—reminding you that this is still L.A. where earthquakes are cheaper by the dozen. Before breaking into Shop-n-Bag, you're best advised to build your strength and score some useful weapons.

1.  **Get loaded right away.** As you emerge from Shop-n-Bag, you're confronted by a row of troopers as the building around you collapses to the ground. Jump to the main parking lot and run to the south end of the downed building to grab the shells near the end of the slope.

2.  **Visit the nearby shops.** Jump over the cyclone fence and slip under the partially raised door of We Store Your Crap at the southeast end. Inside, jump onto the slanted remnants of the downed building and pick up a case of pipe bombs, an atomic health unit, and the night vision goggles. Get out and run directly across to the southwest location. Push open the door and step in to collect a shotgun on top of the highest crate.

3. **Break into Shop-n-Bag.** Now that you're more suitably armed, walk up to the front of Shop-n-Bag and bash the window with your mighty foot.

## In the Dairy and Canned Goods Aisles

The lower south side of Shop-n-Bag has everything you need by way of dairy products and canned goods. But this is also the place where you'll find the blue keycard. Without it, you can't get into the meat section. While in this area, take advantage of this week's specials and stock up on a few useful items, including a Devastator with some ammo, ripper chaingun ammo, and even a shrinker crystal.

1. **Get the Devastator right away.** After breaking into the front window, turn south and blow up the fire extinguisher at the head of the first aisle. Step into the hole in the wall and follow the 90-degree turn to claim the Devastator.

2. **Hop the aisles and continue scoring.** Run the length of the dairy aisle, and stay close to the south wall. Squeeze through the crates to reach the very back of the store. Jump onto the box between the aisles, and from there take another hop onto the top of either set of shelves. Move east, back toward the store's bashed window, and collect the crystal, the Devastator ammo, and whatever else is around.

3. **But most importantly, score the blue keycard.** From the north aisle, jump into the main floor, just before you get to the boxes blocking the way. There, between a box and the wall, is the blue keycard. Now it's yours. It lets you get into the meat market.

## In the Meat Market

The meat market's wide selection of prime cuts is prominently featured in one long aisle in the center of an otherwise mostly-empty room. A quick exploration reveals that you'll need the yellow and the red keycards to press on. The yellow keycard might seem out of reach, there inside the locked butcher shop at the back of the meat market. But a fortunate crawl space provides another way in.

1.  **Storm the meat department.** You needn't linger in the meat area if you know what you came to get. As soon as you enter, blast your way to the crawl space between the first row of aisles to your left.

2.  **Pay the butcher a visit.** Bust the grill and jump into the crawl space, which goes straight west before veering 90 degrees to the north. You'll come out inside the butcher shop.

3.  **Open the butcher's safe box.** Activate any two of the switches around the safe box-like enclosure. It'll yield and offer you the yellow keycard. Take it. Then press the switch next to the metal curtain to get out of the butcher shop.

## Pay the Manager a Visit

You can't possibly check out of Shop-n-Bag without telling the manager just what you really think of his store. But the most pressing reason for going to his office is to find and take the red keycard. There's only a bit of a problem. All gates to the checkout counters are locked. And the manager's office is only accessible from the checkout area. This is where the yellow keycard you obtained at the butcher's shop fits in.

1.  **Open the yellow door.** Use the yellow keycard on the security lock at the south wall of the meat market. The door lifts, but a metal gate still obstructs your way.

2.  **Shoot the gate switch.** Notice the switch on the ceiling just beyond the gate, as shown in Figure 8.10. Aim carefully and hit it. This will cause all the gates to open and grant you access to the registers.

3.  **Cut in line and check out.** Go directly to the last register and assume the

> **TIP**
>
> Be prepared to contend with the assault commander behind the gate. He's in a key position to hover and launch missiles right through the gate. If you prepare for him by pulling out the Devastator, and can connect right on his body a couple of times, he might not even have time to work up a thunderous missile from his protruding bottom orifice.

**FIGURE 8.10:** After unlocking the yellow security lock, shoot the ceiling switch to open the gates to the checkout registers.

position of a checkout clerk. Notice the row of switches in the inside of the counter. Press switches 3 and 4 (from left to right) to unlock the "Employees Only" door.

4.  **Get what you came for.** Fly up the curving stairway right into the manager's office. Ignore the intense hubbub of activity and score the armor, the steroids, the pipe bombs, and RPG ammo. Then when the commotion is over, concentrate on getting the red keycard out of the manager's safe.

5.  **Hit two timed switches and open the safe.** As you have known all along, the red keycard is inside the safe box. It will open only when you activate two timed switches. First push on the switch next to the safe box. Then turn to face the opposing wall and aim quickly at a switch that's become exposed. You might fail the first and second time, but persistence pays off.

6.  **Dash off to the storage area.** With the red keycard in your hot little hands, trail-blaze to the far west side of the store, right past the produce section.

### In the Storage Area

Dark, stuffy, and filled with boxes of many sizes, the storage area is the last remaining major area unexplored. Although you might want to rush in and get it over with quickly, do consider looking and poking around for items like a freezethrower, expander ammo, and an atomic health unit, among other things. Your main job in the storage area is to open the industrial-sized trash compactor, for the exit is found right past it.

1.  **Head in and find the compactor switch.** On opening the storage area with the red keycard, head directly for the set of boxes at the far east wall. Dispose of the pig cop and then climb onto the taller box. Look for the white sign on the wall and then crouch to reach the compactor switch.

2.  **Throw the switch and head for the compactor.** Press the switch and then run back toward the entrance, but turn south quickly when you come to a wide hallway lined with more crates and boxes. After a few steps, you'll hear the heavy piston action of the trash compactor mechanism.

3.  **Unlock a key switch.** Step inside the compacting chamber, heading toward a depression on the metal wall. A sensor causes a plate to slide open and reveal a switch. Back off to avoid burning your feet on the toxic sludge, but fire at the switch to activate it. If you hit it, another plate slides open to reveal a four-position switch.

4.  **Turn off the compactor, one section at a time.** The four-position switch lets you turn off the compactor one unit at a time. You must carefully time each switch so that you stop the piston at its highest point in the pumping action, leaving room for you.

5.  **Scoot in and check out, for good.** Once the compactor sections are stopped and you can move under them, run (or crawl if you must) to reach the east wall, where the red exit switch beckons you.

## COVERT DETAILS

Shop-n-Bag stocks the greatest variety of produce, canned goods, choice cuts, and, naturally, installation secrets. Table 8.6 breaks it all down for you.

## TABLE 8.6: THE SECRETS IN SHOP-N-BAG

| AREA IN LEVEL | SECRET ITEM | HOW TO GET IT |
| --- | --- | --- |
| Hidden corridor at the southeast corner of the store | devastator portable medkit | Blow up the fire extinguisher to open a hole in the wall. Walk inside the narrow corridor, and follow it as it bends, then claim the portable medkit and the Devastator. |
| Boxes stacked to ceiling between aisles 1 and 2 | expander ammo armor | Go behind the boxes between the aisles. Push against the middle box and step inside. |
| Automated teller machine (ATM) in small lobby inside the main entrance of the store | devastator | Press against the ATM on the left side (right below the Federal Loan & Trust sign). Jump behind the screen and grab the Devastator. |
| Pile of crates at the southeast corner of the meat section | ripper chaingun | Detonate a pipe bomb near the pile of small boxes and crawl into the hole. Take the ripper chaingun inside the bottom box. |
| Small alcove south of the trash compactor | RPG ammo protective boots portable medkit | After stopping the second section of the compactor, dash for the section of the south wall where the piston normally comes down. Push against the wall and enter the secret area, where you'll also see Jake the Snake's torso. Supposedly, he escaped from New York. But L.A. is a different story. Obviously, he didn't make it out of New York. |
| Small box in the north end of the storage area | freezethrower pipe bombs NVG | On entering the storage area, hug the wall on the right side, and walk westward until you run into a set of stacked boxes. Jump on the first small box and from there onto the larger pile of boxes. Get inside a small opening between two boxes, and push the cardboard with the arrows pointing up. Enter the small space and take the goods. |
| Large crate in the south end of the storage area | steroids shells RPG ammo | Find the tall wooden crate near the middle of the floor space and push against the crate's surface where an arrow (painted on the crate) is pointing. Step inside the tall crate and grab the stuff. |

# BABE LAND

If you like fun and thrills, you'll *love* Babe Land, an amusement park with something to offer every member of the family. Provided, of course, the family doesn't mind risking

life and limb just to catch a good ride (and that it's not too politically correct or gender-sensitive). And what sorts of fun await you in Babe Land? How about One-Eyed Pete's Shooting Gallery, a dizzying D-Cup ride, and a cruise on a dinghy to witness *Babes of the Caribbean*, a re-enactment of a battle between a Spanish galleon and a heavily guarded fort by the edge of the sea?

How much would you expect to pay for all this fun and excitement? Well, don't mention it, because there's more. The price of admission might be measured in pints of blood. But the memory of this excursion will linger long after the park closes its doors and the aliens retire for the night.

## MAPS AND ROUTE

As shown in Figures 8.11 and 8.12, Babe Land is a thrill-a-minute kind of experience, and one that will certainly leave its mark on you, maybe permanently.

## THE GOODS

Table 8.7 lists all the prizes you can win in Babe Land. If you can find and carry them, they're all yours.

| TABLE 8.7: THE GOODS IN BABE LAND | | |
|---|---|---|
| **WEAPONS** | **AMMO** | **POWER-UPS** |
| 2 shotguns | 4 cases | 1 portable medkit |
| 3 ripper chainguns | 4 cases | 3 atomic health units |
| 3 RPG launchers | 6 cases | 2 holodukes |
| 2 shrinker/expanders | 1 crystal | 2 armors |

*(Continued on next page)*

*(Continued from previous page)*

| WEAPONS | AMMO | POWER-UPS |
|---|---|---|
| 1 devastator | 1 charge | 1 steroid flask |
| 1 freezethrower | | 1 scuba gear |
| 2 laser trip bombs | | 2 NVGs |
| 3 pipe bomb cases | | 1 pair of boots |

## BLAZING THROUGH BABE LAND

To make the most of your day at Babe Land, you must first secure the blue keycard and then the red. Only then will you be able to get on board *Babes of the Caribbean*. Finally, you should board the Spanish galleon and, from there, teleport to the top of the fort across the bay. Survive the alien onslaught, overcome the enemy, fight with much gallantry, and rush for the exit at the end of the narrow hallway behind the door.

### Getting Admission

Babe Land's main entrances are at the northeast side of the installation. Because tickets are extremely hard to come by, you'll have to force your way in. Once inside, you'll be in a rectangular courtyard accentuated by a fountain in its center. From this point, every ride is accessible, at least theoretically. But actually, you can only get in the D-Cup ride. The other rides require you to have a keycard.

1.  **Get inside the box office.** Come out of the sewer pipe and drop into the main ground near Babe Land's box office. Do battle with the troopers and then turn your attention to the box office. Shoot the pig cop inside. Then jump inside the booth and deactivate the force shield blocking the door.

2.  **Step inside the park and take stock of your surroundings.** Before rushing into the D-Cup ride, take a few seconds to collect all the useful stuff around the courtyard. Discard the pig cop near the crates by the entrance. Then hop onto the crates to reach the higher ground. Take the pipe bombs and then jump across the courtyard to land above the fountain. Another skip will land you on top of the pillar with the atomic health unit. A last hop will put you on the west side, in an enclosure above the courtyard, where you can collect more pipe bombs. While up

**FIGURE 8.11:** Mere minutes might be all the time you have to enjoy Babe Land, so make the most of them.

**FIGURE 8.12:** Forget the popcorn and cotton candy—collect the *goodies* you'll need to survive Babe Land.

here, you might as well open the metal shield that blocks the entrance to One-Eyed Pete's Shooting Gallery.

3. **Lift the metal shield to Pete's.** Walk to the computer console and punch the two bottom switches and the switch on the top right corner of the computer screen. Then look in the screen to see the shield lifting and opening the entrance to Pete's.

4. **Get back to the courtyard.** The D-Cup ride holds quite a lot of promise. Truly, a D-Cup's worth.

## Go for the D-Cup Ride of Your Life

Remember the cup ride at the kiddy carnival? Oversized coffee cups spinning on their axis, following each other in circular patterns. All of them, in turn, spinning inside a giant wheel. The cup ride might indeed have been cute and whimsical, and thus considered wimpy by most kids over 6 years old. Not so with the D-Cup ride. You must be tough enough to take this ride if you want to obtain the blue keycard. Without it, you'll never experience One-Eyed Pete's or witness *Babes of the Caribbean*. And who wants to miss *them*? The blue keycard is hidden in the pillar at the axis of this ride. You have to activate three key switches to uncover it.

1. **Hop onto a cup.** Go through the revolving door and fend off the troopers as you proceed to jump onto one of the circling cups.

2. **Execute some daring jumps.** As the cup spins around the room, stand on the ledge and jump onto one of the three platforms on the surrounding walls.

3. **Activate the three switches.** Take the loot from every platform and press each switch. After pressing the last one, the top part of the central column reveals the blue keycard, as you can see in Figure 8.13.

4. **Grab the blue keycard.** Jump back onto a cup and, facing inward, jump on top of the column to claim the blue keycard. You can now proceed to One-Eyed Pete's Shooting Gallery.

**FIGURE 8.13:** Hit all three switches on the platforms above the D-Cup ride to uncover the blue keycard in the pillar at the center.

### At One-Eyed Pete's Shooting Gallery

Your duckies are all lined up and One-Eyed Pete's offers a chance to show off your marksmanship. Not only that, but if you take out two of the targets in close succession, you also get your choice of furry animals and come into contact with the hotly sought-after red keycard—your ticket to *Babes of the Caribbean*. Wow.

1. **Turn in your keycard.** Step inside the booth to the gallery and use the keycard to lower the force shield.

2. **Claim some health and shoot the right targets.** Turn your attention to the floating targets and lose no time in reaching for the atomic health units. Then shoot the second and fourth targets in quick succession. This will cause the secret area behind the stuffed toys to open and reveal the red keycard inside.

3. **Claim your prize.** Waste the pig cop and crouch into the small room to take the red keycard.

Now you'd better dash to *Babes of the Caribbean*. Just cut in line for any hope of a decent seat.

## At *Babes of the Caribbean*

Everyone knows that *Babes of the Caribbean* is the main draw at the Babe Land theme park. And for good reason, too. The dramatic enactment of a seaport battle between a Spanish galleon and defending fort overlooking the bay is worth the horrendous wait. But once you get there, you can't help but be transported straight into the action and battle alongside women who can only exist in a production like *Babes of the Caribbean*. And sailor, you look right handsome in that eye patch.

1. **Get the ammo before you go in.** Step inside the ticket booth to turn off the force field. Pick up the chaingun ammo from the floor and proceed to the ride.

2. **Cut in line and dispose of the protector drones.** There's no reason to linger at the back of the line. Instead, hop over the divisions and have the chaingun ready to pelt the protector drone full of lead, the second you spot him. Deal with his successor in the same way.

3. **Start the ride.** Pick up the pipe bombs and be ready to meet the fire from across the canal, as an area on the wall is triggered open by your proximity. Hop on the dinghy and away you go.

4. **Get off at the first chance.** About halfway down the straight leg of the canal, get near the wall on the right side and jump off as soon as you spot a safe place to land. The triggered explosion could hurt you if you remain on the dinghy.

5. **Uncover a secret.** Blow the door open. Rush in and grab the RPG ammo, which is always most appreciated. Then stand by the edge and wait for the next dinghy so that you can hop on it and continue with the ride.

## Of Human Slavery

The southernmost tip of the toxic canal shows a deplorable sight: actual commerce in human lives. Men and women bound and shackled, being paraded for sale to the highest bidder. Almost like real life in the nine-to-five, humdrum world—but this, you must remember, is only a dramatization. The only reason for stopping here, besides witnessing the sad spectacle, is to cash in on some goods.

1. **Take the chaingun ammo.** Hop off the dinghy and land next to the bound humans. Open the door and take out the pig cop before he knows what hit him between the eyes with a solid hunk of molten American lead. Go past him and take the ammo.

2. **Take the RPG ammo.** Hop over the next higher area where a similar proceeding is under way. Open the next door and give another hot-lead greeting to the snooty pig cop. Get the RPG ammo, and don't pass up the protective boots as you set off in the toxic canal toward the fort near the center of this circuitous ride.

## The Battle in the Bay

As you come on the fort, you'll also come into view of the vicious crew aboard the Spanish galleon. They, too, will see you. You're stepping into the middle of an intense battle. Be prepared to take your chances. Your mission in the bay is to get on board and find a key teleporter. You should then transport to the fort, where you must reach the top floor. Once at the top, you'll find the corridor leading to the exit.

1. **Take out the Battlelord from a distance.** Unload an RPG shot and then hide behind the fort's wall when the Battlelord retaliates. Repeat this procedure until the Battlelord capsizes.

2. **Board the galleon.** Plunge into the waters and swim under the galleon. Emerge into a storage area inside the belly of the vessel, and blow up the powder barrels.

3. **Pick up the shrinker/expander, and beam to the surface of the galleon.** Battle the survivors and then move toward the other end of the vessel. Activate the switch behind the post before climbing next to the wheel. That switch lowers the large gate blocking the entrance to the fort.

4. **Dive into the toxic ooze and trudge over to the fort.** Take a running start into the tepid, fetid waters and slog your way to the shore by the fort.

## At the Fort

The multilevel fort is a heavy structure that you must climb to the top. It offers a breathtaking view of the bay and the encroaching galleon. There are plenty of treasures, from wrecked ships and such, that have made their way to the vaults of the port. You might as well profit from your short stay at the fort.

1. **Comb the ground floor.** Look around for a shotgun and an atomic health unit. Then explore the next level up.

2. **Climb onto the crate and get more stuff.** Climb over the high-tech-looking crate and from there hop onto the second level. Walk the periphery, picking up all the weapons and ammo you can use.

3. **Hop over the gate.** Take a running start to hop over the entrance gate and reach the other half of this plane. Take precautions against the protector drone that will come pouncing out of the metal door at the end of the walkway.

4. **Reach the last level up.** Climb up the platform and emerge at the top of the fort, looking over the vastness of the bay. Collect the jetpack, the holoduke, and the case of pipe bombs.

5. **Uncover the exit tunnel.** Get back indoors. Push the first and third buttons (from left to right) to open a narrow metallic corridor with a pulsating energy gun. You'll also have to contend with a second lizard in this confined space. With the protector drone no longer a threat, step over his carcass, dash to the end of the tunnel, and turn to punch the exit switch.

## COVERT DETAILS

As you'd imagine, a theme park of Babe Land's caliber is bound to have many a surprise and many a secret. Table 8.8 unravels Babe Land's many secrets.

| TABLE 8.8: THE SECRETS IN BABE LAND | | |
|---|---|---|
| **AREA IN LEVEL** | **SECRET ITEM** | **HOW TO GET IT** |
| One-Eyed Pete's Shooting Gallery | shells | Blow a hole in the north wall and crawl inside to claim the shells. |
| One-Eyed Pete's Shooting Gallery | red keycard armor NVG | Shoot the second and fourth circular targets to open a space behind the stuffed prizes. Shoot the furry toys and jump inside the small chamber to collect all the essential items. |
| Blocked corridor by a cell near the southwest side of the toxic canal | RPG ammo | Jump off the dinghy into the cell on the south side wall of the canal. Blow the metal door open, and climb a few steps inside the narrow corridor to get the RPG ammo. |
| Hidden crawl space high above bow of Spanish galleon | atomic health unit | Fly with the jetpack directly above the bow of the ship. Step right through the fake backdrop and reach the crawl space. |

# PIGSTY

"Suuey! Suuuuueeyyy!" Hear those piggies squeal. Pigsty is just another name for the Los Angeles Police Department, also know as L.A.R.D. (or LARD) headquarters, down-town. And you've arrived just as a car slams right into the lobby of the police station, bouncing pig cop bodies to and fro and causing several explosions before coming to a screeching halt near the middle of the floor.

Pigsty is a convenient, one-stop shop for your every need in the criminal justice area. Whether you need to do some time in solitary or simply unwind in an interrogation/torture chamber, Pigsty is a most obliging institution. Pigsty also lets you see things from the other side of the badge. Drop in on detectives Dirty Harry and McLain, watch your tax dollars at work, and chew on a stale doughnut. And if every dog must have its day in court, you can have yours too. Check out Judge Dredd's chambers—if you can find them. And one last thing: Pigsty contains the secret exit that leads to the secret level of The Birth, aptly named Area 51.

## MAPS AND ROUTE

As shown in Figures 8.14 and 8.15, Pigsty is no place to hang out socially, not even when your family throws you out on your butt. The coffee is cold and old, and the doughnuts are rock hard. Besides, the people who drop in are not the kind you'd normally associate with. But you're here for business only. And your business today is to ensure your own survival.

## THE GOODS

Whichever side of the badge you're on, Pigsty is a tough place to be in. Still, it has a few perks for those who can manhandle it and its cast of law-enforcement characters, as Table 8.9 makes all too plain.

### TABLE 8.9: THE GOODS IN PIGSTY

| WEAPONS | AMMO | POWER-UPS |
|---|---|---|
| 1 shotgun | 6 cases | 2 portable medkits |
| 4 ripper chainguns | 3 cases | 4 atomic health units |
| 2 RPG launchers | 2 cases | 1 holoduke |
| 1 shrinker/expander | 2 expanders | 1 armor |
| 1 devastator | 2 cases | 3 steroid flasks |
| 2 freezethrowers | | 1 NVG |
| 2 laser trip bombs | | 1 jetpack |
| 3 pipe bomb cases | | |

## BLAZING THROUGH PIGSTY

True to its namesake, Pigsty is up to its curly little tail in pig cops. Add to the mix a Battlelord sentry and a couple of enforcers and protector drones, and you have all the ingredients for an absolute jailhouse jamboree. The verdict in this level is that you can't cop out, plead *nolo contendere,* or try to strike a deal with the prosecution. You must stand up for your rights and make it to the court on time.

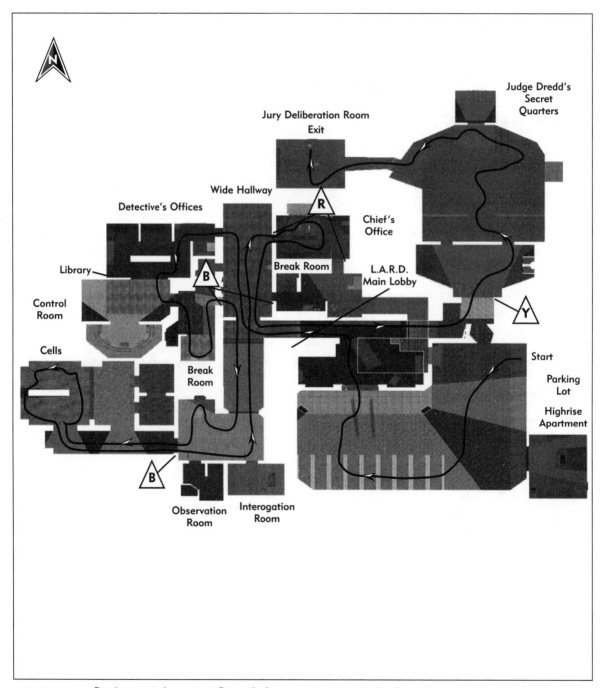

**FIGURE 8.14:** Don't pass judgment on Pigsty before you step in and plead your case.

**FIGURE 8.15:** The only way to beat the system is to infiltrate the system. Pigsty is ready-made for infiltration.

## In the Main Floor of L.A.R.D. Headquarters

Your entry point into Pigsty is by the parking lot at the southeast end. Nearly all the action can take place inside headquarters. As you enter the chaotic scene on the main floor, keep your wits about you and try to get the lay of the land. Although your ultimate destination is the courtroom, you must traverse the entire building before pleading your case in front of a jury. Your immediate concern is to get more ammo, health, and any other useful devices you can find.

1.  **Bust your way inside.** You might meet early resistance from a pig cop tank. Dispose of it in your preferred way and step inside. Run around by the couch under the mug shots and take the shells and armor.

2.  **Get healthy quickly.** Find the on/off lever near the west stairs and flip it on. Then jump over the wrecked vehicle and dash toward the west wall. The phone booths recede to reveal the atomic health unit you want.

## Stop for Coffee, and Don't Forget the Blue Keycard

Once you've got your bearings in the main floor, it's time to proceed with your tour of L.A.R.D.'s headquarters. Your next move should be to locate the blue keycard. Without it, you won't be able to enter the cells, which is where you must get the red keycard.

1.  **Go to the main hallway and score your first heavy weapon.** Ascend the short stairs into the west side, and then turn north toward the wide, dark hallway. Move in and go inside the small utility room halfway down the hall. Take the RPG and then continue to the end.

2.  **Watch the detectives.** Step into the door at the northwest end. You'll be walking into Detective McLain's office. Claim the armor and the portable medkit by the entrance. Don't be deterred by the enforcers and pig cops. Press toward the south side of the bookshelves.

3.  **Proceed to the fresh pot of coffee.** Drop a pipe bomb through the window over a leaping enforcer. Then jump down into a square-shaped floor overlooking an elaborate computer panel in an adjacent semicircular

area. Ignore that for now, and turn eastward toward the coffee, dough-nuts, and blue keycard.

4. **Take two sugars and one blue keycard.** Take the blue keycard from the table and climb up the ramp. Be ready to contend with a contemptuous assault commander. Exit to the hallway and head south toward the cells.

## Grime and Punishment

*Spartan* is perhaps the most emotionally neutral term to describe the cells at the south-west end of Pigsty, but truly they're grim. You must make a forced stop, because the red keycard is found down here.

1. **Plow to the end of the ramp.** Along the way, you'll have to deal with a pig cop tank. Push open the door and contend with yet another pig cop.

2. **Enter the cells.** Use the blue keycard to gain entry to the cells. Watch out for the humorless octabrain warden. Push ahead to the largest cell. You'll be jumped by a merciless assault commander.

3. **Take the red keycard—you're a free man (for now).** Walk around the wall dividing the cell, grab the red keycard, and get back to the main hallway. It's time to meet the Chief of Police in person.

## In the Chief's Quarters

Now that you have the blue keycard, you can enter any room from the main hallway. Even the chief's office—and that's directly where you're going. This is no social visit. The chief, embodied in the hovering torso of the alien assault commander, has some-thing you want. He's keeping the yellow keycard under his watchful eye.

1. **Greet the chief.** Back in the main hallway, stand by the last door on the right. Open the security lock with your red keycard. Mount the RPG launcher on your shoulder, and let one go as soon as you get clear sight of the commander.

2. **Clean out his office.** Jump over the commander's corpse and take the yellow keycard from his desk. While you're here, don't overlook the expander ammo by the potted plant in the corner of the office.

3. **Get ready for the judge.** Come out of the commander's quarters and run back toward the courtroom. Cross the main floor lobby and move westward toward the marble facade.

## Your Day in Court

All you want is an impartial jury that'll stay awake during your trial—but the way things run in Pigsty, you're not likely to get it. With some of the usual suspects roaming freely, two protector drones and a Battlelord sentry, this courtroom is *way* out of order. The situation is highly explosive. But if you make a convincing case, you get to explore a secret level, Area 51, provided that you find Judge Dredd's quarters. Or, if you prefer, the normal exit sends you overnight to Going Postal. You're taking a big chance either way.

1. **Knock in the hall of law.** Open the security lock with your yellow keycard and take out the trooper milling uneasily about.

2. **Take possession of the goods.** Enter the antechamber and grab the shrinker/expander below the solemn portraits of Presidents Jackson and Lincoln. Also, turn your attention to the phone booths on the east side. Pick up the RPG ammo and say an ardent prayer as you enter the actual courtroom.

3. **Open the door and let the fireworks go off.** Stick your nose inside, only to have it nearly blown off (well, you were saving for a nose job anyway). Get off an RPG shot or two and make the best of your fighting ability to subjugate the protector drones and the Battlelord sentry.

Drawing them out the door one at a time and picking them off as they emerge works particularly well.

4. **Take the witness stand.** As you do, a secret wall gives way on the east side of the court-room, releasing a pig cop tank. Grab the atomic health unit and then leap onto the back of the pig cop tank and push its self-destruct switch.

> **TIP**
>
> Hang out by the door to the trial room. Show yourself enough to draw the attention of the prosecution's witnesses, and then pick them off one at a time as they come out.

5. **Sit on the judge's bench.** Jump inside the high seat of the court and notice the single switch in front of you. Push the switch to open a door behind the witness stand on the west side.

6. **Choose an exit.** Follow the tunnel behind the jury box to emerge near the normal exit switch. But if you prefer something weirder, press on President Washington's portrait (behind the judge's bench) and hop into Judge Dredd's quarters. The secret exit switch is in plain view.

## COVERT DETAILS

Pigsty, not unlike other hubs of judicial dispensation, has plenty of secrets it wishes never to be let out. But here they are anyway, in Table 8.10.

### TABLE 8.10: THE SECRETS IN PIGSTY

| AREA IN LEVEL | SECRET ITEM | HOW TO GET IT |
| --- | --- | --- |
| Hidden compartment behind public phones in police station's main lobby | atomic health unit | Find and activate the lever switch on the wall on the right side as you start up the stairs toward the courtroom. Then run back into the main lobby and jump inside the small area now revealed behind the public phones. |

*(Continued on next page)*

*(Continued from previous page)*

| AREA IN LEVEL | SECRET ITEM | HOW TO GET IT |
|---|---|---|
| Hidden area behind the painting in the chief's office | portable medkit | Press against the painting and jump into the hollow space to take the portable medkit. |
| Lower-level interrogation/execution room | ripper chainguns (3) atomic health unit | Find Detective McClain's office in the southeast office at the wide hallway. Push against the bookshelves by the desk. Descend into the lower floor interrogation/execution chamber, where the chainguns and atomic health unit await. |
| Hidden control room inside interrogation chamber at the south end of the wide hallway | atomic health unit | Open the small observation chamber where interrogations are routinely viewed and recorded through the one-way mirror. Press against the large recorder on the table, and then enter the control room that's now visible behind the secret door. |
| Apartment across the street from the police station | freezethrower RPG devastator expander ammo steroids | Get the jetpack from the area near the south interrogation chamber. Fly out through the manhole cover and reach the next-to-top floor on the building across the street. Enter through the window at the far right. |

# AREA 51

If you find yourself in Area 51 at the end of Pigsty, it's because you found Judge Dredd's chamber and the secret exit. Or maybe you just stumbled onto it. (Otherwise you'd be in

the next sequential level, Going Postal.) But regardless of how you got here, consider the words for a second, Area 51. Taken by itself, each of these two words means nothing. "Fifty-one," or "Area." But just say, "Area 51" and people turn their heads. Why? It's only natural. Everyone's heard or told stories about how the military has information and hides it, and even has proof of alien contact with this planet. But all speculation aside, Area 51 is a playful, imaginative level where you get to live your very own close encounter—and maybe even claim back our independence.

## MAPS AND ROUTE

Few places in this country were as off-limits as the secret government facility known as Area 51. But now, you can even consult maps before going inside. Figures 8.16 and 8.17 are now available to anyone for the asking. Of course, very few have the nerve to actually venture in.

## THE GOODS

Besides its imaginative construction, Area 51 also gives you plenty of reasons to pierce the veil of secrecy. Table 8.11 lists each reason for you.

### TABLE 8.11: THE GOODS IN AREA 51

| WEAPONS | AMMO | POWER-UPS |
| --- | --- | --- |
| 2 shotguns | 4 cases | 2 portable medkits |
| 1 ripper chaingun | 5 cases | 3 atomic health units |
| 1 RPG launcher | 2 cases | 2 holodukes |
| 1 shrinker/expander | 4 crystals | 2 armors |
| 1 devastator | 2 charges | 1 steroid flask |
| 1 freezethrower | | 2 NVGs |
| 3 laser trip bombs | | |
| 3 pipe bomb cases | | |

## BLAZING THROUGH AREA 51

Allegedly, Area 51, a government-owned research facility in the New Mexico desert, houses alien aircrafts, artifacts, and even mysteriously preserved alien bodies. But that hardly matters to Duke Nukem, or to anyone now. There's no longer a need to hide the aliens' existence. We all know they've come here to take over our planet and maybe even our souls, too. To be sure, they've taken quite a liking to our chicks.

**FIGURE 8.16:** Until recently, accurate Area 51 maps were nowhere to be found. The alien presence changed all that.

**FIGURE 8.17**: You're about to find out everything about the gruesome alien biology in Area 51.

### Break Into Area 51

You went as far as you could in your trusty Jeep. You jumped over the fence. Now you have to find your way inside Area 51. Naturally, the main gate is heavily guarded and practically impenetrable. Not only that, but even if there were no pig cops, troopers, captains, or pig cops in tanks crawling around, you'd still need to find the blue keycard to get in. So this is your first priority: to get the blue keycard and get inside.

1.  **Blow up the small cement building.** Battle off the few troopers in the area. Then, if you don't have the RPG on you, collect the pipe bombs by the "Danger: Falling Rocks" sign, and toss one by the heavy, squat, building. Stand back a safe distance and *ka-blammm!*

2.  **Open the door to the elevator.** Step into the ruins of the demolished building and activate the red, round switch. Listen for the hiss of the door at the southwest corner as it gives way.

3.  **Ride the first teleporter.** Rush toward the door and grab the case of pipe bombs as you step into the elevator. Go up, get out, grab the chaingun, and step into the teleporter in the corner.

4.  **Blast a fan and drop in.** You emerge on the east side of the main gate, right by an RV. You're surrounded by pig cops, pig cops on RPVs, and even a couple of pig cops in tanks. Do your best to eliminate as many aliens as you can while trying to reach the squat building to the north. Hop on top of the tin roof, put a bullet in the spinning fan, and jump through. Get extra protection by shooting at the floor and collecting the armor in the secret area under your feet.

5.  **Get out of the hole.** Jump on the side of the hole you're in. Look for a small switch by the southeast pillar and press it. The door in front will open to reveal a monitoring room of sorts.

6.  **Waste a couple of pig cops.** Don't run out just yet. Wait for the pig cops inside the monitoring room to come into view. Then let 'em have it. Step inside and spot the blue keycard in front of the control chair.

7. **Take the blue keycard.** But first, drop one or two pipe bombs by each of the flanking doors as you go in. Hold on steady to the detonator. Grab the blue keycard behind the chair, turn around, and, as the pig cops emerge, punch the switch (see Figure 8.18).

8. **Collect the goods and teleport back out.** Enter the small compartment in the northwest corner to take pipe bombs. Then turn 180 degrees and head straight for the other compartment to get into the next teleporter. You'll come out on a cave above the tin-roofed building. Jump down and make a beeline for the main gate of Area 51.

## Access the Shaft

Once you have the blue keycard, you're clear to enter Area 51. However, you'll be dismayed to find that the gate is, once again, under heavy guard. But once you're in, you'll be stepping into a reception room of sorts. As might be expected in a research

**FIGURE 8.18:** Drop pipe bombs by each door, and the second after you grab the blue keycard, detonate them.

facility, the room is sparsely decorated, and there's just one long blue couch. The reception room connects you to an elevator shaft, which is the only way to get to the hub of the installation. From that hub, you can access the various Area 51 chambers, storage areas, and laboratories.

1. **Take over the reception area.** After waging a short war outside with the armed pig cops, troopers, captains, and pig tanks, proceed to use the blue keycard on the main gate of Area 51. Storm inside, taking out the captains and also the enforcer behind a wall partition to one side of the entrance.

2. **Clean out the bottom chambers.** Jump behind the counter and open the door to access the lower chambers. Step through and move down the ramp into a computer control room with various monitors and high-tech machines lining most walls. Deal with the single pig cop down here. Then proceed to another door at the far east side of the chamber. Push it open and enter a narrow metal chamber occupied by a single captain. Snuff him out, and take the laser trip bombs stashed on the divisions by the wall.

3. **Claim an atomic health unit.** Trace your steps back to the computer control room, and find a triangular demarcation on a wall above the computer panels on the south wall. Press it to trigger open a secret compartment for a second or two. The compartment is on the left side of the wall dividing the room. If you run really fast and jump inside the compartment, you'll be 50 percent healthier than you are now.

4. **Get back to the reception area and jump down the shaft.** Walk up to the row of triple switches near the north end of the reception area. Push the middle switch only and you'll see the door in front of you that gives access to the elevator shaft. Jump down and try to land on top of the elevator below. Then slide off the side so that you actually reach the very bottom floor of the shaft. Collect the devastator and hop out the door facing east, to come into view of the central column where all Area 51 chambers, storage rooms, and labs converge.

## Investigate the Laboratory

The diamond shaped, central hub of Area 51 is the place where all the major chambers converge. However, every one of the three paths converging here is blocked by force fields. You can turn off the force fields to chambers 1 and 2. However, the only way to access chamber 3 is through a teleporter in chamber 2. This teleporter is behind a door with a red security lock. Therefore, it makes perfect sense to get the red keycard in chamber 1 before taking on chambers 2 and 3. As you'll find out shortly, chamber 1 is a laboratory where alien life forms have been studied and dissected for some time. Getting the red keycard will entail coming into close contact with some protector drone specimens that are still very much alive . . . and quite ghastly.

1. **Lay a few pipe bombs down by gate 1.** Come out of the elevator shaft and drop a few bombs outside the door labeled "1." Fear not the protector drone inside! The force field keeps him restrained (for the moment).

2. **Climb the central column and deactivate the force field from the lab.** Push against the platform on the west side of the central column to access its top level. Press the switch facing chamber 1, and then press the detonator. If the drone survives, jump below and pepper him with your chaingun or devastator. Then proceed cautiously into the lab.

3. **Blow up the lab.** Firmly gripping the chaingun, step into the lab and open fire when you see the shining-red eyes of the protector drones inside. Sensing the excitement, the drone held in stasis might bust out of its glass cage and attempt to join the fight. So be *very* vigilant and dish out punishment with impunity.

4. **Open the drawer where the red keycard is kept.** Turn your attention to a round switch on the diagonal southeast wall and push it. The nearby white

> **TIP**
>
> Before you deactivate the force field to the laboratory, consider putting down a few LTBs (Laser Trip Bombs) around the main column. Give yourself enough space to climb up into the main column after deploying the LTBs. Then climb to the top of the column and push open switch 1 (see Figure 8.19).

**FIGURE 8.19:** A few strategically placed LTBs will help you overcome this protector drone at the laboratory entrance behind gate 1.

square column will open to reveal a case of shells and some grisly organic remains. Hop over the work area as you pluck the shells. A sensor will cause the drawer near the middle of the west wall to slide open.

5. **Set up some demonic drones.** Before reaching for the red keycard, save yourself serious emotional and physical damage by setting up a couple of drones. The second you grab the keycard, a sensor causes a secret wall to open at the east side of the room, near the entrance. Not one, but two protector drones bounce out like loaded springs. Knowing this, you can make the drones' lives very difficult, not to mention short. Plaster a few Laser Trip Bombs right by the suspect wall. Also, drop as many pipe bombs as you can afford to. Then, and only then, reach for the key while your thumb squeezes the detonator. Should the drones survive, shoot their legs out from under them while still inside the drawer. With the red keycard in hand, you're free to go back to the hub.

### In the Storage Area

The storage area behind the gate labeled "2" contains boxes of equipment, and even one of the original crates from the 1947 Roswell "incident" (as the government euphemistically still calls it). Your main purpose in the storage area is to gain passage to the split-level chamber to the north, gate 3, which, among other things, serves as a hangar to a recovered alien ship.

1. **Open gate 2.** Climb the central column for the second time, and press the switch in front of gate 2.

2. **Take out the enemy and the inventory.** Spray bullets on the troopers and captains who are sure to come flying in pursuit. Then get down and enter the storage room under a shower of bullets you're firing into the rubbery flesh of the octabrains lurking in there. Step inside and climb over the crates to get everything in sight. Turn on the CPU on the corner desk, even if it looks completely wasted. Then run to get inside the large crate at the northeast corner and swipe the scuba gear and armor.

3. **Go north down the ramp.** It's time to push on to the north chamber. Find the ramp at the north end of the wall and run down inside the next chamber, which is, in effect, a hangar.

### In the Hangar

The chamber north of the hub is divided into two main areas. On the east side, there is a strategy room complete with maps and top-secret documents. The yellow keycard is also found here. To the west, a larger chamber houses a recovered alien craft. Once you've obtained the red keycard from the laboratory, your next move is to enter the hangar, unlock the red security lock, and take the teleporter into the adjacent control room. Then, you simply take the yellow keycard and get back to the hangar, where a yellow security lock stands between you and the elusive exit to Area 51.

Of course, you won't be able to simply march inside the north chambers. You'll be facing the toughest opposition yet in this level. The hangar is guarded by protector drones. The yellow keycard in the chamber next door rests under the watchful eye of an assault commander.

1. **Take out the drones.** As you step into the hangar, cut a quick right, past a conveyor belt and crane mechanism, and then turn left to get a view of the captured alien ship. Swing out the chaingun and spray the drone that's sure to spring into action the second his predatorial eyes spot you. You might have to run back into the storage room to seek shelter and regroup. With one protective drone out of the way, walk inside the hangar a little further and deal similarly with the next protective drone.

2. **Open the red security lock.** Find the red lock near the northwest corner of the hangar, unlock it, and step into the awaiting teleporter.

3. **Fight the assault commander and get the yellow keycard.** You'll come out of the teleporter in the very next chamber, the military command center. Be aware that an assault commander is not too far from here. Grab the yellow keycard, and if you're fast enough, race back to the teleporter. (Incidentally, the heads-up display above the yellow keycard is a clue to push the right switches when the time comes to launch the twin rockets.) However, if you can't get away in time, you'll be forced to contend with the commander and maybe even an enforcer.

4. **Access the missile launch control room.** Walk up the ramp at the north end of the hangar and open the yellow security lock. Push the door open and get ready to face the last enemy in Area 51, a Battlelord sentry.

5. **Snuff the Battlelord and launch two rockets.** If your Devastator or freezethrower have any juice left, this is the time to unload whatever's left. Take a few steps into the metallic corridor and open fire. After you've imposed your will on the Battlelord sentry, step into the area in the middle of the T-shaped room.

6. **Start the detonation code.** Push the multiposition switch once. A panel of four switches will rise to your left. Activate the first, second, and fourth switches (from left to right). Then push the multiposition switch a second time. A similar panel of switches will rise to your right. Press the third and fourth switches, and listen to the beep telling you "all systems are go." Also, you'll see two level switches appear, one on each side of the chamber.

7. **Launch the rockets.** Pull the lever on each of these switches to launch both rockets. (Look at the nearby screens to see the thunderous, roaring, metallic, man-made missiles mount into the sky.) After sending off the second rocket, a metal plate gives way, uncovering the glowing red exit switch. *You've done it!* You solved the riddle of Area 51 and, in the process, you've inflicted serious losses on the alien population.

## COVERT DETAILS

No need for any further experimentation in Area 51. Just go for the secrets listed in Table 8.12.

| TABLE 8.12: THE SECRETS IN AREA 51 | | |
|---|---|---|
| **AREA IN LEVEL** | **SECRET ITEM** | **HOW TO GET IT** |
| Tin outdoor building near the north end | armor | Jump on top of the tin building. Kick the fan in and drop through. Fire a bullet at the second fan below your feet in the small circular space where you landed, and uncover a secret space below to take the armor. |
| Reception area near the elevator shaft | portable medkit | Jump behind the counter to the left as you enter the reception area. Press against the computer terminal, and race for the northeast end of the reception area, where a door to a computer panel lifts momentarily to reveal the portable medkit. |
| Storage area | scuba gear armor | Turn on the CPU on the corner desk, even if it looks completely wasted. Then run to get inside the large crate at the northeast corner and swipe the scuba gear and armor. |
| Small cave south of the storage area | expander ammo | Blow a hole in the south wall of the storage room. Step into a cavernous chamber by the edge of the infamous Groom Lake, where, supposedly, a UFO was seen to splash-land and sink to the bottom. Jump in the octabrain-infested waters to get the expander ammo. Take a moment to look through a crack in the wall and spot the sunken intergalactic vessel. (You can blow it up if you have the RPG with you.) |

*(Continued on next page)*

*(Continued from previous page)*

| AREA IN LEVEL | SECRET ITEM | HOW TO GET IT |
| --- | --- | --- |
| Elevated cave at the southeast corner, outside the main gate | RPG | Inside the small cave by Groom Lake, south of the storage room, look for the dark area at the southwest corner. Push against the bloody handprint on the wall, and step inside the teleporter. Emerge on the elevated cave outside, race across the makeshift bridge to a recessed area on the rocks, take the RPG, and run back to the teleporter. |
| Inside captured alien craft | atomic health unit | Stand on the pick-up point on the south side of the hangar and wait for the crane to pick you up and place you on the elevated area on the southwest side. Look for a switch right next to the door as you're dropped into the next conveyor belt. Activate the switch, run to the end of the conveyor, and step inside the small teleporter. You'll emerge into a small teleporter inside the alien ship. Press the round switch to open the teleporter, and take the atomic health unit between the seats. To leave, find the alien hand switch, near the now-hidden teleporter, and press it. Step into the teleporter and beam out. |
| North closet in the monitoring room | atomic health unit | Step inside the closet after taking the blue keycard. Activate the jetpack to reach the ceiling. Step inside the small wall recess marked with the yellow stripes and take the atomic health unit. |
| Lower-level computer control room | steroids | Open the door behind the counter of the reception area. Walk down the ramp into the lower-level computer control room. Jump on top of the computer consoles at the entrance of the ramp. Grab the holoduke in plain view and continue toward the northwest corner of the room, while still walking on top of the computer consoles. Push against every corner of the room. Enter the secret compartment and take the steroids. |
| Lower-level computer control room | atomic health unit | Climb over the computer panel on the southeast wall. Then run back to crawl inside a receding computer panel in the southwest side of the room. |

# GOING POSTAL

You're overworked and underappreciated. Your girlfriend is seeing your best friend (behind your back). Your car payment is two months behind. *Dogs* don't like you. Why, it's enough to make you "go postal." (Insert the sound of maniacal, sinister laughter here.)

Going Postal takes you behind the scenes and gives you a first look at the many reasons why dropping a piece of mail in the slot at the post office is the same as dropping it into a black hole. When you come to this post office, getting a simple book of stamps is like pulling teeth with your bare hands, or a crowbar at best. And if you ask anyone for help, you might get shipped out in separate boxes, postage due.

After visiting the post office, you might not have a better understanding or appreciation of the postal service, but you'll begin to understand why people here tend to go seriously "postal."

## MAPS AND ROUTE

As shown in Figures 8.20 and 8.21, Going Postal is efficiently arranged to move people and packages expediently. Never mind that the packages might carry human body parts. Or that the security is totally lax and the morale of the place is best characterized as intensely hostile. Never mind that the wild-haired guy in shredded clothing standing next to you in line looks like the Unabomber.

## THE GOODS

Even if the package you've been expecting doesn't arrive, you can still walk out of Going Postal with your life intact and a great many weapons and power-ups, as shown in Table 8.13.

**FIGURE 8.20**: Don't expect the aliens posing as postal workers to wish you a nice day after you blow up the mail.

**LOCKERS**
Armor
△ Blue Keycard

RPG Ammo (2)
Atomic Health Unit

Steroids

Chaingun

**(IN DUCT)**
△ Red Keycard
Portable Medkit

Portable Medkit

RPG
Shotgun
Atomic Health Unit

Shotgun

Chaingun Ammo (3)
Pipe Bombs
Shells
Armor
Devastator

Pipe Bombs

Shotgun

Holoduke

△ Yellow Keycard
Devastator Ammo

Expander Ammo

Pipe Bombs

Laser Trip Bombs (2)

Atomic Health Unit

Atomic Health Unit

Devastator

Shotgun

Devastator Ammo

Armor
Atomic Health Unit

Freezethrower Ammo

Protective Boots
Devastator

**FIGURE 8.21:** This level is particularly draining on your health, so be sure to capitalize on the abundance of atomic health units.

**TABLE 8.13: THE GOODS IN GOING POSTAL**

| WEAPONS | AMMO | POWER-UPS |
|---|---|---|
| 2 shotguns | 3 cases | 3 portable medkits |
| 2 ripper chainguns | 4 cases | 5 atomic health units |
| 1 RPG launcher | 4 cases | 1 holoduke |
| 1 shrinker/expander | 1 crystal | 3 armors |
| 3 devastators | 2 cases | 2 steroid flasks |
| 1 freezethrower | 1 charge | 1 NVG |
| 2 laser trip bombs | | 1 pair of boots |
| 4 pipe bomb cases | | |

## BLAZING THROUGH GOING POSTAL

More than half the area in Going Postal is taken up by a parking lot and a couple of side streets. The post office itself has various rooms where the mail and packages are sorted out and processed for delivery (or for *disposal*, others would argue). Before leaving the post office, you must claim the blue, red, and yellow keycards. Then you're set to overcome one of the toughest onslaughts in the whole of The Birth episode as you make the final, heroic stretch to reach the exit switch.

### In the Parking Lot

The wide-open parking lot is flanked by the zigzag facade of the post office and by a tall building on the other side. Except for a fire truck, the parking lot is completely empty. Take advantage of the relative calm out here, and score some major weapons and some serious health points while you're at it.

1. **Get some goodies before going in.** Jump inside the dumpster to collect a case of pipe bombs. Then dash for the side of the 451 fire truck—incidentally, this is the burning temperature for paper—and push against its hoses. Do your best to avoid getting hit by the turret outside the post office as you slip through its window behind the fire truck.

2. **Score a heavy weapon and some major health points.** Do your best to stand the heat in the burning room, and collect both a pair of protective

boots and the Devastator in the corner of the room. Find the switch low on the right side of the entrance, push it, and jump out.

3. **Hop on the fire truck.** Emerging from the burning room, jump on top of the fire truck and take the atomic health unit. Then race across the parking lot and kick through a window to get inside the post office.

## The Front Office

The post office's front office houses a scalloped wall of private postal boxes and the major customer service area. Set out to locate the blue keycard. Of course, grab every opportunity to fortify yourself and build your arsenal as you go. Pig cops and troopers will keep you occupied in the front office. But the tension soon mounts exponentially, as you penetrate to the mail rooms.

1. **Check out your post office box.** Stepping inside the post office, look for a dog paw-mark on the wall. Push on it and watch your post office drawer slide open. Crawl inside to get the shotgun. Then proceed toward the customer service area.

2. **Pause for expansion.** Before walking into the customer area, stop in the small room with the vending machines. The machine to the left will dispense a pipe bomb. There's also ammo for the expander in this small partition. Don't pass it up.

3. **Take over the customer area.** Turn inside the customer area and open fire at the pig cop behind the counter. There might also be a couple of pesky troopers and captains you'll want to dispense with promptly. Jump behind the counter and push the button below the register. The slots for mail and packages will widen so that you can slip through and access the mail rooms in the back.

## In the Mail Collection and Locker Rooms

The mail room is the area where tons of mail are processed routinely, never to be seen by human eyes again. But your foray into the mail collection rooms and the adjoining locker room is intended to do more than mock the overburdened postal institution. You're going in here to obtain the blue keycard and, time permitting, to vent a little steam.

1. **Drop through the slot.** Jump inside either of the slots and prepare your chaingun. The small mail collection room below has a few alien eggs, a couple of enforcers, and a pig cop to boot. Douse the eggs with your chaingun before stepping inside. Then run in, take the RPG launcher, and turn it on the pig cop and the enforcer. Also, boost your energy with the atomic health unit.

2. **Proceed to the lockers.** Leave the collection room and head east. Follow the bending hallway. You'll reach a point where you can only turn left or right. The entrance to the mail rooms is to the right; to the left are the lockers. You'll have to contend with a protector drone in this section of the hallway. So be ready to hit him with everything you have before he gets dangerously close.

3. **Ransack the lockers.** Turn right at the end of the hallway into the lockers, and stomp out the pig cops before turning your attention to the lockers. Every locker has something to offer. The third locker (from the left) has the blue keycard. Take everything and go out toward the south end of the hallway. You're ready to enter the conveyor chambers.

## In the Mail Processing Chambers

This post office has three mail processing chambers, interconnected by a network of conveyor belts. This state-of-the-art system is responsible for all those unsolicited catalogs threatening to break your coffee table under their combined weight. Normally, it doesn't make sense to shoot the messenger for the bad news, but as you reach the mail processing chamber, you'll want to leave no envelope unturned. You really have to *want* the red keycard badly. A couple of protector drones seriously complicate matters in the chambers.

1. **Ride the first belt.** Use the blue keycard on the security lock and step down onto the first conveyor belt. Stay on the belt and fend off the levitating captains and troopers.

2. **Get off in the middle chamber.** As soon as you enter the second chamber, jump off the belt. Climb over the crate and take the Devastator. Then run into the small passage to the third, and smallest, of the mail processing chambers.

3. **Hop on the belt again.** But first, grab the pipe bombs in the corner of the room. Crouch down to get through the elevated passage. Stay on the belt as it turns in 90-degree angles and brings you into a recessed area where the red keycard awaits you. Clutch the keycard, and come out of the conveyor belt back inside the first and largest of the mail processing chambers (see Figure 8.22).

4. **Ride the first belt again.** If you get the feeling you're going around in circles, then you're doing all right. Take the ride on the conveyor belt all the way to the second chamber. Then take on the protector drone that likes to lurk on the south side of the chamber. When you have an opportunity, activate the red security switch. Then you can venture out into the east side streets.

## In the East Side Street

At first, the street flanking the post office on the east side looks rather ordinary. But the overturned post office vehicle and the scattered fires burning reveal more than a hint of riotous behavior. Of course, the predator protector drones outside *live* to riot. Your objective is to reach the fortified area in the cul-de-sac around the corner. Once there, you must wage a brutal battle as you wait for the timed door to open and expose the yellow keycard.

1. **Slip out and slip back fast.** Crouch under the garage door and drop off a couple of bombs. Roll back in and detonate the bombs when the protector drones get near. Stand inside and shoot their legs from under them.

2. **Raid the postal truck.** Run out and go through the truck nearby to get a couple of laser trip bombs. Then jump over the overturned truck and head toward the cul-de-sac around the corner.

Mail Processing
Chambers

**FIGURE 8.22**: The path you must follow to get the yellow security card might appear rather circuitous . . . and it is.

## In the Cul-de-Sac

The scene in the cul-de-sac is just plain climactic. First you have to take over the fortified area at its end. This means going through a couple of protector drones and terminating some determined enforcers. After that, you have to step into the area to trigger a timed door and, thus, expose the yellow keycard. However, when you step inside the fortified area, you also release waves of troopers, captains, enforcers, pig cops, pig cop tanks, and even a couple of Battlelord sentries. In other words, you unleash all holy hell on yourself.

1. **Pound the cul-de-sac from afar.** As soon as you make visual contact with the walled area at the end of the cul-de-sac, open fire with a long-range weapon like the RPG launcher.

2. **Plant a good many pipe bombs.** Before taking possession of the walled area, and in anticipation of the droves of enemies you know will material-ize as soon as you step inside, drop a decent number of pipe bombs around the outside of the wall.

3. **Take possession and blow every-one away.** With the remote deto-nation switch in your hand, step into the walled area. Almost instantly, you'll hear the growls of captains and the whirring of their jetpacks. To inflict maximum damage, don't pull the trigger just yet—steady on.

> **TIP**
>
> Drop as many bombs and place as many LTBs as you can before stepping into the walled area at the cul-de-sac. You're about to be ambushed by an angry mob of aliens who have gone beyond "postal." When you set foot on the area, wait for the crowd to reach the critical area, and then detonate your pipe bombs. Let the LTBs take care of any sur-vivors. Also, don't forget there are cannons mounted on the walls to either side of the dead-end street. You'll need all the explosive power you can muster.

4. **Activate the side-mounted cannon.** Reach and activate the switch to the left side as you face the stampeding enemies. This causes the cannon mounted on the left wall to fire powerful blasts into the crowd. Then, detonate the pipe bombs. The combined blasts should be enough to completely massacre everyone in the cul-de-sac. Use the switch on the right side to annihilate any remaining survivors (see Figure 8.23).

5. **Snatch the yellow keycard.** By now the chamber directly due east of your position should be wide open. The yellow keycard is now within

**FIGURE 8.23:** Stand your ground and fight like a Duke Nukem should.

your grasp; but first, you can't simply ignore the irate Battlelord sentry. Pound him well and avoid getting hit. Then race for the yellow keycard.

6. **One more Battlelord sentry to go.** Start running south toward the exit. When you reach the overturned postal truck, you'll also come in close contact with the second Battlelord sentry. Take him down. Then march resolutely to the exit hall, and leave your days of Going Postal behind.

## COVERT DETAILS

Going Postal houses a good deal of surprises and secrets. Table 8.14 details them for you.

## TABLE 8.14: THE SECRETS IN GOING POSTAL

| AREA IN LEVEL | SECRET ITEM | HOW TO GET IT |
|---|---|---|
| Postal Rifle Association | chaingun<br>shotgun<br>2 RPG ammos<br>atomic health unit<br>portable medkit | In the locker room, walk through the second locker into the adjoining meeting room/lounge for members of the Postal Rifle Association, who share a common hatred for canines. Two protector drones serve cocktails behind the bar. Eliminate them. Step behind a wooden block, take aim at the doggie target, hit a bull's-eye, and claim the RPG ammo and the atomic health unit from the wall. |
| Burning office | protective boots<br>devastator | Press the side of the fire truck with the hoses. Jump inside the burning office. The boots and the Devastator are to the right. To get out, press the low switch on the other side. |
| Large mail sorting chamber | freezethrower | On entering the largest mail-sorting chamber, jump over the narrow conveyor belt on the east side. Then walk toward the middle pillar, and crouch down to walk right into the lower part of the pillar inside a secret metal duct with the freezethrower at the far end. |
| Post office front office | pipe bomb case | Press the picture of the alleged Unabomber and climb inside the enclosure to grab the pipe bomb case. |

# XXX-STACY

It's not every day that you get to go behind the cameras of a movie production meant for adults. Of course, it's not every day that you're likely to *die* on a cheap movie set, either. But regardless of your stand on explicit, adult content, XXX-Stacy puts you in the silent shoes of a voyeur and lets you experience, first-hand, what it's like to be in close proximity to lustful starlets in the making. XXX-Stacy makes you realize, more than other *Duke Nukem 3D: Atomic Edition* levels, that the aliens' fascination with humans might transcend physical domination into areas that are perhaps too painful to discuss.

## MAPS AND ROUTE

Figures 8.24 and 8.25 bare the naked truth about XXX-Stacy. This is the kind of place your mom might have warned you about. With any luck, she won't be around for your imminent tour de force.

## THE GOODS

Other than the obvious goods, there are many other nice pieces you can claim as your own in XXX-Stacy. Table 8.15 shows you these goods.

| TABLE 8.15: THE GOODS IN XXX-STACY | | |
|---|---|---|
| **WEAPONS** | **AMMO** | **POWER-UPS** |
| 1 shotgun | 5 cases | 2 portable medkits |
| 1 ripper chaingun | 2 cases | 2 atomic health units |
| 2 RPG launchers | 1 case | 1 holoduke |
| 1 shrinker/expander | 1 charge | 1 armor |
| 1 devastator | | 1 steroid flask |
| 1 freezethrower | | 1 scuba gear |
| 2 laser trip bombs | | 1 pair of boots |
| 2 pipe bomb cases | | 1 NVG |

## BLAZING THROUGH XXX-STACY

Besides what some might consider eye candy, XXX-Stacy offers plenty of action in a more traditional sense. Penetrating the movie production house won't be easy. But once you manage to slip through, you must contend with all manner of deviant aliens bent on enslaving and humiliating you. The line between pleasure and pain really begins to blur in XXX-Stacy. You must remain spiritually strong to make it to the east side of XXX-Stacy, where, again, you must battle for your life. But even when you're just mere yards away from the exit, you'll have to subdue a gang of protector drones to get final clearance.

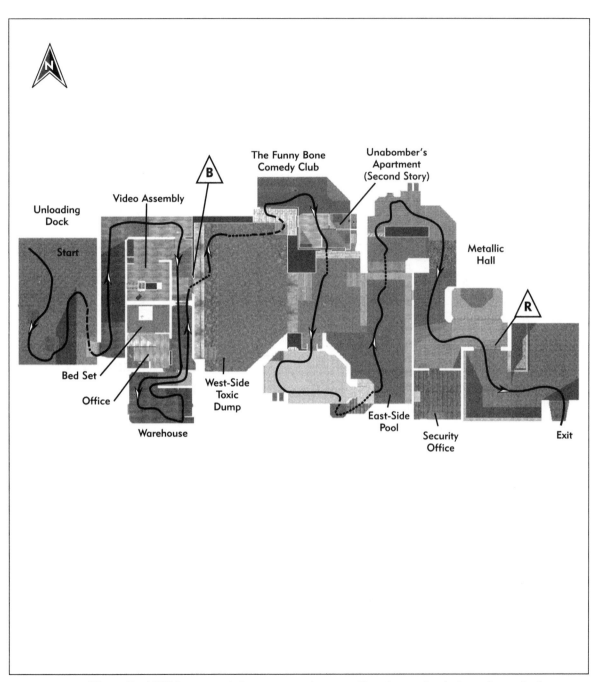

FIGURE 8.24: Places like XXX-Stacy aren't for everyone, but try telling that to the deviant aliens who have taken over the set.

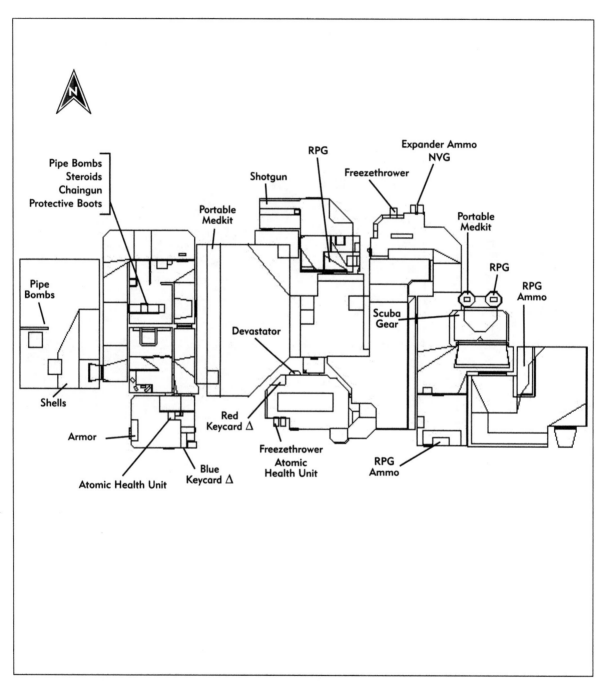

**FIGURE 8.25:** After only a few minutes in XXX-Stacy, you begin to realize that pleasure and pain are two sides of the same coin.

## Dropping In on the Set

The west wing of this level is nothing less than XXX-Stacy Video Productions. This company produces what they call erotic videos, which, incidentally, are also taped in-house. Whether you consent or not, you must still go inside and find the blue keycard. With it, you'll be able to reach the central area and have a chance for a bit of levity at the Funny Bone (a comedy bar).

1.  **Enter only if you're not easily offended.** Take the pipe bombs and shoot the captains and troopers milling about. Shoot one of the trash cans and score some shells quickly. Then, climb the ramp, open the door, and kill the next captain. Force your way past the pig cops and turn into the first door.

2.  **Check out the promo office.** Turn into the first office by the water fountain. Collect a ripper chaingun from behind the wall divider. Also, cash in on the protection boots inside the narrow cooler. Notice the piece of equipment in the middle of the floor churning out copies of XXX-Stacy's latest flick, "Sister Act III." Kick the trash can to take some pipe bombs.

3.  **Do you want to see how it's done?** Enter the editing room next. Then go around the wall division to the actual set. Shield your eyes if you're a minor. Consider this only an educational experience, for there isn't much booty (at least, in the way of weapons or power-ups) to score here.

4.  **At last, take the key with a big bang.** Coming at the end of the hallway, you'll run into a room that is completely lined with highly explosive C-9 tanks. Simply throw a pipe bomb into the room, back off as far as you can, and detonate the bomb. When the rumblings subside, run back to the storage room and collect an armor, the blue keycard, and an

atomic health unit. Also, there's a freezethrower hidden in the crate above the blue keycard.

### In the Central Area

The central area of XXX-Stacy is quite colorful. It consists of two rectangular pools (one on the east side and one on the west side), a couple of buildings, and even a comedy bar. The pool on the west side is completely toxic. The pool in the east, however, is totally safe. Its water level can be raised or lowered through the proper switches. Your main reason for passing through the central area is to locate the red keycard, which in turn, will let you out of XXX-Stacy and into pure bliss.

1. **Open the window to the cesspool.** Open the security lock to raise the window overlooking the green, slimy, toxic pool. Take out the pig cops and sentry drone before stepping over into the ledge.

2. **Cross the slime.** Jump down into a narrow walkway. Then wait for the shrinking sparks to pass. (These are shrinker charges that can render you miniature if you come into contact with them.) Run over to the pool, and jump on top of the crate at the northeast end. You might hear the sinister laugh of an assault commander nearby. In a few seconds, you could be his private joke.

3. **Tickle the Funny Bone.** Blow away the pig cop by the window to the Funny Bone and then step inside. Grab a shotgun from the other side of the bar and move toward the stage as you mow down the troopers and captains lounging there.

4. **Reach the storage area.** Locate the shielded window at the south end of the Funny Bone and open it. You must now contend with the hovering assault commander.

5. **Get the red keycard.** Dash toward the metallic-looking building. Open its door and placate the leaping, hyperactive enforcers. Then proceed to take the red keycard. Also look in the narrow closets. One has freezethrower ammo; the other, an atomic health unit.

### In the Eastern Wing

Once you've collected the red keycard, your next toughest proposition is to actually get to use it. The eastern wing of XXX-Stacy includes a computer control room, a small nesting site for alien eggs, and a parking lot. Near the nesting site, a gang of protector drones, barely contained by a triggered door, waits like tightly wound springs ready to pounce on you. The door will open whenever you come near. It's obvious somebody in XXX-Stacy doesn't want you to leave—at least not alive, not for awhile.

> **TIP**
>
> Before you go dashing to get the red keycard, you might collect some heavy dividends by storming the alleged Unabomber's apartment, which sits right on top of the Funny Bone. See Table 8.16 for full details on how to access the Unabomber's pad.

1. **Take a plunge.** Still in the rusty building, open the door to the west, pick up a stray pipe bomb, and examine the water level. Raise it by pushing the switch near the door. Then take a deep breath and plunge into the water hole inside the enclosure.

2. **Storm the computer control area.** Dive and look for an opening leading west and then follow the body of water northward. Emerge to catch your breath but continue moving north. You will come upon a metallic computer control room manned by various troopers and captains. Blast them all. Then lower the water level again with a similar switch by the door. Turn around and grab the freezethrower that's revealed behind one of the computer panels.

3. **Beat some eggs.** Before starting up the darkened corridor covered with alien webbing, shoot one of the C-9 tanks and back away quickly. Then continue moving in.

4. **Make some protector drone guacamole.** Before setting off the trigger that releases the protector drones, stand a short distance out in the hallway. From this key position, throw as many pipe bombs as you can near the metallic door containing the protector drones. Then step in just

enough to cross the trigger and back away quickly. As you hear the shriek of the first protector drone in pursuit, detonate the bombs.

5. **Be on your way.** With the protector drone blitzkrieg safely squelched, turn back around and use the red keycard on the door facing south. Step out to beat on the pig cop tank like an old can of beans. Then open the garage door on the southeast corner. Run in, hit the exit switch, and leave XXX-Stacy behind.

## COVERT DETAILS

Although boasting a wide open attitude, XXX-Stacy is not without its share of secrets. Table 8.16 exposes the juiciest of them.

| TABLE 8.16: THE SECRETS IN XXX-STACY | | |
| --- | --- | --- |
| **AREA IN LEVEL** | **SECRET ITEM** | **HOW TO GET IT** |
| Storage room south of the bedroom set inside XXX-Stacy Video Productions | freezethrower | Blow up the C-9 tanks from a safe distance. Then rush in to collect all manner of weapons and power-ups. Push the crate above the blue keycard to grab the freezethrower inside. |
| Unabomber's apartment, above the Funny Bone | chaingun ammo devastator RPG launcher pipe bombs | Coming out of the Funny Bone into the crate storage area, climb over the crate next to the east wall. Then hop on top of the wall, which separates the crate area from the east-side pool. Stand at the end of the wall and fire a single shot inside the window of the apartment right above the Funny Bone, and brace yourself for the ensuing explosion. (The place holds multiple C-9 tanks.) Then make a running start into the same window. Inspect the Unabomber's apartment and collect all the loot. The Devastator is inside the trash can. |
| Computer control room, just north of the clear pool | freezethrower | When you lower the water level of the pool (with the switch by the door), a panel opens up in the computer wall, revealing the green glow of the freezethrower. |

# CRITICAL MASS

Today, our galaxy—like billions of other galaxies—continues to travel away from its point of origin, the Big Bang where it all began. But scientists theorize that some day in the unimaginable future, the universe will cease to expand. At precisely that moment, what's called critical mass will be achieved as gravity starts to assert itself and begins to rejoin all the celestial bodies into a common point. Sounding more like science fiction than an actual scientific theory based on empirical evidence, this might seem altogether inconceivable. But the truth can be more bizarre than what any pulp writer could ever conjure. In the *Atomic Edition*, Critical Mass also marks a turning of sorts. From this point on, the levels get intricately more complex, the puzzles more perplexing, and the structures more challenging.

## MAPS AND ROUTE

Figures 8.26 and 8.27 lay out the highly modular structure of Critical Mass.

## THE GOODS

You have plenty of weapons and power-ups at your beck and call in this level. If you value your life and want to fulfill your mission, you'll be ever so grateful for each small mercy. Look at Table 8.17 and count your blessings.

| TABLE 8.17: THE GOODS IN CRITICAL MASS | | |
| --- | --- | --- |
| **WEAPONS** | **AMMO** | **POWER-UPS** |
| 2 shotguns | 2 cases | 2 portable medkits |
| 2 ripper chainguns | 4 cases | 4 atomic health units |
| 1 RPG launcher | 1 case | 1 holoduke |
| 1 shrinker/expander | 1 crystal | 1 scuba gear |
| 1 devastator | 1 case | 2 armors |

*(Continued on next page)*

*(Continued from previous page)*

| WEAPONS | AMMO | POWER-UPS |
|---|---|---|
| 1 freezethrower | 1 charge | 1 steroid flask |
| 2 laser trip bombs | | 1 NVG |
| 2 pipe bomb cases | | 1 pair of boots |

## BLAZING THROUGH CRITICAL MASS

Highly compartmentalized and perilous in the extreme, Critical Mass is strung together from myriad types of rooms and enclosures. This rather eclectic level lies adjacent to the ocean. In Critical Mass, you'll find everything from crate warehouses and exploding rooms, to a crushing spiral staircase and even a pool equipped with huge pressing metal plates designed to flatten anything or anyone that happens to fall in. There's also a large power generator that is half sunk in liquid chemicals. Finally, if you survive and manage to make it to the outside, you'll get to view a large cruiser not too far from shore. The cruiser is your ticket out of Critical Mass and onto the next level.

> **TIP**
> To reach the chaingun ammo, you'll have to climb the highest crate in the middle of the floor, and then hop from there. To reach the Devastator ammo, climb the same crate, but jump toward the crate in the southwest corner (by the staircase).

### Storm the Crate Room

The unloading dock to the north is your entry point into Critical Mass. You are about to step inside a dark storage area guarded by fearless pig cops and an enforcer or two. Even if your arsenal is somewhat depleted, you'll soon have a chance to stock up on some first-necessity items. That's your intended goal in the storage area. Get all the goods you can.

1. **Clean out the parking lot and get in.** Be sure, especially if your ammo is low, to get the pipe bombs. And of course, don't ever pass up on the armor. Activate the switch near the door on the far right. Be prepared to drop a bomb at the feet of the enforcer, back away, and detonate.

2. **Grab everything in sight.** Work your way around and over the various crates, and take everything that's rightfully yours: an atomic health unit, a couple of laser trip bombs, and chaingun and Devastator ammo.

**FIGURE 8.26**: Plan your moves carefully, learn where to find the goods you need, and avoid the multiple traps in Critical Mass.

Pipe Bombs

Armor

Atomic Health Unit

Chaingun Ammo

Pipe Bombs NVG

RPG Ammo

Δ Red Keycard

Shrinker Crystal

Freezethrower

RPG

Atomic Health Unit

Devastator Holoduke Expander Ammo

Yellow Keycard Δ

Blue Keycard Δ

Chaingun Ammo

Chaingun Ammo Armor Shells

Laser Trip Bombs (2)

Portable Medkit

Protective Boots

Steroids

**FIGURE 8.27:** Critical Mass reaches intensity plateaus not seen before in other versions of *Duke Nukem*.

3. **Climb the circular stairs.** Once you've cleaned out the storage area, proceed to the staircase at the south end. Ready for some heat?

## Living Through a Massive Explosion

The next room in Critical Mass is the first in a series of perilous passages, where you stand to get seriously hurt and possibly die—if not by the onerous onslaughts of your enemies, then by the cleverly set traps located at various points. Once you open up the door at the end of the spiral staircase, you can't turn back. You must step up the action as the heat goes mercurial.

1. **Step in if you dare.** Push the door open decisively, and step inside a room bathed in red light with computer panels on its north and south walls.

2. **Don't panic, but run like a Duke.** Ignore the shaking floor and the rumbles of imminent explosions. Take the chaingun and start firing at the enforcer as you dash toward the east end of the room. As you run across the room, heavy explosives go off, completely destroying the room and engulfing it in flames. Once the explosions start, you have scarce sec-

   onds to reach the east side of the room, where a thick metallic door is beginning to close. Sneak under the door and shield yourself from the danger.

3. **Don't sing victory yet.** Apparently sealed off from the world, you won't be lonely for long. After you've had a second or two to catch your breath, a protector drone pops up from behind a door on the north side. Be ready for him. If you managed to get the chaingun earlier, you can simply douse him with loads of lead the instant you see his likeness.

## Getting Through a Tight Squeeze

Having survived the exploding passage and the protector drone's rage, you can continue southward on your trek. But you must keep your senses sharp because the next two areas are filled with treachery and imminent danger. First, there's the green pool. The second you step in, two gigantic metal slabs start to close in on you. Your only escape is to activate a sunken switch that opens a door along the wall, letting you escape. Then there's the matter of the metallic corridor. It seems dead calm at first, but once you reach the end, the lights go out and the protector drones come out to play.

1. **Jump through the grill.** Crouch along the floor and find the metal grill at the south end. It will be completely dark, unless you have the NVGs handy. Throw caution to the wind and jump in. Feeling like a morsel at the end of a hook, you'll immediately bait the octabrains to come to you.

2. **Don't fight them, just get out.** Normally you could take on the octabrains. But you can't stop the encroaching slabs. So, instead, look for the switch along the bottom of the north wall. Activate it and then swim as fast as you can in the opposite direction. Surface, and jump inside the door, hopefully just in time to turn around and see the slabs come together and hear the squish of flattened alien flesh.

3. **Reap a few goods for your trouble.** Look around the small enclosure you entered. Waste no time in taking the scuba gear and the pipe bombs. Then open the door to an eerily quiet, long metallic corridor.

4. **Ready your weapon and weather another protector drone storm.** Walk toward the end of the corridor and take the chaingun ammo. In a second or two, the lights will go off and the walls of the corridor will come open to let out a couple of lithe and lethal protector drones. Turn your chaingun on them uninterruptedly until they're both lying in their own green fluids.

## Move West and Get the Blue Keycard

The path ahead of you is certainly shorter now, but still not uncomplicated. You must reach the computer room at the far southwest corner of Critical Mass to score the blue keycard, the first one of the level.

1. **Cross the electrical field room.** Open the door at the end of the corridor into a room lit by a buzzing current flowing from the ceiling to the electrically charged floor. You might experience health drains if an electrical discharge goes through your body. So, take refuge in either of the computer panel areas on the sides. While there, collect the protective boots and a holoduke.

2. **Raid another storage room.** Ride the small elevator at the end of the electrical room. Get out in the darkened storage space, and begin your alien butt-kicking routine. Be sure to grab the laser trip bombs, the steroids, and the portable medkit.

3. **Reach the computer room, and get the blue keycard.** Open the folding gate into a bright hallway. The sight out of the windows is that of a red sky and a dark sea. Walk past the windows into a white tile room with computer consoles covering one wall. Pause to take the shotgun, grab the armor, and kick the trash can to collect even more chaingun ammo. Then liberate the blue keycard.

4. **Press the right switches.** Find the row of four switches on the north side of the room. Activate the first, third, and fourth switches (from left to right). Then push the small compartment to the right and take the blue keycard.

## Going for a Plunge in the Central Reactor

The central reactor is the largest part of Critical Mass. The half-submerged, churning apparatus is the only object you can see in the large cylindrical enclosure. It glows with the characteristic greenish power halo of much of the alien machinery. Besides housing the reactor, this enclosure also holds an alien nest. And where there are eggs, you can count on at least a few egg nannies—the dreadful octabrains. The red keycard is submerged at the bottom of the reactor, as is an atomic health unit. You need them both.

1. **Blow away the eggs and octabrains.** Use the blue keycard to open the door and, although it's hard to see, aim to the south and then to the north walls. You're likely to hit eggs and octabrains. The NVGs would be a true blessing in these conditions. Cut your work in half by blowing up

the C-9 tanks on the north wall. Get the RPG launcher from the north wall, near where the C-9 tanks blew up.

2. **Explore the depths.** Jump in. Take the ripper chaingun from the hub of the reactor. Then dive for the bottom. Look for a row of circular switches. Time your movement with the circling reactor columns. Then activate all three switches.

3. **Clutch the yellow card, and absorb the atomic health unit.** Wait a few seconds as the reactor's column ascends slowly. Under each column, you'll find what you came here to get.

4. **Emerge and head north.** Surface and start north. You're close to the end, but you must still find the red keycard.

## In Search of the Red Card

The last leg of this journey is under way. There are only a couple of places to explore now. Still, you'll be contending with the overly ebullient protector drones, an assault commander, and some vengeful enforcers. Defeat the protector drones in the hallway. Violate the commander's quarters. Then, once you get past the last of the enforcers, you're free to sail to other ports.

1. **Duel the protector drones.** Grab the freezethrower in the small booth before opening the lock at the north end of the hallway. Wage war on the protector drones. Just freeze and shatter them. Then it's on to the commander's quarters.

2. **Salute the commander.** Use the yellow keycard, and don't let the commander pull rank on you. If you have any ice left, ice him. Otherwise dispose of him as you best see fit. Take the red keycard from the bookshelves and the shrinker crystal from the ex-commander's desk.

### Your Boat Has Come In

A small reception-type area is all that's between you and the sea. You only have but to open a couple of doors and then step out to smell the salty air and feel the gentle sea breezes.

1.  **Annihilate the enforcers.** You've come too far to let an enforcer or two stand in your way. Open the door with the red keycard and pummel anything that moves. Face the last door and open it.

2.  **Crouch under the door and run for your life.** The second you cross the threshold, the entire structure will collapse. Perhaps you caused this by raising the reactors earlier. Who knows? Who cares! But there's going to be a spectacular display of pure destructive power in a second. So dash off for safety.

3.  **Spot the boat and wave good-bye.** Crawl among the rubble and find the beckoning red exit switch atop a large slab of cement. Take a running jump onto the slab. Look searchingly at the boat, and then smash the switch without a second thought.

## COVERT DETAILS

The gravity of the situation in Critical Mass can't be overly stated. Learn a few of its secrets and lessen the weight on your shoulders. Table 8.18 lifts the veil from the secrets.

### TABLE 8.18: THE SECRETS IN CRITICAL MASS

| AREA IN LEVEL | SECRET ITEM | HOW TO GET IT |
| --- | --- | --- |
| Small metallic room between the pool and the corridor at east end | portable medkit | Push the computer console and take the portable medkit from the secret compartment. |
| Central reactor | RPG launcher | Blow up the C-9 tanks at the north end of the walkway circling the reactor. Crawl into the hole made by the explosion and take the heavy gun. |

*(Continued on next page)*

*(Continued from previous page)*

| AREA IN LEVEL | SECRET ITEM | HOW TO GET IT |
|---|---|---|
| Reactor room | freezethrower devastator ammo | You must have the jetpack from your exploits in a previous level, as there are no jetpacks in Critical Mass. Enter the reactor room and activate the jetpack. Fly over the pool of ooze below to reach a small flat area along the east side, high up on the wall. |
| Booby-trapped control room | Sector 7-G | This is a small, secret room directly across from the spiral staircase. The door opens automatically after the explosions and seconds before the ceiling starts caving in. To reach this room, first run to the east end to shield yourself from the explosions. Then sneak out under the closing door, and dash to the southwest corner of the control room, where the Sector 7-G secret door should be open. Get inside before the ceiling falls in on you. |

# DERELICT

At the end of Critical Mass, you spot a huge ship in the distance. Here, in Derelict, you get to board it. But don't expect a leisurely cruise or a guest appearance on the *Love Boat*. In fact, by the looks of the black, gooey ocean, and the name "Valdeez-2" stenciled on the side of the ship, this is an enormous, leaky oil tanker. Indeed, you're about to discover that conditions are less than ship-shape aboard this hardly seaworthy vessel.

The back area of the Valdeez-2 consists of five overlapping floors of varying dimensions. The first three floors all have storage spaces, but the top floor houses the navigation bridge. The floor next to the bottom is designated for the captain's quarters, the barracks, and the mess hall. At the bottom of all this lies the large engine room.

Pushing forward, you find a drum-processing area complete with a conveyor belt network. Finally, the front section of the ship contains a pool of highly toxic chemicals on the port (left) side and a pool of crude oil on the starboard (right) side. As for the crew, they're murderous . . . and mutinous. You'll have to watch your butt at every turn. Remember, everybody around is posing as a sailor. Ahoy! Hit the deck fighting.

## MAPS AND ROUTE

Because of its multiple overlapping floors, a wire frame image of Derelict would be confusing at best. For simplicity and clarity, Figure 8.28 shows you the top, bottom, and middle portions of Derelict's Valdeez-2. And to help you locate weapons and power-ups, consult Figure 8.29. It shows you different slices and views of the floors you'll visit.

## THE GOODS

Although the Valdeez-2 is no pirate ship, it contains enough booty in Derelict to keep you searching for a good while. And you'll need everything you can get. Table 8.19 lists the booty up close.

### TABLE 8.19: THE GOODS IN DERELICT

| WEAPONS | AMMO | POWER-UPS |
|---|---|---|
| 3 shotguns | 12 cases | 2 portable medkits |
| 4 ripper chainguns | 11 cases | 11 atomic health units |
| 3 RPG launchers | 4 cases | 1 holoduke |
| 2 shrinker/expanders | 10 crystals | 1 scuba gear |
| 1 devastator | 3 charges | 4 armors |
| 1 freezethrower | | 4 steroid flasks |
| 2 laser trip bombs | | 3 NVGs |
| 4 pipe bomb cases | | 2 pairs of boots |

## BLAZING THROUGH DERELICT

Derelict pushes the design envelope by re-creating a cross section of a large industrial oil tanker. Its multifloor levels are intricate and sophisticated. To solve the puzzle of

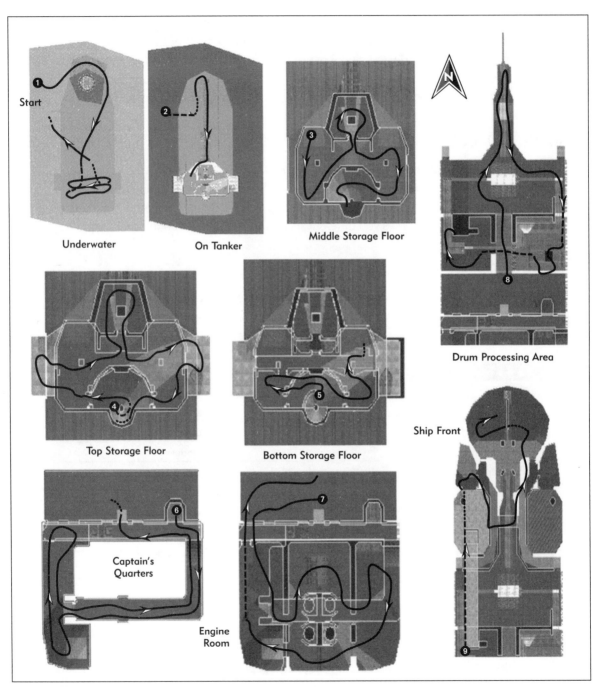

Start

Underwater

On Tanker

Middle Storage Floor

Drum Processing Area

Top Storage Floor

Bottom Storage Floor

Ship Front

Captain's Quarters

Engine Room

FIGURE 8.28: Study your maps, plot your path, and keep from walking the plank.

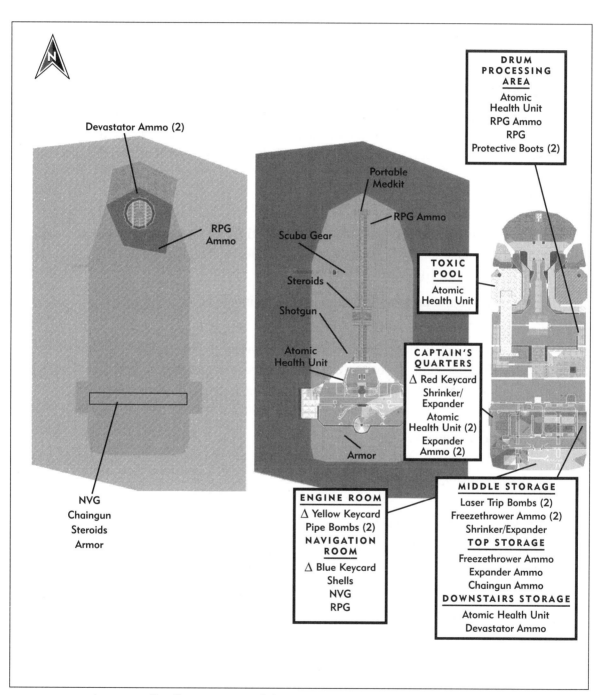

**DRUM PROCESSING AREA**
Atomic Health Unit
RPG Ammo
RPG
Protective Boots (2)

Devastator Ammo (2)

RPG Ammo

Portable Medkit

RPG Ammo

Scuba Gear

Steroids

Shotgun

Atomic Health Unit

**TOXIC POOL**
Atomic Health Unit

**CAPTAIN'S QUARTERS**
Δ Red Keycard
Shrinker/Expander
Atomic Health Unit (2)
Expander Ammo (2)

Armor

NVG
Chaingun
Steroids
Armor

**ENGINE ROOM**
Δ Yellow Keycard
Pipe Bombs (2)
**NAVIGATION ROOM**
Δ Blue Keycard
Shells
NVG
RPG

**MIDDLE STORAGE**
Laser Trip Bombs (2)
Freezethrower Ammo (2)
Shrinker/Expander
**TOP STORAGE**
Freezethrower Ammo
Expander Ammo
Chaingun Ammo
**DOWNSTAIRS STORAGE**
Atomic Health Unit
Devastator Ammo

**FIGURE 8.29:** Arm yourself well at every step of the way to avoid a most embarrassing spill in Derelict.

Derelict, you'll have to visit practically every chamber and run from the bow to the stern and from port to starboard.

## Scrape the Bottom

You start Derelict splashing in the thick slick created by the leaking Valdeez-2. Your first concern is to get on board and get cranking. But, if your ammo and weaponry are somewhat low, you can dive for more. You can, in fact, board a narrow enclosure under the hull of the ship, where some useful stuff might help make your cruise just a bit more survivable.

1. **Swim toward the front of the ship and then go under.** To help guide you, look for the large, glowing, green pillar that connects the ship to the floor of the ocean.

2. **Scrape the bottom.** Swim around the column's base to get some Devastator ammo and an RPG launcher.

3. **Swim below the stern rear area.** Kick toward the rear end of the ship. (If you're running low on air, you might want to surface for a breath.) Locate a small entry point by the light it projects in the otherwise pitch-black waters.

4. **Get the goods.** Jump up into the narrow space. Take the armor, chain-gun, steroids, and NVG. Then dive back into the water and get back near the point where you started Derelict.

## Get On Board and Then Inside

Now that you're better armed, you can try to get on the ship. Without a jetpack, there's only one other way of doing it. And once on board, the inside of the ship will seem air-tight and impenetrable. *It is*. Until you find one of the two secret entrances.

1. **Let the crane lift you aboard.** Find a small square space on the port side of the ship. Float in place and wait for the crane to pluck you from the tepid waters and drop you onto the deck.

2. **Reach the front side of the bridge.** First, run all the way forward and jump on top of the platform at the very beginning of the long network of pipes and tubing that splits the deck right down the middle. Take the portable medkit and run toward the rear until you reach the bridge area.

3. **Get inside.** Jump around the corner of the bridge to land on the elevated area above the deck's port side. Then just jump through the window. You're in the middle of three nearly identical floors. You'll soon visit the top and bottom chambers. But for now, explore the middle floor.

## The Middle Floor

After breaking inside the ship, you'll find yourself in the middle of three nearly identical floors connected by a spiral staircase. Like the other two floors, the middle floor has plenty of storage space. Unlike the other two levels, the ceiling here is comparatively low. To help you keep your bearings, refer to Figure 8.29.

1. **Clean up on the middle floor.** Run around the port and starboard sides to collect two laser trip bombs. Also look inside the enclosure toward the bow end. There are two expander ammo packs and a shrinker/expander.

2. **Get out and climb the stairs.** Take one of the small side doors to reach a semicircular area with a staircase that continues both above and below your floor. You want to go up to the top floor and get the blue keycard.

## The Top Floor

Were it not for the fact that the bridge is actually on this floor, the top chamber is a virtual replica of the middle floor. And, speaking of the bridge, you must blast your way there to get the blue keycard. With this key, you'll be able to reach the bottom floor and the captain's quarters.

1. **Explore the wings.** Besides the blue keycard, there are a few choice items in each of the wings on this floor. To the port side, you'll find freezer ammo (on top of the crates) and expander ammo as well. The

large crate on the starboard side is surrounded by C-9 tanks. Blow up the entire crate and take the chaingun.

2. **Storm the bridge and take the blue keycard.** Find the small doorway to the bridge and enter. The blue keycard is right behind the wheel (see Figure 8.30). While you're here, take the shotgun and the NVGs on top of the computer console. The partition on the starboard side hides an RPG launcher on top of an improvised bed. Run toward the bottom floor when the bridge inspection is over.

### The Bottom Floor

The bottom floor is dingy and dark, serving no other purpose besides storage. However, the narrow hallway outside this floor connects you to an elevator that works only if you have the blue keycard. The elevator descends into a large area consisting of the captain's quarters, the barracks, and the main hall. The captain's quarters contain the red keycard, which you must have to enter the engine room, even farther below.

**FIGURE 8.30:** The navigation bridge houses the blue keycard and other useful items.

1. **Take what you can.** Come out onto the bottom floor and look in the port side for the holoduke, hidden behind the oil drums. Look for some expander ammo on the starboard side too.

2. **Get to the hallway.** Use either door on the port or starboard sides to enter the narrow hallway and go forward, toward the front of the ship.

3. **Unlock the elevator.** Unlock the security lock with the blue keycard. Your next step is to assault the captain's quarters on the floor below.

## The Captain's Quarters

The floor sandwiched between the three storage chambers and the engine room encompasses the captain's quarters, the barracks, and the mess hall. The captain keeps the red keycard under watchful vigilance. You must enter his plush pad and take the card. Along the way, you can enter the mess hall and the barracks for some spirited fighting and to get a few useful items.

1. **Take the long hallway.** Coming out of the elevator, look for the ascending stairs. Follow the L-shaped hallway past the barracks and the mess hall entrances.

2. **Grab the red keycard.** Step into the carpeted room. In the bedroom to your left, you'll find an armor. The entertainment area has a wet bar, a desk, and a cushy couch. Pick up the shells as you move toward the desk, and reach for the red keycard.

3. **Score big behind the tomes.** Push against the wall clock over the desk. Then look behind you at the receding bookshelf. Behind it, you'll find nothing less than the shrinker/expander, two atomic health units, and two expander packs. Take the loot and go use your newly acquired red keycard to access the engine room below.

## In the Engine Room

The engine room at the very bottom of the rear section houses the heart, such as it is, of the Valdeez-2. A set of enormous thumping pistons and a massive engine block dominate the central area. On the starboard side, you find a storage area with a few crates and oil drums. This is also where the yellow keycard is hidden, among the crates. With the yellow card, you'll be ready to penetrate into the drum-processing area.

1. **Get down in the engine.** Open the red security lock and step onto a ramp leading to the bottom. Climb over the engine block to score a chaingun.

2. **Get the yellow keycard.** Run around into the storage area, and climb among the boxes. The yellow keycard is on the second tier of boxes. On the top crate, you'll find two cases of pipe bombs. Get back upstairs and head for the elevator in the middle of the hallway. You're going into the drum-processing area.

## In the Drum-Processing Area

The drum-processing area—an automated system of conveyor belts, pulleys, and cranes moving oil drums from one place to another—spans most of the mid-section of the Valdeez-2. The drum-processing area is itself divided into two halves. The forward half (toward the bow), except for the conveyor and cranes running down its middle, is completely open. The back half (toward the stern) has two distinct areas. On the starboard side, there are various crates piled together. On the port side, there's a slightly elevated area. This is the area you ultimately want to reach. To get there, you can simply ride the cranes and belts, or take a few shortcuts. Once you reach the port side of the drum-processing area, you'll soon be on your way toward the front part of the ship, and you hope, to the end of a hard, long ride in a leaky boat.

1. **Raid the place.** Open the yellow security lock and pounce into action. Run forward toward the end of the conveyor belt, straight ahead toward the front of the processing area. You'll find an atomic health unit. Get it, and on the way back, pick up the RPG ammo as well.

2. **Reach the crates.** Run to the starboard side and hop on the conveyor belt. Let the crane pick you up and deposit you near the crated area. Climb over the crates and find the hidden space over the top crate, where you can get an RPG launcher and a pair of protective boots.

3. **Reach the port side.** In two jumps you should be able to reach the elevated port side. From the crates, hop onto the dividing wall with the yellow and black stripes. From there, it's just another jump.

4. **Find the chemical aqueduct.** Look for the protective boots near the end of the conveyor belt. This cue tells you're steps away from the highly noxious chemicals that you must traverse to reach your final destination (see Figure 8.31).

## In the Front End of the Ship

A steep duct carrying deadly chemicals provides the only access forward. And that's exactly where you want to go. Therefore, you have no choice but to endure some temporary discomfort, and possibly a very painful—but mercifully fast—death if you ever want to leave your Valdeez-2 days behind. The port side in this area is dominated by

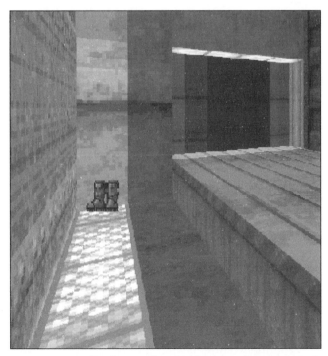

**FIGURE 8.31:** Don't set a foot inside the noxious chemicals aqueduct without appropriate footwear. Didn't your mother always tell you to wear your galoshes?!

a highly toxic, greenish pool of extremely dangerous chemicals. A similar pool on the starboard side holds crude oil. Your goal is to reach the switch that unlocks the front end. Then it's up to your skill and fighting ability to see you through.

1.  **Don the boots and go, go, go.** Slip your boots on and crawl through the small space by the conveyor belt. You'll be trudging into a steep current of very deadly chemicals. So hasten your step.

2.  **Drop into the pool but get out just as quickly.** At the top of the steep climb, there's a sudden drop-off. Fall into the life-draining liquid and do your best to move forward to reach an area where you can stand.

3.  **Go starboard to reach the key switch.** Move into the adjacent hallway, and follow its path as it goes aft and then veers toward the starboard side. Turn forward and stay in the hallway, going past the pool of crude, until you come upon a door with a switch and a barrel blocking the way. Blow up the barrel, push the switch, and step onto a narrow platform overlooking a large empty space, the very front end of the Valdeez-2.

> **TIP**
>
> Before taking the perilous ascent into the noxious chemical ramp, check your health status. If it's below 80, you'll want to jump into the pool and get out just as fast. However, if your health is higher than 80, you can probably risk losing some health to get the atomic health unit at the bottom of the pool of noxious chemicals.

4.  **Reach the floor level and wave good-bye.** Stand on one of the two small elevators by the edge of the walkway and activate it. Fight your way inside the small water opening. Sink to the very bottom, and look for the exit switch. This ship is sinking, but you don't have to go down with it.

## COVERT DETAILS

Even for the environmentally indifferent, a ride in the Valdeez-2 is no pleasure cruise. On the other hand, a ship this size is bound to contain a few interesting passages and secrets. Table 8.20 makes you aware of what these are.

## TABLE 8.20: THE SECRETS IN DERELICT

| AREA IN LEVEL | SECRET ITEM | HOW TO GET IT |
|---|---|---|
| TV room near the bar racks in the stern | shotgun | Jump behind the broken television set to pick up a chaingun. Then jump on top of the TV. A metal panel behind the armchair opens momentarily to make a shotgun available. |
| Captain's quarters | atomic health units (2) shrinker/expander expander pack | Climb over the captain's desk and punch the clock on the wall. Then grab the goods from behind the sinking bookshelves. |
| Crates area in the drum processing section | protective boots RPG launcher | Climb over the crates and drop by the south side. You'll find the RPG launcher and boots next to an open crate. |
| Narrow storage space under tanker | armor (2) chaingun steroids NVG | Swim under the tanker and kick toward the back of the ship. Look for a small opening in the hull. Access the narrow space and score. |
| Kitchen in the mess hall | portable medkit | Crouch down by the stove and activate the switch. A wall next to the stove will open so that you can take the portable medkit. |

# THE QUEEN

So *that's* who's been laying all those eggs—the alien's very own matriarch and mother queen. She who can lay protector drones by the droves. She whose sole motivation is nothing less than to see her species and its allies spread vast and wide to the far corners of the galaxy. Is she to be *blamed* for following a mother's instincts and nursing her nefarious offspring?

The maddening drive to survive and procreate, even if it means the extinction and decimation of other species, is something humankind can easily relate to. Maybe the aliens and their queen are doing nothing more than serving as mirrors. Could they be showing us an extreme outcome of what could happen to us when our desire goes unabated as we divide, conquer, and destroy everything we don't understand?

Perhaps Duke Nukem can find the strength and the tenacity to see this mission to the end. You wonder and can only hope that, as Duke Nukem, *you* can rise to the title of savior of humanity and all-around cool guy.

## MAPS AND ROUTE

The Queen's symmetry and balance are almost perfect. So your moves, execution, and bravado should elevate several notches for you to contend with the mother of all aliens. Figures 8.32 and 8.33 show you what you're in store for if you choose to visit the queen in her own palace.

## THE GOODS

Given the fact that you're about to face the mother of all aliens, you'll be glad to know the supply of armament and weaponry is up to par to help you meet the formidable task before you. Table 8.21 shows you the instruments at your disposal.

### TABLE 8.21: THE GOODS IN THE QUEEN

| WEAPONS | AMMO | POWER-UPS |
|---|---|---|
| 1 shotgun | 11 cases | 3 portable medkits |
| 2 ripper chainguns | 13 cases | 5 atomic health units |
| 4 RPG launchers | 10 cases | 1 scuba gear |
| 2 devastators | 18 cases | 3 jetpacks |
| 1 freezethrower | 3 charges | 5 armors |
| 2 laser trip bombs | | 1 steroid flask |
| 8 pipe bomb cases | | 3 pairs of boots |

## BLAZING THROUGH THE QUEEN

The Queen spreads symmetrically from a long, oval-shaped network of corridors and tunnels into eastern and western octagonal chambers where some horrific battles await you. Your entire energies must be focused on securing passage to The

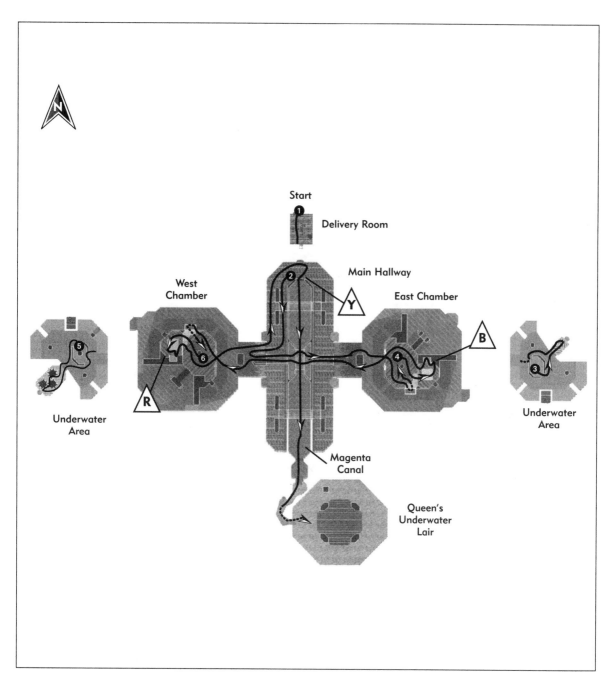

**FIGURE 8.32:** The layout and design of The Queen might look simple and straightforward, but wait until you set foot in it.

**FIGURE 8.33**: While you might not be dressed for this royal encounter, you can accessorize with the proper power-ups.

Queen's underwater breeding grounds. After that, use any energy left in your reserves to dethrone the queen and destroy the evil alien empire. Easily said, isn't it?

### In the Main Hall

Your main purpose during your initial run of the main hall is simply to build your arsenal so that you can go do battle and reap the secrets from the wings. Oriented north and south, the main hall is really four narrow, undulating hallways. A magenta canal runs down the middle through the entire length. The canal is toxic in the extreme. It can render a pair of protective boots useless in seconds. But the canal also leads to the queen's burrows. The magenta canal will remain inaccessible until you activate the right switches in each of the wings, provided you find the right keys.

1. **Beam to the main hall.** At the start of The Queen, you'll find yourself in a vaguely familiar room. Yes, you remember! This is the same alien delivery room the undercover military operative filmed before his demise. No use waiting for someone to give you a cigar and announce it's a boy. Head straight for the teleporter at the south side of the room.

2. **Reach the blocked entrance to the west wing.** Materializing at the north end of the main hall, race around the east hallway, killing, maiming, and otherwise disposing of the scores of troopers, captains, and enforcers. Eventually, you'll run into what looks like an opening into the west wing. You'll notice that access is denied just as the east wing, too, is momentarily out of reach. Find the narrow door with the glowing blue spots and go up the stairs.

3. **Reach the central column, and unlock the access to the east wing.** Proceeding east in the elevated corridor, you will come on a small, unassuming column smack dab in the center of the main hall and, for that matter, of the entire installation. Look for the set of three switches on the east side of the column and activate the second and third ones (from left to right). Then dash for the east wing, which is now accessible.

### In the East Wing

Roughly octagonal, the east wing poses a major challenge because of the quantity and the quality of alien folk who make this their home. The central structure sits surrounded by water on almost all sides. This structure houses two key chambers and gives access to the underwater area. The blue keycard lies in the depths below, behind an impenetrable metal door. Your first task is to unlock that door. Then you need to make your way below, and get past two heavy pistons to reach the blue keycard. With it, you'll be able to access a chamber above, where by simply throwing a switch, you'll remove one of the barriers blocking the magenta canal.

1. **Dominate the periphery.** Alien greeters will be at your neck the second you step into the east wing. Placate the troopers, captains, and enforcers so that you can concentrate on entering the central structure. But do take a little time to visit an elevated duct in the northeast corner. It's crammed full of weapons and ammo. You'll need them all.

2. **Open the main door and get ready for the fireworks.** The heavy adversaries inside the chamber include a Battlelord sentry and a protective drone. You might do best if you battle them from the outside, but the drone could retreat underwater to guard the keycard.

3. **Uncover the door to the blue keycard.** When you're able to go inside, climb onto the platform at the south end and open the large door in front of you. Deal with the enforcer and then hop inside the small rectangular pool. Sinking near the bottom, you'll find a recessed area. Throw the square

**N O T E**

The duct also connects to the inside of the chamber. From the inside, you can also get out through the same duct, but you won't see it, as it becomes an illusory wall.

metallic switch, and then look to your right along the wall for a circular organic switch. Activate it (see Figure 8.34). If you look north through the dirty glass of the pool, you'll see a large area come open on the opposing wall. Climb out of the pool.

4. **Get the blue keycard.** Run for the central wet area and dive in. Head straight for the area you uncovered below. Of course, you'll encounter serious opposition from the many octabrains and slimers in the pool. On reaching the entrance, you'll be able to see a narrow enclosure where the blue keycard is kept. However, blocking your progress are two massive pillars moving up and down, threatening to flatten you the second you step in. Notice, too, the set of switches along the sides of the wall. Time your advance into the room with the pumping action of the pillars to get near each switch and activate them all. This will cause the keycard's enclosure to widen enough so that you can actually slip through and get it. After grabbing the keycard, get back to the surface.

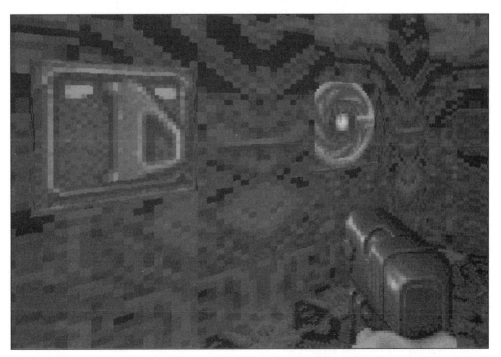

**FIGURE 8.34:** Activate these submerged switches to open the underwater chamber where the blue keycard is kept.

5. **Use the blue keycard if you dare.** Walk up to the chamber on the southeast side, inside the central structure; climb onto the narrow platform; and throw open the door. Back off immediately, as you will be awakening a Battlelord sentry. Use the pillar in the middle of the structure to guard against his onslaughts and retaliate in kind. Then get up on the elevated chamber and use the blue keycard. Another smaller chamber will open up. Walk in there and activate the switch by the monitor, which, incidentally, shows a barrier as it lifts in the magenta canal. Now it's time to conquer the west wing.

## Back in the Main Hall

1. **Reach the central column again.** Trace your steps back into the main column above the magenta canal in the main hall. Then look on the west side of the column and activate switches two and three (from left to right). Use the nearby monitor to see the doors lift from the west wing chamber.

2. **Get to the west wing.** As you hear the heavy door lifting, run across the corridor to get inside the west wing.

## In the West Wing

Like its eastern counterpart, the west wing also is octagonal, has a central structure surrounded by water, and sits above a deep underwater area. Your mission here is similar in nature. Penetrate an underwater room and collect the red keycard. Then get back inside the main chamber where you can use it and thus uncover the yellow keycard. You also have the opportunity to press the switch that removes the last barrier in the magenta canal, which grants you access to the queen's lair. The yellow keycard will let you open the canal.

1. **Take over the circumference.** Secure the peripheral areas, and collect every useful item you can get your hands on. Visit the elevated duct at the southwest corner to score a mini-arsenal. Then turn your attention toward the central structure.

2. **Demolish the insiders.** Open the structure's gate, and dispense every form of punishment you're capable of.

3. **Go for a dunk in a small pool.** Locate the narrow platform along the north wall and open it. Just as in the east wing, hop into the small square pool, and activate two switches below. You're opening the gate to the submerged room where the red keycard lies unclaimed. Get out and dive again by the wet area in the middle of the structure.

4. **Reach the red keycard's underwater chamber.** Pound on the octabrains mercilessly, and try to conserve your air for the careful maneuvering required of you to get the red keycard. Coming on the entrance of the chamber, you'll see a series of spinning cogs making the entry almost impossible (see Figure 8.35). Not only that, but you'll notice that the enclosure where the keycard is kept isn't wide enough for you to swim through. That's where the switches along the walls of the spinning cogs come in.

**FIGURE 8.35:** Negotiate the cogs and turn on all switches to widen the opening to the compartment containing the red keycard.

5. **Get the red keycard.** Being very careful not to get caught in the cogs, get as close as you can to each of the switches on the left and right sides and activate them. Then back up a little bit and advance into the cogs when you see a gray area where a cog *tooth* is missing. Moving inside this space and swimming steadily forward, you'll reach the other side of the chamber. Activate the last of the remaining switches, and slip through the widening enclosure to claim the red keycard.

6. **Surface and use the red keycard.** Get back above water, and climb the narrow platform on the northwest side of the central structure. Open the door to face the wrath of another Battlelord sentry. Step above and use the red keycard on the security lock to open an adjacent chamber. Step in, grab the yellow keycard, and push the last switch to remove all blockages from the entrance to the queen's domain. Knowing what awaits, lose not another second and scramble back to the main hall.

### Up the Magenta Canal

With all the keycards in your possession and having pushed all the right switches, you're headed for the last and most daring stretch: an actual showdown with the Missus and, boy, are you in for it. Once back in the main hall, the yellow keycard will open the door into the magenta canal. The rest is up to you. Until now, humanity has counted on you. Why should it be any different today?

**WARNING**

Make your time in the magenta canal as brief as you can. The viscous substance is lethal beyond any level encountered before. Flying or jumping won't help. The protective boots will last you a couple of breaths, perhaps.

1. **Use the yellow keycard.** At the north end of the main hall, near your original entry point, place the yellow keycard squarely in its socket. Then turn around and watch the magenta canal radiate its noxious glow.

2. **Traverse the canal as fast as your boots can carry you.** As soon as your big toe touches the magenta substance, you'll see and feel the

liquid eating right through your boots. Your boots were made for walkin', but in this case, you must practically fly to the end of the canal if you want to have a shred of health left and be somewhat presentable when you make the queen's acquaintance.

### The Final Showdown

At the end of the magenta canal, you'll run into a rocky cave with a few goods in it. Also, you'll notice a little corner where water seeps through. This is the start of the queen's chambers. Once you submerge and reach the end of the tunnel, the nightmare will have only just begun and you'll have no choice but to let it all hang out.

1. **Swim to meet the queen.** Follow the broken rocky path to the point where you see a small water hole. Dive in and swim to the end of the underwater tunnel. Grab your heaviest weapon and wait a second or two for the wall in front of you to raise and reveal the queen in all her glory.

2. **Make the queen say, "Hail to the king."** As soon as the queen spots you, she'll begin pacing and working up energy blasts to lay a protector drone fetus. The fetus will sit still only for a second before springing into action at her mother's beckoning. Expect this pattern to repeat ad nauseam. Pound the queen as much as you can, while fending off the newborn drones. You might find a bit of respite in one of two cavities on the ceiling of the underwater chamber. The one near the northeast end even has an atomic health unit, a portable medkit, and a few rounds of ammo. Thank God for small mercies.

Eventually, get down before the chamber is thick with bouncing baby drones, and make your peace once and for all with the queen—which is a nice way of saying, "Blast her and her unborn to a very bloody hell!"

## COVERT DETAILS

Every castle has its share of secret doors and passageways. The Queen is no different in that respect. But the secrets in The Queen, as shown in Table 8.22, come at a mighty high price, which includes, but is not limited to the value of your own life.

## TABLE 8.22: THE SECRETS IN THE QUEEN

| AREA IN LEVEL | SECRET ITEM | HOW TO GET IT |
|---|---|---|
| Air duct at the northeast corner of the eastern chamber | pipe bombs<br>shotgun ammo<br>RPG ammo<br>devastator ammo<br>chaingun ammo | Jump inside the organic-looking orifice into the airduct and collect all the good things. |
| Air duct at the southwest corner of the western chamber | RPG ammo<br>pipe bombs<br>shotgun ammo<br>devastator ammo<br>chaingun ammo | Jump inside another organic-looking orifice into the airduct to claim the substantial loot. |
| Small cave on ceiling of Queen's underwater lair | atomic health unit<br>armor<br>portable medkit | Swim along the ceiling just east of the central kiosk-like structure. Look for a small square opening in the ceiling. Jump in and step out onto a small cave holding the precious items. |
| Look-out post on the north side of the entrance to the western chamber | devastator ammo (2) | Use the jetpack to lift yourself above the column and reach the look-out post. |
| Look-out post on the south side of the entrance to the western chamber | shotgun ammo (2) | Use the jetpack to lift yourself above the column and reach the look-out post. |
| Look-out post on the north side of the entrance to the east chamber | chaingun ammo (2) | Use the jetpack to lift yourself above the column and reach the look-out post. |
| Look-out post on the south side of the entrance to the east chamber | RPG ammo (2) | Use the jetpack to lift yourself above the column and reach the look-out post. |

# PART

# III

# Duke Nukem Cognoscenti

Now that you've blown your way through the dicey levels in the *Atomic Edition*, you might consider designing and creating your own ominous levels for Duke Nukem to conquer. In Part III, you get a cursory glimpse at the map and art editing tools, which the game's producers are all too happy to place in your hands—so long as you have the registered versions of *Duke Nukem 3D* and *Duke Nukem 3D: Atomic Edition*. To assist your learning as you play the game's levels or design your own, this part includes a list of all the game's cheat codes.

This section also gives you a chance to get up close and personal with Apogee and 3D Realms' real life bosses, Scott Miller and George Broussard. We have industry insider Geoff M. Keighley to thank for gracefully conducting and then sharing his insightful, no-holds barred interview with us. The interview was originally published online in *GameSlice Weekly* (SM) magazine. (Geoff is a writer and consultant in the publishing, television, and online industries who also serves as editor of *GameSlice Weekly*. He can be contacted through e-mail at: editor@gameslice.com.)

# Modifying Level Maps, Cheating, and Using Command Line Parameters

This chapter provides a brief introduction on using the game's Build engine to modify or create level maps; its counterpart, ArtEdit, for modifying the game's art elements; and cheat codes that allow you to play the game with immortality, so that you can delve even more deeply into the world of *Duke Nukem 3D*—if you dare!

You will also find a list of command line parameters that you can use to set up a variety of game options. A new and exciting feature in the *Atomic Edition* is AI play, in which you can inhabit levels with computer-generated and computer-controlled likenesses of Duke Nukem.

## MODIFYING LEVEL MAPS

The makers of the *Atomic Edition*, the ingenious, even wacky, programmers and developers at 3D Realms, want you to have fun. That's the primary reason why they breathed life into *Duke Nukem 3D* and the *Atomic Edition*. Taking fun one step further, they'd like you to be the master of your own gaming environment. That's why 3D Realms includes two programs—Build and ArtEdit—with the registered version of *Duke Nukem 3D* and the *Atomic Edition*. This chapter briefly describes Build and ArtEdit and provides some basic information for getting started with these sophisticated programs.

# WHAT IS BUILD?

Think of Build as a design or modeling tool that lets you create brand-new *Duke Nukem 3D* levels, essentially by modifying existing ones. Build is the front-end to 3D Realms' acclaimed Build engine, the powerhouse behind *Duke Nukem 3D*. This same engine will soon be deployed in upcoming games from 3D Realms, including *Shadow Warrior* and *Blood*.

While Build will appeal mostly to those with more than a passing interest in programming and level design, you can—if you have the patience and dedication—use Build to create your own levels and share them with your friends, or upload them for other dedicated Nukem gamers. Build lets you work in both 2D (top-down) and 3D views. The 2D view is ideal for laying out a level, which is composed mainly of walls, ceilings, and floors. Use this view to create sectors and other level divisions. The 3D view is better suited for working with textures and bitmaps. It lets you see your creations and changes immediately in real time. Although modifying levels can become quite complex, rudimentary adjustments, such as raising or lowering a wall, are fairly simple—as are other seemingly complex level-design operations.

## What Is ArtEdit?

ArtEdit is a useful program for viewing, importing, and altering the game's bitmap images. Although ArtEdit can be used as a stand-alone utility, it's typically called from Build whenever you press V to view the existing tiles for any given level.

# USING BUILD

Like all disciplines in the real world, including the fine arts, level-building in *Duke Nukem* might take a while to master. But those who feel the calling will find that, after some practice, the Build tool is extremely useful and fun. Maybe your creations won't hold a candle to the Eiffel Tower or surpass the Roman Coliseum, but you *might* surprise yourself and gain the admiration of your friends.

Your registered CD-ROMs for *Duke Nukem 3D* or *Duke Nukem 3D: Atomic Edition* contain an extensive help file, called BUILDHLP, that covers the fundamentals and some advanced techniques for using Build. It walks you through the first steps in creating a sector, and then it builds from that point. Although you will definitely need assistance from the help file to get started with Build, nothing will stop you from discovering the joy of building levels from scratch or modifying existing levels once you're familiar with the tool. Read Build's help file, and follow some of the examples to begin. And remember, 3D Realms is always looking for good talent!

# CHEAT CODES

Even the most daring players might need a little bit of help from time to time. That's why 3D Realms provides the cheat codes for the game. After all, why allow your frustration level to interfere with your fun? Like all good things, use the cheat codes sparingly. Save them for those moments when you really need them. Just keep in mind that some cheat codes really don't have a tremendously beneficial effect. They simply cause amusing messages to appear, or some interesting effects to occur. Cheat codes are also useful when you're play-testing your own levels while perfecting them.

To use the cheat codes, simply type the appropriate characters as you're playing a level. To turn off a cheat code, just type the code a second time. (The cheat codes are toggles.) Table 9.1 lists the various cheat codes you can use when playing *Duke Nukem 3D*.

## TABLE 9.1: THE *DUKE NUKEM 3D* CHEAT CODES

| CHEAT CODE | EFFECT |
| --- | --- |
| DNKROZ (or DNCORNHOLIO) | This code puts you in God mode. In this mode, you're in effect completely invulnerable and can face off opponents with no fear or danger of losing your life. Your health status will remain at a constant 100 percent the entire time. |
| DNSTUFF | This code gives you every weapon, power-up, and all the ammo you can carry. In addition, you get all of the keycards. |
| DNCLIP | Lets you walk through walls and other solid surfaces. Type DNCLIP a second time to turn "clipping" back on. |
| DNITEMS | This code gives you every power-up and keycard, but no weapons or ammo. |
| DNSCOTTY # ## | This code lets you warp to any episode and level. For example, DNSCOTTY 3 03 puts you in Flood Zone, the third level in Shrapnel City. (The spaces are important.) |
| DNHYPER | This code gives you steroids, so that you can run around like a madman and kick like a mule. |
| DNVIEW | This code turns on the *chase* view, where you can see yourself from behind, as though you were placing a camera behind you. |
| DNCASHMAN | After typing this code, press the spacebar to throw dollar bills around. This cheat code may not help you overcome your enemies or solve levels, but it infuses you with a lovely false sense of financial security. |

| CHEAT CODE | EFFECT |
|---|---|
| DNBETA | This code shows the message "Pirates Suck!" This is obviously an inside jest among the 3D Realms developers. |
| DNALLEN | This code shows the message "Buy Major Stryker," a not-so-subliminal message to promote a game in which level designer Allen Blum had a major part. |

# COMMAND LINE PARAMETERS

There are 22 commands you can use to alter the performance and the game play in *Duke Nukem 3D*. These command line parameters or *switches* let you tweak anything from speeding up the game and turning off the music, to adding computer-controlled Duke Nukem enemies. Because you must type these commands at the DOS prompt, they are called *command line parameters*.

As an example, consider this command line parameter to turn off the monsters: /m. To issue this command line parameter, you type it on the same line as the command to start the

> **NOTE**
> Be sure to run the program called DN3DHLP.EXE, included with the *Atomic Edition*, to read more in-depth information about the command line parameters.

game, which is DUKE3D. So, to start *Duke Nukem 3D* and turn off the monsters during play, you can type the following command at the DOS prompt:

```
duke3d /m
```

After you press Enter, the game begins as usual, but the aliens will all be out to lunch. You can roam freely throughout levels without any resistance by the alien invasion. All of the command line parameters listed and described in Table 9.2 are entered the same way as in this example.

### TABLE 9.2: *DUKE NUKEM 3D* COMMAND LINE PARAMETERS

| PARAMETER | FUNCTION |
| --- | --- |
| /? or simply ? | Opens a help screen that lists all the command line parameters and brief descriptions of their functions. |
| /l# | Starts the game at a specific level denoted by a number from 1 to 11 that you type in place of the #. |
| /v# | With the registered version of *Duke Nukem 3D* or the *Atomic Edition*, starts the game at a specific volume (episode) denoted by a number from 1 to 3 or 1 to 4, depending on the game's version. |
| /s# | Starts the game at a specific skill level, with 1 being the easiest, Piece of Cake skill level, and 4 being the hardest, the Damn I'm Good skill level. |
| /r | Turns on the demo recording feature, so you can record your play as a demo. You can watch your recorded demo the next time you start the game. It plays back automatically as the background demo you see before you start a game. |
| /dFILE | Starts the game using the demo file you specify. For instance, if you have recorded a demo called Mydemo.dmo, you can type duke3d /dMYDEMO to see the demo before you start the game. Notice that you don't have to include the file's extension. |
| /m | Turns off all monsters. |
| /ns | Turns off the sound effects completely, but not the music. |
| /nm | Turns off the music completely, but not the sound effects. |
| /t# | Starts the game with selected respawning game elements, denoted by a number or letter. Type 1 for respawning monsters, 2 for respawning weapons, 3 for respawning power-ups, or x if you want everything to respawn. |
| /c# | Starts a specific type of multiplayer game, denoted by a number. Type 1 for DukeMatch, 2 for Co-op, or 3 for DukeMatch without respawning players. |
| /q# | Starts a game with fake multiplayers. You can specify up to eight of them. Besides the presence of Duke's cool striking figure, this line parameter has no real value in a game. However, it can be used during level design to set up respawn locations. |
| /a | Applies artificial intelligence to any fake multiplayers you set up with the /q# parameter. The computer assumes control of the highly maneuverable and very fast fake Duke enemies. They are virtual clones of yourself, but their brains are silicon based. |
| /i# | Network mode is 1 for any number of players. |

| PARAMETER | FUNCTION |
|---|---|
| /f# | Sends fewer packets during multiplayer mode over a network or a modem. You should not use this command normally. It is intended for multiplayer networks such as TEN, which use fewer packets due to heavy traffic. |
| /gFILE | Starts a game with a specified "group" file to use for game play. The group file contains all the art, sound, and map elements that allow the environments to exist. The default group file is DUKE3D.GRP. |
| /u########## | Starts a game with a specified favorite weapon ordering. When a weapon runs out of ammo, the game checks and switches to the next most favorite weapon that contains ammo. The default order is 3425689071. |
| /# | Starts the game and loads and runs a previously saved game from one of the ten game slots. |
| /z | Allows the game to run when the computer has low memory (heavy disk input/output). |
| -map FILE | Starts a game with a specified user map. |
| -name NAME | Starts a multiplayer game with a specified player name. |
| -net | Informs the game to initiate a true multiplayer. |

# The Bosses of Apogee and 3D Realms Come Clean

Writer's Note: The following interview was conducted by Geoff M. Keighley, who besides writing and consulting in the interactive industry, serves as editor-in-chief of *GameSlice Weekly*, one of the best online game magazines to date, available on CompuServe (GO GAMESLICE) and on the Internet (http://www.gameslice.com). *GameSlice Weekly* includes new features updated every Monday morning, including the latest game reviews and previews, as well as interviews with leading interactive developers, and special contests. Besides offering articles on this unique online experience, you'll also be able to download still images and video clips of new games, such as *Duke Nukem 3D: Atomic Edition*.

This refreshingly frank interview originally appeared on *GameSlice Weekly* as a part of their continuing series of interviews with leading game developers. George Broussard and Scott Miller, Apogee and 3D Realms presidents and partners, sit down to talk to Geoff about the games, the interactive industry, and, naturally, about Duke Nukem.

# MILLER AND BROUSSARD REVEAL THEIR INNER CHILDREN

**KEIGHLEY:** What has been the crowning achievement for Apogee/3D Realms since inception?

**MILLER:** *Duke 3D* is the game we're the most proud of because it's the first game done exactly how we wanted it to be done, and we think we did a pretty good job.

**BROUSSARD:** Agreed. *Duke 3D* is the first product we really did internally, without outside developers. As a result, we had more control and I think a better product emerged.

**KEIGHLEY:** *Duke 3D* is probably your best selling game in the history of the company, but is it the best game you've ever produced in terms of quality, as quality does not always dictate quantity of sales?

**BROUSSARD:** I think *Duke 3D* is the best game we've ever done. Period. That goes for everything from gameplay and design to packaging and advertising. It was the culmination of all our experience in one product.

**MILLER:** If you define quality in terms of quality-of-content, then *Duke 3D* is our best effort. If you define quality in terms of quality-of-gameplay, then we have several games I rate very highly along with *Duke 3D*, including *Death Rally*, *Stargunner*, *Monster Bash*, *Raptor* and *Commander Keen*.

**KEIGHLEY:** With the success of *Duke*, has there been one purchase (a car, etc.) that either of you have made that really made you feel like you had earned your success? For id, a Ferrari equaled success, but for 3D Realms?

**MILLER:** No. George and I went through our big buying phase back when *Wolfenstein 3D* was the "big hit" of 1992, and we bought nice houses and cars. When you have everything you want already, there's nothing much to do with extra money except reinvest it back into the company, which is what we're doing. Todd Replogle, *Duke*'s lead programmer, bought a black Ferrari after trading in his Viper, though. And Allen Blum, *Duke*'s lead mapper and assistant designer, bought a bright red Mazda RX-7.

**BROUSSARD:** I think to some extent we're beyond the doing this for money point. Sure, the money is great, but we also think we have something to prove, and just want to make hit game after hit game. I think that's what drives us all the most: making great games. I have no doubt that a lot of the *Duke* team will be buying more "stuff" now though.

**KEIGHLEY:** Are there any plans to take Apogee or 3D Realms public, or do you still wish to maintain 100 percent private ownership?

**BROUSSARD:** We get approached all the time from people wanting to buy us, or take us public. The bottom line is that we don't care. We make more than enough money now and have 100 percent control over the company. We do what we like, when we like, without reporting to shareholders, or a parent company. There may be a point at which we go public, or sell, but that is still a long way off, as we like what we are doing now.

**KEIGHLEY:** Does id Software make better 3D games than 3D Realms? Are you appealing to the same market?

**MILLER:** I think we're appealing to the same market, just like *Warcraft* and *Command & Conquer* appeal to the same market. Our 3D games are different in many ways to id's games, though. For example, we put a lot of emphasis on the character and giving that character a personality. We also like to put lots of interaction within the game that may or may not have an effect of gameplay, just to make the environment more interesting. id likes to keep their environments free of any clutter and free of anything absolutely nonessential to gameplay. We just have different styles, and players can pick whichever style they prefer. There's really no right or wrong way.

**KEIGHLEY:** If there were five adjectives you'd use to describe the gameplay in *Duke*, what would they be?

**MILLER:** Raw, frenetic, surprising, humorous, and dangerous.

**BROUSSARD:** I'd boil it down to one adjective: fun.

**KEIGHLEY:** With so many hit games under your belts, you must be very close to perfecting the formula for a great game. What do you think are the key ingredients needed to separate the kings from peasants in terms of software?

**MILLER:** I don't think anyone has the formula for making a hit game every time [Smiles]. However, there are certain keys that are typically important: A game must be innovative in some manner, otherwise it's just a clone of something already released. And a lot of work must be put into fine-tuning and polishing the gameplay, and trying to get it just right. This is probably what separates all great games from good games. We know the value of this polishing phase and spend months on it.

**BROUSSARD:** The bottom line is just being a fun game that people want to play. That's fairly easy to achieve if the game is being made by a team of die-hard gamers. You just try to bring something new to the equation in terms of engine capabilities or gameplay, such as the interactive environment in *Duke*. From there, you just hammer on the game until everyone in the office likes it better than the competition's. If you can't get people to stop playing *DOOM* and play *Duke 3D* in the office, then how can you expect the rest of the world to? So, we kept at *Duke* until everyone dropped *DOOM* forever and moved on.

**KEIGHLEY:** You've had some dry spells in the history of the company—including a backlog of EGA games that came out much too late in the early 90s—but what's been the most embarrassing moment or the most regretted decision in the history of Apogee/3D Realms?

**MILLER:** Well, some of those EGA games were actually great games, such as *Monster Bash*, which I still think is one of the best platform-style games ever for the PC. But, because we spent too long on getting the gameplay perfect, those games came out too late to be in EGA mode. I can't think of a most embarrassing decision, though. Most decisions we felt were good at the time, and only looking back in hindsight did some turn out bad. Probably our worst mistake was trying to develop too many games during 1992 and 1993, rather than focus on a few games and make sure they were done right. This is a trap that fast growing companies often fall into, and we were no exception. Luckily, we realized this mistake in 1994 and climbed out of the trap (and also dropped several games so that we could focus on just a few).

**BROUSSARD:** Like Scott said, the only mistake we ever made was in trying to make too many games at a time. All that does is dilute your quality. It's happening to some of the larger retail publishers now. They try to do a hundred games a year, when 25 would be fine, with the net result being better games. The bottom line is that 20 lame games won't make as much as one top 5 game, so we changed our direction. Now we only work on two or three big games at a time and focus on quality and gameplay. We have also moved nearly all development in-house, so as to further insure quality. *Duke 3D* is the first game created with this new direction.

**KEIGHLEY:** It's not often that two names share the top tier of the masthead for a company, but it seems both of you have shared the power at Apogee relatively equally. What's the secret to not constantly bickering with each other? Does this relationship result in a better end product?

**BROUSSARD:** We've been friends for 15 years or so. We know each other very well and constantly keep the other in check. I think this method is the best, because it keeps you "grounded". We aren't run by one guy that will get a big head, live in an ivory tower and think we can do no wrong. By having two of us, we insure that things stay balanced. Plus it's real good to have the ability to point the finger at the other guy when things go wrong. [Grins.]

**MILLER:** In addition to what George said, I can't imagine trying to run a company of this size without a partner—it's really a perfect situation to have two people in charge. What makes it work so well is that George and I have been friends since spending countless hours at the arcades in the late 70s and throughout the 80s. We have the same goals and beliefs in game design, so there's not much bickering at all.

**KEIGHLEY:** Did you expect *Duke Nukem* to do any worse than it has? When it went out the door, did you know that "this is going to be huge!?"

**MILLER:** We thought it'd be a top 10 game for certain, but it surprised us by rocketing to #1 and staying there for so long. It has out-sold our expectations by a factor of two or three.

**BROUSSARD:** We knew *Duke* was going to be big. [Pauses.] Maybe. To tell you the truth, by the end of the game's development cycle, we were all so burnt out, we had no objectivity left. We just let it go, knowing it was a cool game to us and did more than any other 3D game out there. We hoped players would flock to it, and they did. I think we're a little surprised at the game's staying power. We half expected people to drop it when *Quake* came out, but it just goes to show that engine superiority isn't everything. *Duke* still does things other 3D games don't and that's all that matters to the players.

**KEIGHLEY:** What can you tell us about the next *Duke Nukem* game? Can we expect a sequel for Holiday 1997?

**BROUSSARD:** There will be a sequel to *Duke Nukem 3D*. We are deciding now what technology we will use. It is likely we will do one more 25–30 level game with an improved Build engine. Possibly with polygon characters, but we are still in the fact finding stages. I do expect to be in full production in a sequel to *Duke* by X-mas 1996.

**MILLER:** Geoff, we are also making *Duke Nukem Forever*, which will be out next Christmas for sure. *DN Forever* is not a sequel though, rather it's simply another episode in the life of *Duke*, just like each episode of Star Trek is not a sequel to the previous episode. *DN Forever* will be a side-scrolling platform game similar to the original two *Duke* games, but with far better technology and graphics. We're using the same Duke model from *Duke Nukem 3D* and adding dozens of new frames. Duke will climb chains, poles, ladders, walk hand-over-hand along wires and pipes, do midair flips, and ride several vehicles, including a jet ski and a Harley.

The graphics will be very realistic and dark in style, and not cartoonish like the first two Duke platform games. Duke will have several familiar weapons, like the shotgun, RPG, and Ripper, plus several new weapons. And, of course, he'll have his legendary attitude and Duke Talk™ [Smiles.] (The ™ is a joke, by the way. [Laughs.]

**KEIGHLEY:** Scott, we know that there has been an on-going legal hassle between MicroStar and GT Interactive/3D Realms with regards to *Duke 3D* add-on packages. What is Apogee/3D Realms' position on this matter?

**MILLER:** We're not very happy about companies that basically leech off our efforts and success. In Micro Star's case, they violated our copyrights by including too many screen shots of our copyrighted graphics on the box, plus they included our graphics on their CD-ROM. This is why the court ruled against them.

**KEIGHLEY:** id Software called *Quake* a "Ferrari," and said the interactive nature of Duke is akin to "vanity mirrors" and "cup holders" in a car. Do you agree with that assessment of your product?

**BROUSSARD:** id can call Duke what they want to, but I see Duke as a Lamborghini. [Smiles.] It has raw power and speed, plus all the amenities that a Ferrari doesn't. I see no reason why a game can't have it all. Why limit yourself?

**MILLER:** Whether I agree or not is not that important. All you need to do is read the Internet newsgroups to see that most players love the interactive environment in Duke. I hope id keeps their philosophy and leaves this style of gameplay for us to exploit by ourselves. [Grin.]

**KEIGHLEY:** Is *Quake* the best 3D game on the market today? If so, how long will it maintain its reign?

**MILLER:** *Quake* and *Duke* both have strong and weak points. I think that if *Duke* had not been released, then *Quake* would have been much more appreciated. *Duke*, though, raised the bar in several areas (character personality, realistic, and recognizable locations, interactive environment, humor) that *Quake* did not reach. And conversely, *Quake* has many features not in *Duke* (true 3D levels and characters, Internet WAN play). So, it's hard to say which game is truly number #1, and frankly, that doesn't concern me. *Duke* is already such an amazing success that I couldn't be happier.

**BROUSSARD:** I think *Quake* has the most technically advanced engine on the market. As for "best" 3D game? I think the players will decide that, and I think the jury's still out. I see a big split on-line between gamers on the issue of *Duke* vs. *Quake*. I think it's all kind of silly to compare anyway. They are both awesome, fun 3D games. I play them both, as I expect most gamers do. There is room for more than one game.

**KEIGHLEY:** When you look at *Quake*, do you ever think to yourself that id had great technology, but they really fell a few yards short in terms of gameplay and interactivity?

**MILLER:** I don't think they fell short—I think they made this decision and they're happy with it. *Quake* is the game they intended to make. I spoke with John Romero last week and he said that one of the reasons he split from id is that he liked *Duke* so much and wanted to add some of *Duke*'s stuff to *Quake*, but the others at id didn't want to do so. I have heard a lot of people within the game industry make your comment, though.

**KEIGHLEY:** John Romero recently left id, and I know both of you are good friends with him—in fact Tom Hall, a former 3D Realms employee, is now working with John at ION Design. Do you think Romero departure from id will negatively affect their output and quality in the future?

**MILLER:** I don't see how it can't affect id's future games. He was the heart of those games, and made sure they were finely polished and perfected. It's as if the Beatles lost Paul—can they still be the same in the future? I don't see how, but then id has surprised me many times before. I wish them good luck.

**BROUSSARD:** Also, I think John left because he "couldn't" affect games at id anymore, or else he likely wouldn't have even left.

**KEIGHLEY:** When I look at the 3D first-person action market today, it seems many magazines and consumers are getting stuck on the technology aspect of games. For instance, we are talking about *Prey* years before its release when there really isn't much of a game to talk about. Does this fascination with 3D technology bother you as an individual, and/or as a company?

**MILLER:** Technology is exciting. Players always want to hear about the next new thing. But really, the technology behind a game doesn't affect sales nearly as much as the game's content and gameplay. Case in point: Capstone released three games using the same Build engine used in *Duke Nukem 3D*, but none of those three games sold over 50,000 copies. That's because the content and playability of those three games was weak. And look at how little *Quake*'s release has affected the appeal of *Duke*, even though *Quake* has the superior engine. Overall, I think far too much emphasis is placed on game technology. "It's the content, stupid" should be the battle cry for gamers.

**KEIGHLEY:** If you were to put 3D technology and gameplay on a see-saw, in order to create the perfect game, which side would have to be heavier—and no, they can't be equal in weight. [Smiles.]

**MILLER:** On a scale, technology gets 30 percent and content gets 70 percent.

**BROUSSARD:** I think content and gameplay are way more important than technology. Look at *Duke* and *Quake*. By all rights, *Duke* should have been crushed by *Quake*'s better engine, but no, *Duke* happily moves along at the top of games on the market today. So I think the bottom line is that gameplay can save a game, regardless of technology. But if you have great technology and crappy gameplay, you are dead in the water.

**KEIGHLEY:** Moving onto this summer, it certainly was a very active time for Apogee and 3D Realms. Nevertheless, let's deal with some of the issues: First and foremost, we know that a number of your developers left in August. Why?

**MILLER:** Tom Hall left because he had an incredible opportunity to team up with his long-time friend, John Romero and have ownership in ION Design. This was a good move for Apogee, too, because Tom really didn't want to make *Prey* as hard-core as we want *Prey* to be. Tom's forte is strategy, playful, character-oriented games and now he'll have an opportunity to do exactly the game he wants. Some of the others, Richard [Grey], Mark [Dotcherman] and Jim [Dose] left because they wanted more control over their game. I've heard they also think we were treating them unfairly, royalty-wise, but I don't think they'll find another company that pays higher royalties than we do, unless they start their own company—which is a very risky proposition. Another group of developers—the *Raptor* team—left us several years ago to do the same thing and created *Strife*. Some of those developers have asked to come back to work for us again. [Grins.]

**BROUSSARD:** The other guys, besides Tom, left because they were control freaks. That's the bottom line. They had sweet deals and wanted more. So, they split and started their own gig. That's fine with us, and we wish them well. We had over 30 developers and three left, so I don't see any core problems on our end.

**KEIGHLEY:** Without going into specifics, does 3D Realms compensate their employees reasonably? I've heard that despite the success of 3D Realms, you do not share your profits with the majority of the workforce. Is this fact or fiction?

**MILLER:** Absolute fiction. Try to find another company that pays its developers a percent of gross revenues as high as we do, including revenues for merchandising. Most publishers do not pay any royalties to their developers. Still, four out of the five people who left (only three of the five were developers, by the way) were not key developers of *Duke*, so they didn't get a royalty. I think they expected to share in the profits on games they were not involved with.

**BROUSSARD:** Well, I'd like to hear about artists at other companies nearing six figures a year. The bottom line is you've got to produce a hit game. We have *Duke 3D* people driving Ferrari's now. So if a game is a flop, we all pay the price, and if it's a hit, we all share in the success. The ones who left were unwilling to put the time in on *Prey*, and thought they could do better elsewhere.

**KEIGHLEY:** id said that Hipnotic Interactive, the team that is currently creating a *Quake* add-on pack, is comprised of the best developers "3D Realms had," who left your company in August. Were these developers the cream of the crop at 3D Realms?

**BROUSSARD:** I have to laugh at the statement that they were the "best talent."[Laughs.] What a joke. The *Duke* team produced the biggest 3D game of 1996, so I'd have to say they are in the running for the "best." The guys that left were talented, but easily replaced. We've already hired two new mappers and a new *Prey* producer. We have several hot technology programmers coming in for interviews over the next few weeks as well. All in all, we're a lot more happy now, and the rest of the company is more happy, without the "boat rockers."

**KEIGHLEY:** When all is said and done, what net result has this defection had on the future of 3D Realms and Apogee?

**BROUSSARD:** The net result equals zilch. *Duke Plutonium PAK* got done without a glitch and *Prey* is now much better off, with more motivated people on it now.

**KEIGHLEY:** In the past six months, many new 3D game companies have started development on their own engines and products, including firms such as ION, Hipnotic, and others. Since it really doesn't take significant resources to release shareware games, are you concerned that some of these companies will significantly reduce your market share in the coming years?

**BROUSSARD:** Not worried in the least. We know we can make killer 3D games, so there will always be a market for us. As things get more and more crowded, people get squeezed out the bottom as fast as they enter through the top, so I think it all stays pretty balanced. There are way too many people just jumping on the 3D action bandwagon, thinking they can pump put a game in less than a year and have it hit #1. Guess again. Those people will be broke soon and the rest of us will be happily chugging along, working on the next game.

**KEIGHLEY:** *Duke 3D* has really had a lot of glory and excitement surrounding it from the get-go, but what about *Shadow Warrior* and *Blood*? Do you still expect them to be a strong force in the market?

**MILLER:** Yes. These games will have new tricks up their sleeves. Of course, it's silly to predict these games will have the amazing success that *Duke* had, but we think they'll be hits.

**KEIGHLEY:** For the many players and fans of *Duke Nukem 3D*, will they be just as content playing *Shadow Warrior* when it is released? What new and exciting features does it have for those players growing tired of *Duke 3D*?

**BROUSSARD:** Shadow Warrior will have things like rooms above rooms (like in *Quake*); vehicles to drive like tanks, forklifts, boats; and more! When all is said and done, we think there will many new things to "do" in *Shadow Warrior* which other 3D games don't let you do. Just as we polished *Duke* before it went out the door, *Shadow Warrior* will go through that same process.

**KEIGHLEY:** I think it would be safe to say that Apogee has expanded, then recently contracted the number of projects you work on. Are you now more focused on producing titles based on quality, rather than quantity?

**MILLER:** Exactly correct. To make games right, you can't be spread too thin.

**BROUSSARD:** Like Ford, quality is Job one. [Ducks from the bad joke.] All we care about now is making top games and forgetting the rest. We are totally devoted to this, as are all the people here.

**KEIGHLEY:** Speaking of *Prey*, with it now being a 1998 release, what can you tell us about the game that we haven't heard before? What will help *Prey* "break through the clutter" of 3D games?

**MILLER:** Content. That's what will matter most. We recently hired Paul Schuytema, formally lead designer at FASA for *Mechwarrior 3*, and a technology writer for Computer Gaming World, to lead this project. He understands exactly what we're trying to accomplish with *Prey* and we're excited to have his talent at our disposal. Between Paul and George, *Prey* can't help but have innovative and awesome content.

**KEIGHLEY:** Finally, you've had a great year in some regards (*Duke 3D*), and a disappointing one in others (the delay of *Prey*). In a sentence, sum up 1996, so far, for Apogee and 3D Realms.

**BROUSSARD:** It's been our best year yet, as has each of our year's before. We've never had a year that did worse than the previous one, and we don't want to start now. So back to work we go.

**MILLER:** We couldn't be happier. If only every year could be this success filled and exciting. [Smiles.]

# Installation and Setup

Whether you are starting out with *Duke Nukem 3D: Atomic Edition* or

simply upgrading your existing registered version of *Duke Nukem 3D*

(version 1.3d) with the *Plutonium PAK*, this is where you find out how

to install and set up your system.

# INSTALLATION OF *DUKE NUKEM 3D: ATOMIC EDITION* OR THE *PLUTONIUM PAK*

The installation directions that follow depend on which version of the game you want to install. If you're upgrading to the *Atomic Edition* with the *Plutonium PAK*, then you'll want to refer to the section, "Upgrading to the *Atomic Edition* with the *Plutonium PAK*." If you're installing *Duke Nukem 3D: Atomic Edition* for the first time, see the section "Installing *Duke Nukem 3D: Atomic Edition*." After you install either version of the program, refer to the section "Setting Up *Duke Nukem 3D*."

## UPGRADING TO THE *ATOMIC EDITION* WITH THE *PLUTONIUM PAK*

If you're upgrading to the *Atomic Edition* with the *Plutonium PAK* because you already have a registered version of *Duke Nukem 3D* (v1.3d) installed, follow these instructions:

1. Insert the *Plutonium PAK* CD-ROM into your CD-ROM drive.

2. At the DOS prompt for the CD-ROM drive, type install and press Enter. You will be prompted for a destination directory (folder) where the

*Plutonium PAK* patch will be applied. The program will suggest C:\DUKE3D as the default directory.

3. To accept the default directory, simply press Enter. But if your Duke Nukem 3D directory is different than the destination the program suggests, type the appropriate path and then press Enter.

   The install program will begin copying the necessary files to the directory for the game. The process will take under five minutes. When the installation is complete, you will see a confirmation message.

4. Press any key to continue with the setup procedure.

Refer to "Setting Up *Duke Nukem 3D*" to prepare the game to recognize and interface with your system's components.

## INSTALLING *DUKE NUKEM 3D: ATOMIC EDITION*

If you purchased *Duke Nukem 3D: Atomic Edition*, follow these instructions to install it in your system:

1. Insert the *Atomic Edition* CD-ROM into your CD-ROM drive.

2. At the DOS prompt for the CD-ROM drive, type `install` and press Enter. You will be prompted for a destination directory (folder) where the Atomic Edition will be installed. The program will suggest C:\DUKE3D as the default directory.

3. To accept the default directory, simply press Enter. To install in a different directory or drive, type the appropriate path and then press Enter.

   The install program will begin copying the necessary files to the directory for the game. The process will take under eight minutes. When the installation is complete, you will see a confirmation message.

4. Press any key to continue with the setup procedure.

Refer to "Setting Up *Duke Nukem 3D*" to set up the game for your system's components.

# SETTING UP *DUKE NUKEM 3D*

You can run the setup procedure immediately after you install the game or anytime
later. When you install the *Atomic Edition* rather than the *Plutonium PAK*, the Install
program runs the setup procedure automatically. When you're ready to set up the
game, access the directory for the game. Then follow these steps:

1. Type setup and
   press Enter. The
   initial setup Main
   Menu is displayed
   (see Figure A.1).

**TIP**

To postpone the setup procedure, press the
Esc key.

2. Use the arrow
   keys to select the option you want to adjust and press Enter. Depending
   on the option you choose, the program will present you with related
   screens so that you can make the appropriate selections.

```
                    Main Menu

  Current  Filename  (  DUKE3D.CFG  )

   Sound Setup
   Screen Setup
   Controller Setup
   Network Game
   Modem Game
   Serial Game
   TEN Game
   See The Duke Nukem 3D Help File
   Select User Level
   Change Setup Filename
   Save and launch Duke Nukem 3D

     Esc Exits   ↑↓ Move   ⏎ Selects
```

**FIGURE A.1:** The setup Main Menu lets you choose several options, to adjust for your system.

## SOUND SETUP

If you choose Sound Setup, you'll see another screen where you can choose the various sound settings for your system.

To set up your system's sound card so that you can hear the game's sound effects, do the following:

1.  Select Choose Sound FX Card and press Enter. Another screen will show you the available options.

2.  After you choose your sound card, you can also adjust its various settings. Figure A.2, for example, shows the adjustments you can make for a Sound Blaster card.

```
              Sound Blaster Configuration

Current Address      [ 0x220 ]
Current Type         ( Sound Blaster or Compatible )
Current Interrupt    [ 5 ]
Current 8-bit DMA    [ 1 ]
Current 16-bit DMA   [ 5 ]

Use These Settings and Continue...

Change Address
Change Sound Card Type
Change Interrupt
Change 8-bit DMA Channel
Change 16-bit DMA Channel

        Esc Exits   ↑↓ Move   ⏎ Selects
```

FIGURE A.2: The top portion of the screen shows the current settings. Select the option you want to change from the bottom.

Other options you can adjust for your sound card include:

- Number of mixing voices
- 8- or 16-bit mixing
- Mixing rate

## SCREEN SETUP

If you choose Screen Setup from the Main Menu, you can choose between normal or VESA modes. You can get the best screen resolution using VESA modes, but your system must be equipped with a graphics card that supports the VESA standard. In VESA modes, you can specify resolutions of up to $800 \times 600$.

## CONTROLLER TYPE

The Controller Type option lets you choose the device you will use to control the action. The default setup is Keyboard and Mouse. In addition, you can also make other adjustments to your controlling device by selecting other setup options shown on this screen.

## OTHER SETUP OPTIONS

The remaining options you can set up during the setup procedure are summarized in Table A.1.

**TABLE A.1: SETUP OPTIONS**

| OPTION | DESCRIPTION |
| --- | --- |
| Network Game | This option lets you set up and run multiplayer games over networks using the IPX protocol. |
| Modem Game | This option lets you run multiplayer games over your modem. |
| Serial Game | This option lets you run multiplayer games with two computers linked through a null modem adapter. |
| TEN Game | This option lets you dial up the Total Entertainment Network, so you can play multiplayer games over the Internet. |

| OPTION | DESCRIPTION |
| --- | --- |
| See the *Duke Nukem 3D* Help File | This option lets you display the extensive help file that comes with *Duke Nukem 3D*. |
| Select User Level | This option lets you start a game using a level designed by you or another third party. |
| Change Setup Filename | This option lets you rename the setup file so that you can use a second setup file that contains different settings. |
| Save and launch *Duke Nukem 3D* | Use this option to save any adjustments you have made and to start *Duke Nukem 3D*. |

# Multiplayer Tips and Online Resources

Multiplayer mode games include games over an IPX network, modem games, and games over computers that are serially connected. Up to eight players can play the *Atomic Edition* (provided that each player has a registered version of the software). This appendix does not cover the instructions for launching multiplayer matches. That information is covered extensively in the help file called DN3DHLP that comes with your CD-ROM. Instead, this appendix covers a few tips for making you a fearsome adversary in DukeMatch games or a better teammate in Co-Op play.

# GENERAL MULTIPLAYER TIPS

One of the most important aspects of multiplayer play actually occurs before the game is ever started. Selecting a configuration that is both comfortable and well thought out is paramount to playing well. For the keyboard, assign commonly used functions to keys that are close to one another.

## CONFIGURATION TIPS

It's important in combat to not take your eyes off the screen when you want to change from one weapon to another or to activate the steroids before making a hasty escape. Doing so means losing sight of your opponent, which could possibly lead to the ultimate loss—of the battle itself. By clumping functions next to one another, your fingers can quickly move off your "home keys" and onto others, and then quickly reposition themselves without your ever having to look down. Try this technique with your favorite weapons. Your opponent will be amazed at how quickly you can switch between them while remaining in action.

Another useful configuration trick is to double-assign keys and buttons. When in battle, you may think it is a good idea to get the medkit into action as your health dips below 100 percent. The *last* thing you want to do, however, is move your fingers off your main control keys to rejuvenate your health. Chances are, your opponent will take advantage of this short pause to end your life before you have a chance to increase it.

A better choice is to double-assign keys that are normally used in battle—such as strafe, jump, or crouch—to also include activating the medkit. You can even repeat the assignment of the same function across several keys to make sure that you don't miss it when it really counts. For example, while you're dancing around your opponent, you're automatically activating your portable medkit (if it's in your inventory) without having to remember or move your hands around the keyboard. You can use this same technique for other functions, such as opening doors, using night vision goggles, and so on.

## CONTROLLER TIPS

Now that you've got the configuration set up, it's time for practice. There are many good keyboard-only players, but the excellent players *always* use the mouse. With the mouse, you get a greater level of precision and rotational speed that just can't be matched by the keyboard. The down side is the learning curve. Chances are, for the first few days of mouse use, you'll do more damage to yourself than good (sort of like doing brain surgery on yourself). Then, with a little persistence, a breakthrough is achieved.

Use the mouse to run, turn, and fire. If you have a three-button mouse, you can even assign one of the buttons to mouse aiming, which is useful for knocking your aggressors out of their hiding places above and below you. Leave the strafing to your other hand by assigning left and right strafing to the keyboard. To become proficient at this two-handed maneuver, stand at one end of a long street, such as the one in Episode 1, Hollywood Holocaust. Turn on the crosshair, and aim at a fixed point at the opposite end of the street. Now start running forward and, while keeping the crosshair on the *target*, begin strafing to the left and then the right. This left-right motion will later be used to dodge your opponents' RPGs, while sending your own forget-me-nots in return.

Another good exercise is to find a stationary object that is open on all sides. Keep your crosshair glued on the object and begin strafing to the left or right, completely encircling it. With a little practice, these maneuvers will become simple techniques that you'll employ in every battle.

## TIPS FOR BATTLE

With bootcamp behind you, it's time to march into battle. To help you FNGs (Freakin' New Guys) live for more than a few seconds, here are some tips that will help you to be more than someone else's chew toy:

- Exercise caution when entering areas that can't be seen before reaching the entry point. If you make a habit of charging into places full-speed-ahead, you may run headlong into a web of laser trip bombs or perhaps a nest of pipe bombs. Some players are more direct: they'll just camp out in a certain vantage spot and launch a salvo of RPGs at you when you unexpectedly dash in.

- If you find that your opponent's play strategy resembles a scene out of *True Grit,* begin wallpapering the walls with laser trip bombs. First choose the ideal spot; blind corners and places that you have to jump up or down to are best. Now start setting traps. Place the laser trip bombs high and low, and fairly close to one another. All it takes is for just one to be triggered, and the entire lot will blow in a chain reaction. The beauty of laser trip bombs is that they remember who set them. If you set a bomb and are subsequently killed, you will still get credit for a kill if your opponent is unfortunate enough to stumble into one. Just remember *where* you set them. Forgetting could lead to a rather embarrassing loss in the form of a frag.

> **TIP**
>
> If you're not sure whether someone's awaiting your arrival just around the corner, use the peek-a-boo trick. Stop short just shy of an entrance or corner and *peek* into the room by using the Insert and Delete keys. Quickly strafing into and out of the area, to draw enemy fire, is also a safe and effective maneuver.

- Never stop moving! Don't be a sitting duck for chaingun fire; instead, evade damage by strafing, jumping, and flying. Quick, erratic movements work best. If you're running low on health, try to pick up health items while you continue battle. Remember to keep your aim fixed on the enemy!

- When using the RPG launcher, it's not always necessary to directly hit your opponent to hurt him. If you can't seem to hit a player, aim at a wall or other object very close to your opponent. The concussion from the explosion will deal a lot of damage.

- By the same token, don't stand next to walls or objects when being fired upon by RPGs. Stay in open areas to prevent your aggressor from knocking precious chucks of health off you from indirect hits. Force your opponent to make a direct hit.

- Use NVGs in dark areas. In areas where you can control the lighting, a good technique is to turn the lights off and activate your goggles. With any luck, your opponent will stumble into the area without goggles, giving you a chance for an easy kill.

- When in trouble, retreat! Don't be afraid to run and fight another time. If you're taking heavy damage, make a fast retreat, and replenish your health as quickly as safety will permit. If someone is hot on your tail, zigzag left and right, jump, repeatedly activate your holoduke, and sharply turn and hide around corners until your opponent runs past you. Then quickly backtrack down the same path that led you there, while your opponent tries to figure out where you went. If outside, you can also jetpack straight up and very high to a point that's out of sight of your opponent. If you have pipe bombs, drop them as you run, and try to time the detonation to coincide with your opponent's reaching the same spot. It's *very* rewarding to kill your opponent, who definitely has the upper hand on you, by cleverly using this tactic.

- Shut . . . up . . . and . . . listen. You can easily get a bead on your opponents by listening to what they are doing. You may recognize certain sounds: a particular door opening, an elevator in motion, the bubbling sound of someone swimming, the "Ohhh" heard as someone takes damage jumping out of a high window, or the "Ahhh" made when the portable medkit is used to replenish health. These sounds will tip you off to your opponent's location. If you run there in a hurry, you might be able to catch him unexpectedly, leaving your opponent amazed at your ability to always show up at the same place he does. Turning off ambient sounds (TV, your little sister), music, and Duke talk may help you to hear better.

- Teleporters not only teleport people, they also teleport certain weapons and projectiles. Throw pipe bombs or shoot RPGs through teleporters before entering them. If someone is standing on the other side, you'll clear the way with your little surprise.

- Don't, for heaven's sake, stand in front of teleporters! If you know the teleporter trick mentioned previously, chances are that someone else does too. If you engage in battle through the teleporters, always stand to the side and fire away.

- Each level has its own set of respawning points. These are particular areas in a map where a player will respawn after dying. Once you do your opponent in, run to the closest respawning points. If you're lucky and the opponent is there, his handgun and lack of shields and extra health will be no match against your chaingun, shrinker/expander, shotgun, Devastator, or RPG launcher.

- If you just fought a grueling battle that left you holding the short end of the stick, but you conveniently find yourself respawned near your opponent, don't be afraid to open up on the opponent with the handgun, especially at longer ranges. If you did a lot of damage to him in the previous battle, pumping a number of handgun rounds into his tattered body will quickly do him in.

- If you just fought a winning battle that left you barely alive, stay away from the respawning points and seek out health.

- Get into your opponents' heads. Part of being a good player is learning how to intimidate your opponents. Anticipate their moves, take shortcuts to head them off, mesmerize them with unbelievable moves and control, and, when you put them to rest, give them a few Remote Ridicules to think about. You can get opponents so rattled and jumpy that they'll end up fraggin' themselves every time they see you coming.

🔥 Use the old bait-and-switch technique. You can usually pull this off only once or twice a game, but when it works, it's beautiful. *Pretend* to be in possession of only less-damaging weapons, by firing off a few rounds, and then retreating with your opponent in hot pursuit. Run to an area that will provide temporary protection from return shots, do a 180-degree turn, switch to your money weapon, and wait. As soon as your opponent enters the area, let him have it. Knowing that you just made a sucker of your opponent is a pleasure second to none.

🔥 When possible, always enter into battle with 200 percent health, 100 percent shields, and the portable medkit. With these levels, you'll survive even a direct shot with an RPG—once. Between two equally skilled players equipped with the same weapon, the results of a battle are often determined by nothing more than who entered into it with the most health and shields. Learn where health is distributed, especially atomic health units, as well as shields and medkits. After your opponents barely escape battle with heavy damage, run to the health caches and try to wipe them out as they attempt to repair their damage.

🔥 When the respawn indicators are on, pay close attention to them. If they're red and spinning slowly, clear the area—it's not worth the wait. If they're green and spinning quickly, payday is near; stick around for the goodies.

🔥 Dead men don't tell tales, but they sometimes leave nice shiny weapons behind for the taking. Now and then when you kill opponents, they give up one of their weapons. If you see something lying next to the corpse of what used to be your enemy, run over, pick it up, and use it to your advantage. And make sure to *thank* them for the free RPGs! This is especially helpful when playing with the No Respawn option.

🔥 When playing with no respawns, always keep a portable medkit in your inventory. Once a level has been played for a while, it'll be the only source of additional health.

## CO-OP MODE TIPS

Most Co-Op games eventually degrade into DukeMatch games anyway. But in general, just try not to kill the other guy. Also, help your opponents fight battles, and never leave them in a room full of monsters. You may want to separate and send one guy after a keycard, while the others clear a path toward a certain part of the level or a door.

# ONLINE RESOURCES

Thousands of *Duke Nukem 3D* enthusiasts will find extensive support and resources from various online platforms. Besides the official and established channels, there is also a growing brew of home-spun Web home pages where users congregate to exchange useful information.

Here is a short list of the more recognized online resources *for Duke Nukem 3D*:

- 💣 **CompuServe:** Issue the command Go REALMS.

- 💣 **America Online:** Use the keyword "3D Realms."

- 💣 **3D Realms' official Web site:** Point your browser to www.3drealms.com

- 💣 **Software Creations Web BBS:** Point your browser to www.swcbbs.com

In addition, you can also hook up with other *Duke Nukem 3D* players and issue or accept multiplayer mode challenges over the Internet.

## ONLINE PLAY THROUGH TEN

*Duke Nukem 3D* is also available for multiplayer gaming exclusively on Total Entertainment Network (TEN). Stop playing *Duke Nukem 3D* by yourself! You can play it on the Internet with gamers across the country on TEN. At any hour of the day or night, there could be dozens of other *Duke Nukem 3D* fans on TEN playing brutal DukeMatches. Why miss out? If you want to know more, check out TEN's Web page at http://www.ten.net. You can also phone TEN at 800-8040-TEN, or e-mail them at questions@ten.net.